AUDUBON GUIDE
to the National Wildlife Refuges

Northern Midwest

AUDUBON GUIDE
to the National Wildlife Refuges

Northern Midwest

Illinois · Indiana · Iowa · Michigan
Minnesota · Nebraska · North Dakota
Ohio · South Dakota · Wisconsin

By John Grassy and
Tom Powers

Foreword by Theodore Roosevelt IV

Series Editor, David Emblidge
Editor, Donald Young

A Balliett & Fitzgerald Book
St. Martin's Griffin, New York

AUDUBON GUIDE TO THE NATIONAL WILDLIFE REFUGES: NORTHERN MIDWEST. Copyright © 2000 by Balliett & Fitzgerald, Inc.

National Audubon Society® is a registered trademark of the National Audubon Society, Inc.

Cartography: © Balliett & Fitzgerald, Inc. produced by Mapping Specialists Ltd.
Illustrations: Mary Sundstrom
Cover design: Michael Storrings and Sue Canavan
Interior design: Bill Cooke and Sue Canavan

Balliett & Fitzgerald Inc. Staff
Sue Canavan, Design Director
Maria Fernandez, Production Editor
Alexis Lipsitz, Executive Series Editor
Rachel Deutsch, Associate Photo Editor
Kristen Couse, Associate Editor
Paul Paddock, Carol Petino Assistant Editors
Howard Klein, Editorial Intern
Scott Prentzas, Copy Editor

Balliett & Fitzgerald Inc. would like to thank the following people for their assistance in creating this series:
At National Audubon Society:
    Katherine Santone, former Director of Publishing, for sponsoring this project
    Claire Tully, Senior Vice President, Marketing
    Evan Hirsche, Director, National Wildlife Refuges Campaign
At U.S. Fish & Wildlife Service:
    Richard Coleman, Chief, Division of Refuges, U.S. Fish & Wildlife Service
    Janet Tennyson, Outreach Coordinator
    Craig Rieben, Chief of Broadcasting & Audio Visual, U.S. Fish & Wildlife
        Service, for photo research assistance
    Pat Carrol, Chief Surveyor, U.S. Fish & Wildlife Service, for map information
    Regional External Affairs officers, at the seven U.S. Fish & Wildlife Service
        Regional Headquarters
    Elizabeth Jackson, Photographic Information Specialist, National
        Conservation Training Center, for photo research
At St. Martin's Griffin:
    Greg Cohn, who pulled it all together on his end, as well as Michael
        Storrings and Kristen Macnamara
At David Emblidge—Book Producer:
    Marcy Ross, Assistant Editor
Thanks also to Theodore Roosevelt IV and John Flicker.

ISBN 0-312-24315-4
First St. Martin's Griffin Edition: March 2000

10 9 8 7 6 5 4 3 2 1

CONTENTS

Appendix

Foreword

America is singularly blessed in the amount and quality of land that the federal government holds in trust for its citizens. No other country can begin to match the variety of lands in our national wildlife refuges, parks and forests. From the Arctic Refuge on the North Slope of Alaska to the National Key Deer Refuge in Florida, the diversity of land in the National Wildlife Refuge (NWR) System is staggering.

Yet of all our public lands, the National Wildlife Refuge System is the least well known and does not have an established voting constituency like that of the Parks System. In part this is because of its "wildlife first" mission, which addresses the needs of wildlife species before those of people. That notwithstanding, wildlife refuges also offer remarkable opportunities for people to experience and learn about wildlife—and to have fun doing so!

The Refuge System was launched in 1903 when President Theodore Roosevelt discovered that snowy egrets and other birds were being hunted to the brink of extinction for plumes to decorate ladies' hats. He asked a colleague if there were any laws preventing the president from making a federal bird reservation out of an island in Florida's Indian River. Learning there was not, Roosevelt responded, "Very well, then I so declare it." Thus Pelican Island became the nation's first plot of land to be set aside for the protection of wildlife. Roosevelt went on to create another 50 refuges, and today there are more than 500 refuges encompassing almost 93 million acres, managed by the U.S. Fish & Wildlife Service.

The Refuge System provides critical habitat for literally thousands of mammals, birds, amphibians and reptiles, and countless varieties of plants and flowers. More than 55 refuges have been created specifically to save endangered species. Approximately 20 percent of all threatened and endangered species in the United States rely on these vital places for their survival. As a protector of our country's natural diversity, the System is unparalleled.

Setting NWR boundaries is determined, as often as possible, by the needs of species that depend on the protected lands. Conservation biology, the science that studies ecosystems as a whole, teaches us that wildlife areas must be linked by habitat "corridors" or run the risk of becoming biological islands. The resulting inability of species to transfer their genes over a wide area leaves them vulnerable to disease and natural disasters. For example, the Florida panther that lives in Big Cypress Swamp suffers from a skin fungus, a consequence, scientists believe, of inbreeding. Today's refuge managers are acutely aware of this precarious situation afflicting many species and have made protection of the System's biodiversity an important goal.

Clearly, the job of the refuge manager is not an easy one. Chronic underfunding of the System by the federal government has resulted in refuges operating with less money per employee and per acre than any other federal land-management agency. Recent efforts by some in Congress to address this shortfall have begun to show results, but the System's continued vulnerability to special interests has resulted in attempts to open refuges to oil drilling, road building in refuge wilderness areas, and military exercises.

The managers of the System have played a crucial role in responding to the limited resources available. They have created a network of volunteers who contribute tens of thousands of hours to help offset the lack of direct financing for the Refuge System. Groups like refuge "friends" and Audubon Refuge Keepers have answered the call for local citizen involvement on many refuges across the country.

I hope Americans like yourself who visit our national wildlife refuges will come away convinced of their importance, not only to wildlife but also to people. I further hope you will make your views known to Congress, becoming the voice and voting constituency the Refuge System so desperately needs.

—*Theodore Roosevelt IV*

Preface

Thank you for adding the *Audubon Guide to the National Wildlife Refuge System* to your travel library. I hope you will find this nine-volume series an indispensable guide to finding your way around the refuge system, as well as a valuable educational tool for learning more about the vital role wildlife refuges play in protecting our country's natural heritage.

It was nearly 100 years ago that Frank Chapman, an influential ornithologist, naturalist, publisher and noted Audubon member, approached President Theodore Roosevelt (as recounted by Theodore Roosevelt IV in his foreword), eventually helping to persuade him to set aside more than 50 valuable parcels of land for the protection of wildlife.

Because of limited funding available to support these new wildlife sanctuaries, Audubon stepped up and paid for wardens who diligently looked after them. And so began a century of collaboration between Audubon and the National Wildlife Refuge System. Today, Audubon chapter members can be found across the country assisting refuges with a range of projects, from viewing tower construction to bird banding.

Most recently, National Audubon renewed its commitment to the Refuge System by launching a nationwide campaign to build support for refuges locally and nationally. Audubon's Wildlife Refuge Campaign is promoting the Refuge System through on-the-ground programs such as Audubon Refuge Keepers (ARK), which builds local support groups for refuges, and Earth Stewards, a collaboration with the U.S. Fish and Wildlife Service and the National Fish and Wildlife Foundation, which uses refuges and other important bird habitats as outdoor classrooms. In addition, we are countering legislative threats to refuges in Washington, D.C., while supporting increased federal funding for this, the least funded of all federal land systems.

By teaching more people about the important role refuges play in conserving our nation's diversity of species—be they birds, mammals, amphibians, reptiles, or plants—we have an opportunity to protect for future generations our only federal lands system set aside first and foremost for wildlife conservation.

As a nation, we are at a critical juncture—do we continue to sacrifice wetlands, forests, deserts, and coastal habitat for short-term profit, or do we accept that the survival of our species is closely linked to the survival of others? The National Wildlife Refuge System is a cornerstone of America's conservation efforts. If we are to leave a lasting legacy and, indeed, ensure our future, then we must build on President Theodore Roosevelt's greatest legacy. I invite you to join us!

—John Flicker, President, National Audubon Society

Introduction
to the National Wildlife Refuge System

He spent entire days on horseback, traversing the landscape of domed and crumbling hills, steep forested coulees, with undulating tables of prairie above. The soft wraparound light of sunset displayed every strange contour of the Badlands and lit the colors in each desiccated layer of rock—yellow, ochre, beige, gold.

Theodore Roosevelt was an easterner. As some well-heeled easterners were wont to do, he traveled west in 1883 to play cowboy, and for the next eight years he returned as often as possible. He bought a cattle ranch, carried a rifle and a six-gun, rode a horse. North Dakota was still Dakota Territory then, but the Plains bison were about gone, down to a scattering of wild herds.

The nation faced a new and uneasy awareness of limits during Roosevelt's North Dakota years. Between 1776 and 1850, the American population had increased from 1.5 million to more than 23 million. National borders were fixed and rail and telegraph lines linked the coasts, but Manifest Destiny had a price. The ongoing plunder of wildlife threatened species such as the brown pelican and the great egret; the near-total extermination of 60 million bison loomed as a lesson many wished to avoid repeating.

Despite the damage done, the powerful landscapes of the New World had shaped the outlooks of many new Americans. From Colonial-era botanist John Bartram to 19th-century artists George Catlin and John James Audubon, naturalists and individuals of conscience explored the question of what constituted a proper human response to nature. Two figures especially, Henry David Thoreau and John Muir, created the language and ideas that would confront enduring Old World notions of nature as an oppositional, malevolent force to be harnessed and exploited. The creation in 1872 of Yellowstone as the world's first national park indicated that some Americans, including a few political leaders, were listening to what Thoreau, Muir, and these others had to say.

Roosevelt, along with his friend George Bird Grinnell, drew upon these and other writings, as well as their own richly varied experiences with nature, to take the unprecedented step of making protection of nature a social and political cause. Of his time in the Badlands, Roosevelt remarked "the romance of my life began here," and "I never would have been president if it had not been for my experiences in North Dakota." As a hunter, angler, and naturalist, Roosevelt grasped the importance of nature for human life. Though he had studied natural history as an undergraduate at Harvard, believing it would be his life's work, Roosevelt owned a passion for reform and had the will—perhaps a need—to be effective. Rather than pursuing a career as a naturalist, he went into politics. His friend George

Barren-ground caribou

New England Region
Middle Atlantic Region
Southeast Region
Northern Midwest Region
South Central Region
Southwest Region
Rocky Mountains Region
Alaska and Pacific Northwest Region
California and Hawaii Region

Migratory Flyway

G r e a t   L a k e s

Minnesota

Michigan

Wisconsin

New Hampshire
Vermont
Massachusetts

Maine

New
York

Iowa

Illinois

Indiana

Ohio

Pennsylvania

Rhode
Island
Connecticut

New Jersey
Delaware
Maryland

Missouri

Kentucky

West
Virginia

Virginia

North
Carolina

Tennessee

Arkansas

Mississippi

Alabama

Georgia

South
Carolina

Atlantic
Ocean

Louisiana

Florida

Puerto
Rico

Gulf of Mexico

Bird Grinnell, publisher of the widely read magazine *Forest and Stream,* championed all manner of environmental protection and in 1886 founded the Audubon Society to combat the slaughter of birds for the millinery trade. Fifteen years later, TR would find himself with an even greater opportunity. In1901, when he inherited the presidency following the assassination of William McKinley, Roosevelt declared conservation a matter of federal policy.

Roosevelt backed up his words with an almost dizzying series of conservation victories. He established in 1903 a federal bird reservation on Pelican Island, Florida, as a haven for egrets, herons, and other birds sought by plume hunters. In eight years, Roosevelt authorized 150 million acres in the lower 48 states and another 85 million in Alaska to be set aside from logging under the Forest Reserve Act of 1891, compared to a total of 45 million under the three prior presidents. To these protected lands he added five national parks and 17 national monuments. The NWR system, though, is arguably TR's greatest legacy. Often using executive order to circumvent Congress, Roosevelt established 51 wildlife refuges.

The earliest federal wildlife refuges functioned as sanctuaries and little else. Visitors were rare and recreation was prohibited. Between 1905 and 1912 the first refuges for big-game species were established—Wichita Mountains in Oklahoma,

Atlantic puffins, Petit Manan NWR, Maine

the National Bison Range in Montana, and National Elk Refuge in Jackson, Wyoming. In 1924, the first refuge to include native fish was created; a corridor some 200 miles long, the Upper Mississippi National Wildlife and Fish Refuge spanned the states of Minnesota, Wisconsin, Illinois, and Iowa.

Still, the 1920s were dark years for America's wildlife. The effects of unregulated hunting, along with poor enforcement of existing laws, had decimated once-abundant species. Extinction was feared for the wood duck. Wild turkey had become scarce outside a few southern states. Pronghorn antelope, which today number perhaps a million across the West, were estimated at 25,000 or fewer. The trumpeter swan, canvasback duck, even the prolific and adaptable white-tailed deer, were scarce or extirpated across much of their historic ranges.

The Depression and Dust-bowl years, combined with the leadership of President Franklin Delano Roosevelt, gave American conservation—and the refuge system in particular—a hefty forward push. As wetlands vanished and fertile prairie soils blew away, FDR's Civilian Conservation Corps (CCC) dispatched thousands of unemployed young men to camps that stretched from Georgia to California. On the sites of many present-day refuges, they built dikes and other

Saguaro cactus and ocotillo along Charlie Bell 4WD trail, Cabeza Prieta NWR, Arizona

water-control structures, planted shelterbelts and grasses. Comprised largely of men from urban areas, the experience of nature was no doubt a powerful rediscovery of place and history for the CCC generation. The value of public lands as a haven for people, along with wildlife, was on the rise.

In 1934, Jay Norwood "Ding" Darling was instrumental in developing the federal "Duck Stamp," a kind of war bond for wetlands; hunters were required to purchase it, and anyone else who wished to support the cause of habitat acquisition could, too. Coupled with the Resettlement Act of 1935, in which the federal government bought out or condemned private land deemed unsuitable for agriculture, several million acres of homesteaded or settled lands reverted to federal ownership to become parks, national grasslands, and wildlife refuges. The Chief of the U.S. Biological Survey's Wildlife Refuge Program, J. Clark Salyer, set out on a cross-country mission to identify prime wetlands. Salyer's work added 600,000 acres to the refuge system, including Red Rock Lakes in Montana, home to a small surviving flock of trumpeter swans.

The environmental ruin of the Dust bowl also set in motion an era of government initiatives to engineer solutions to such natural events as floods, drought, and the watering of crops. Under FDR, huge regional entities such as the Tennessee Valley Authority grew, and the nation's mightiest rivers—the Columbia, Colorado, and later, the Missouri—were harnessed by dams. In the wake of these and other federal works projects, a new concept called "mitigation" appeared: If a proposed dam or highway caused the destruction of a certain number of acres of wetlands or other habitat, some amount of land nearby would be ceded to conservation in return. A good many of today's refuges were the progeny of mitigation. The federal government, like the society it represents, was on its way to becoming complex enough that the objectives of one arm could be at odds with those of another.

Citizen activism, so integral to the rise of the Audubon Society and other groups, was a driving force in the refuge system as well. Residents of rural Georgia applied relentless pressure on legislators to protect the Okefenokee Swamp. Many other refuges—San Francisco Bay, Sanibel Island, Minnesota Valley, New Jersey's Great Swamp—came about through the efforts of people with a vision of conservation close to home.

More than any other federal conservation program, refuge lands became places where a wide variety of management techniques could be tested and refined. Generally, the National Park system followed the "hands off" approach of Muir and Thoreau while the U.S. Forest Service and Bureau of Land Management, in theory, emphasized a utilitarian, "sustainable yield" value; in practice, powerful economic interests backed by often ruthless politics left watersheds, forests, and grasslands badly degraded, with far-reaching consequences for fish and wildlife. The refuge system was not immune to private enterprise—between 1939 and 1945, refuge lands were declared fair game for oil drilling, natural-gas exploration, and even for bombing practice by the U.S. Air Force—but the negative impacts have seldom reached the levels of other federal areas.

Visitor use at refuges tripled in the 1950s, rose steadily through the 1960s, and by the 1970s nearly tripled again. The 1962 Refuge Recreation Act established guidelines for recreational use where activities such as hiking, photography, boating, and camping did not interfere with conservation. With visitors came opportunities to educate, and now nature trails and auto tours, in addition to beauty, offered messages about habitats and management techniques. Public awareness of wilderness, "a place where man is only a visitor," in the words of long-time advocate Robert Marshall of the U.S. Forest Service, gained increasing social and political attention. In 1964, Congress passed the Wilderness Act, establishing guidelines for designating a host of federally owned lands as off-limits to motorized vehicles, road building, and resource exploitation. A large number of refuge lands qualified—the sun-blasted desert of Arizona's Havasu refuge, the glorious tannin-stained waters and cypress forests of Georgia's Okefenokee Swamp, and the almost incomprehensible large 8-million-acre Arctic NWR in Alaska, home to vast herds of caribou, wolf packs, and bladelike mountain peaks, the largest contiguous piece of wilderness in the refuge system.

Sachuest Point NWR, Rhode Island

Nonetheless, this was also a time of horrendous air and water degradation, with the nation at its industrial zenith and agriculture cranked up to the level of "agribusiness." A wake-up call arrived in the form of vanishing bald eagles, peregrine falcons, and osprey. The insecticide DDT, developed in 1939 and used in World War II to eradicate disease-spreading insects, had been used throughout the nation ever since, with consequences unforeseen until the 1960s. Sprayed over wetlands, streams, and crop fields, DDT had entered watersheds and from there the food chain itself. It accumulated in the bodies of fish and other aquatic life, and birds consuming fish took DDT into their systems, one effect was a calcium deficiency, resulting in eggs so fragile that female birds crushed them during incubation.

Partially submerged alligator, Anahuac NWR, Texas

Powerful government and industry leaders launched a vicious, all-out attack on the work of a marine scientist named Rachel Carson, whose book *Silent Spring*, published in 1962, warned of the global dangers associated with DDT and other biocides. For this she was labeled "not a real scientist" and "a hysterical woman." With eloquence and courage, though, Carson stood her ground. If wild species atop the food chain could be devastated, human life could be threatened, too. Americans were stunned, and demanded an immediate ban on DDT. Almost overnight, the "web of life" went from chalkboard hypothesis to reality.

Protecting imperiled species became a matter of national policy in 1973 when President Nixon signed into law the Endangered Species Act (ESA), setting guidelines by which the U.S. Fish & Wildlife Service would "list" plant and animal species as *threatened* or *endangered* and would develop a program for their recovery. Some 56 refuges, such as Ash Meadows in Nevada and Florida's Crystal River, home of the manatee, were established specifically for the protection of endangered species. Iowa's tiny Driftless Prairie refuge exists to protect the rare, beautifully colored pleistocene land snail and a wildflower, the northern monkshood. Sometimes unwieldy, forever politicized, the ESA stands as a monumental achievement. Its successes include the American alligator, bald eagle, and gray wolf. The whooping crane would almost surely be extinct today without the twin supports of ESA and the refuge system. The black-footed ferret, among the rarest mammals on earth, is today being reintroduced on a few western refuges. In 1998, nearly one-fourth of all threatened and endangered species populations find sanctuary on refuge lands.

More legislation followed. The passage of the Alaska National Interest Lands Conservation Act in 1980 added more than 50 million acres to the refuge system in Alaska.

The 1980s and '90s have brought no end of conservation challenges, faced by an increasingly diverse association of organizations and strategies. Partnerships now link the refuge system with nonprofit groups, from Ducks Unlimited and The Nature Conservancy to international efforts such as Partners in Flight, a program to monitor the decline of, and to secure habitat for, neotropical songbirds. These cooperative efforts have resulted in habitat acquisition and restoration, research, and many new refuges. Partnerships with private landowners who voluntarily offer marginally useful lands for restoration—with a sponsoring conservation group cost-sharing the project—have revived many thousands of acres of grasslands, wetlands, and riparian corridors.

Citizen activism is alive and well as we enter the new millennium. Protecting and promoting the growth of the NWR system is a primary campaign of the National Audubon Society, which, by the year 2000, will have grown to a membership of around 550,000. NAS itself also manages about 100 sanctuaries and nature centers across the country, with a range of opportunities for environmental education. The National Wildlife Refuge Association, a volunteer network,

Coyote on the winter range

keeps members informed of refuge events, environmental issues, and legislative developments and helps to maintain a refuge volunteer workforce. In 1998, a remarkable 20 percent of all labor performed on the nation's refuges was carried out by volunteers, a contribution worth an estimated $14 million.

A national wildlife refuge today has many facets. Nature is ascendant and thriving, often to a shocking degree when compared with adjacent lands. Each site has its own story: a prehistory, a recent past, a present—a story of place, involving people, nature, and stewardship, sometimes displayed in Visitor Center or Headquarters exhibits, always written into the landscape. Invariably a refuge belongs to a community as well, involving area residents who visit, volunteers who log hundreds of hours, and a refuge staff who are knowledgeable and typically friendly, even outgoing, especially if the refuge is far-flung. In this respect most every refuge is a portal to local culture, be it Native American, cows and crops, or big city. There may be no better example of democracy in action than a national wildlife refuge. The worm-dunker fishes while a mountain biker pedals past. In spring, birders scan marshes and grasslands that in the fall will be walked by hunters. Compromise is the guiding principle.

What is the future of the NWR system? In Prairie City, Iowa, the Neal Smith NWR represents a significant departure from the time-honored model. Established in 1991, the site had almost nothing to "preserve." It was old farmland with scattered remnants of tallgrass prairie and degraded oak savanna. What is happening at Neal Smith, in ecological terms, has never been attempted on such a scale: the reconstruction, essentially from scratch, of a self-sustaining 8,000-acre native biome, complete with bison and elk, greater prairie chickens, and a palette of wildflowers and grasses that astonish and delight.

What is happening in human terms is equally profound. Teams of area residents, called "seed seekers," explore cemeteries, roadside ditches, and long-ignored patches of ground. Here and there they find seeds of memory, grasses and wildflowers from the ancient prairie, and harvest them; the seeds are catalogued and planted on the refuge. The expanding prairie at Neal Smith is at once new and very old. It is reshaping thousands of Iowans' sense of place, connecting them to what was, eliciting wonder for what could be. And the lessons here transcend biology. In discovering rare plants, species found only in the immediate area, people discover an identity beyond job titles and net worth. The often grueling labor of cutting brush, pulling nonnative plants, and tilling ground evokes the determined optimism of Theodore and Franklin Roosevelt and of the CCC.

As the nation runs out of wild places worthy of preservation, might large-scale restoration of damaged or abandoned lands become the next era of American conservation? There are ample social and economic justifications. The ecological justifications are endless, for, as the history of conservation and ecology has revealed, nature and humanity cannot go their separate ways. The possibilities, if not endless, remain rich for the years ahead.

—*John Grassy*

How to use this book

Local conditions and regulations on national wildlife refuges vary considerably. We provide detailed, site-specific information useful for a good refuge visit, and we note the broad consistencies throughout the NWR system (facility set-up and management, what visitors may or may not do, etc.). Contact the refuge before arriving or stop by the Visitor Center when you get there. F&W wildlife refuge managers are ready to provide friendly, savvy advice about species and habitats, plus auto, hiking, biking, or water routes that are open and passable, and public programs (such as guided walks) you may want to join.

AUDUBON GUIDES TO THE NATIONAL WILDLIFE REFUGES

This is one of nine regional volumes in a series covering the entire NWR system. **Visitable refuges**—over 300 of them—constitute about three-fifths of the NWR system. **Nonvisitable refuges** may be small (without visitor facilities), fragile (set up to protect an endangered species or threatened habitat), or new and undeveloped.

Among visitable refuges, some are more important and better developed than others. In creating this series, we have categorized refuges as A, B, or C level, with the A-level refuges getting the most attention. You will easily recognize the difference. C-level refuges, for instance, do not carry a map.

Rankings can be debated; we know that. We considered visitation statistics, accessibility, programming, facilities, and the richness of the refuges' habitats and animal life. Some refuges ranked as C-level now may develop further over time.

Many bigger NWRs have either "satellites" (with their own refuge names) separate "units" within the primary refuge or other, less significant NWRs nearby. All of these, at times, were deemed worthy of a brief mention.

ORGANIZATION OF THE BOOK

■ **REGIONAL OVERVIEW** This regional introduction is intended to give readers the big picture, touching on broad patterns in landscape formation, interconnections among plant communities, and diversity of animals. We situate NWRs in the natural world of the larger bio-region to which they belong, showing why these federally protected properties stand out as wild places worth preserving amid encroaching civilization.

We also note some wildlife management issues that will surely color the debate around campfires and

ABOUT THE U.S. FISH & WILDLIFE SERVICE Under the Department of the Interior, the U.S. Fish & Wildlife Service is the principal federal agency responsible for conserving and protecting wildlife and plants and their habitats for the benefit of the American people. The Service manages the 93-million-acre NWR system, comprised of more than 500 national wildlife refuges, thousands of small wetlands, and other special management areas. It also operates 66 national fish hatcheries, 64 U.S. Fish & Wildlife Management Assistance offices, and 78 ecological services field stations. The agency enforces federal wildlife laws, administers the Endangered Species Act, manages migratory bird populations, restores nationally significant fisheries, conserves and restores wildlife habitats such as wetlands, and helps foreign governments with their conservation efforts. It also oversees the federal-aid program that distributes hundreds of millions of dollars in excise taxes on fishing and hunting equipment to state wildlife agencies.

congressional conference tables in years ahead, while paying recognition to the NWR supporters and managers who helped make the present refuge system a reality.

■ **THE REFUGES** The refuge section of the book is organized alphabetically by state and then, within each state, by refuge name.

There are some clusters, groups, or complexes of neighboring refuges administered by one primary refuge. Some refuge complexes are alphabetized here by the name of their primary refuge, with the other refuges in the group following immediately thereafter.

■ **APPENDIX**

Nonvisitable National Wildlife Refuges: NWR properties that meet the needs of wildlife but are off-limits to all but field biologists.

Federal Recreation Fees: An overview of fees and fee passes.

Volunteer Activities: How you can lend a hand to help your local refuge or get involved in supporting the entire NWR system.

U.S. Fish & Wildlife General Information: The seven regional head-quarters of the U.S. Fish & Wildlife Service through which the National Wildlife Refuge System is administered.

National Audubon Society Wildlife Sanctuaries: A listing of the 24 National Audubon Society wildlife sanctuaries, dispersed across the U.S., which are open to the public.

Bibliography & Resources: Natural-history titles both on the region generally and its NWRs, along with a few books of inspiration about exploring the natural world.

Glossary: A listing of specialized terms (not defined in the text) tailored to this region.

Index

National Audubon Society Mission Statement

PRESENTATION OF INFORMATION: A-LEVEL REFUGE

■ **INTRODUCTION** This section attempts to evoke the essence of the place, The writer sketches the sounds or sights you might experience on the refuge, such as sandhill cranes taking off, en masse, from the marsh, filling the air with the roar of thousands of beating wings. That's a defining event for a particular refuge and a great reason to go out and see it.

■ **MAP** Some refuges are just a few acres; several, like the Alaskan behemoths, are bigger than several eastern states. The scale of the maps in this series can vary. We recommend that you also ask refuges for their detailed local maps.

■ **HISTORY** This outlines how the property came into the NWR system and what its uses were in the past.

■ **GETTING THERE** General location; seasons and hours of operation; fees, if any (see federal recreation fees in Appendix); address, telephone. Smaller or remote refuges may have their headquarters off-site. We identify highways as follows: TX14 = Texas state highway # 14; US 23 = a federal highway; I-85 = Interstate 85.

Note: Many NWRs have their own web pages at the F&W web site, http://www.fws.gov/. Some can be contacted by fax or e-mail, and if we do not provide that information here, you may find it at the F&W web site.

■ **TOURING** The **Visitor Center**, if there is one, is the place to start your tour. Some have wildlife exhibits, videos, and bookstores; others may be only a kiosk. Let someone know your itinerary before heading out on a long trail or into the backcountry, and then go explore.

Most refuges have roads open to the public; many offer a wildlife **auto tour,** with wildlife information signs posted en route or a brochure or audiocassette to guide you. Your car serves as a bird blind if you park and remain quiet. Some refuge roads require 4-wheel-drive or a high-chassis vehicle. Some roads are closed seasonally to protect habitats during nesting seasons or after heavy rain or snow.

Touring also covers **walking and hiking** (see more trail details under ACTIVITIES) and **biking.** Many refuge roads are rough; mountain or hybrid bikes are more appropriate than road bikes. When water is navigable, we note what kinds of **boats** may be used and where there are boat launches.

■ **WHAT TO SEE**

Landscape and climate: This section covers geology, topography, and climate: primal forces and raw materials that shaped the habitats that lured species to the refuge. It also includes weather information for visitors.

Plant life: This is a sampling of noteworthy plants on the refuge, usually sorted by habitat, using standard botanical nomenclature. Green plants bordering watery places are in "Riparian Zones"; dwarfed trees, shrubs, and flowers on windswept mountaintops are in the "Alpine Forest"; and so forth.

Wildflowers abound, and you may want to see them in bloom. We give advice about timing your visit, but ask the refuge for more. If botany and habitat relationships are new to you, you can soon learn to read the landscape as a set of interrelated communities. Take a guided nature walk to begin.

(Note: In two volumes, "Plants" is called "Habitats and Plant Communities.")

Animal life: The national map on pages 4 and 5 shows the major North American "flyways." Many NWRs cluster in watery territory underneath the birds' aerial superhighways. There are many birds in this book, worth seeing simply for their beauty. But ponder, too, what birds eat (fish, insects, aquatic plants), or how one species (the mouse) attracts another (the fox), and so on up the food chain, and you'll soon understand the rich interdependence on display in many refuges.

Animals use camouflage and stealth for protection; many are nocturnal. You may want to come out early or late to increase your chances of spotting them. Refuge managers can offer advice on sighting or tracking animals.

Grizzly bears, venomous snakes, alligators, and crocodiles can indeed be dangerous. Newcomers to these animals' habitats should speak with refuge staff about precautions before proceeding.

■ **ACTIVITIES** Some refuges function not only as wildlife preserves but also as recreation parks. Visit a beach, take a bike ride, and camp overnight, or devote your time to serious wildlife observation.

Camping and swimming: If not permissible on the refuge, there may be federal or state campgrounds nearby; we mention some of them. Planning an NWR camping trip should start with a call to refuge headquarters.

Wildlife observation: This subsection touches on strategies for finding species most people want to see. Crowds do not mix well with certain species; you

---

A NOTE ON HUNTING AND FISHING Opinions on hunting and fishing on federally owned wildlife preserves range from "Let's have none of it" to "We need it as part of the refuge management plan." The F&W Service follows the latter approach, with about 290 hunting programs and 260 fishing programs. If you have strong opinions on this topic, talk with refuge managers to gain some insight into F&W's rationale. You can also write to your representative or your senators in Washington.

For most refuges, we summarize the highlights of the hunting and fishing options. You must first have required state and local licenses for hunting or fishing. Then you must check with refuge headquarters about special restrictions that may apply on the refuge; refuge bag limits, for example, or duration of season may be different from regulations elsewhere in the same state.

Hunting and fishing options change from year to year on many refuges, based on the size of the herd or of the flock of migrating birds. These changes may reflect local weather (a hard winter trims the herd) or disease, or factors in distant habitats where animals summer or winter. We suggest what the options usually are on a given refuge (e.g., some birds, some mammals, fish, but not all etc..). It's the responsibility of those who wish to hunt and fish to confirm current information with refuge headquarters and to abide by current rules.

COMMON SENSE, WORTH REPEATING

Leave no trace Every visitor deserves a chance to see the refuge in its pristine state. We all share the responsibility to minimize our impact on the landscape. "Take only pictures and leave only footprints," and even there you'll want to avoid trampling plant life by staying on established trails. Pack out whatever you pack in. Ask refuge managers for guidance on low-impact hiking and camping.

Respect private property Many refuges consist of noncontiguous parcels of land, with private properties abutting refuge lands. Respect all Private Property and No Trespassing signs, especially in areas where native peoples live within refuge territory and hunt or fish on their own land.

Water Protect the water supply. Don't wash dishes or dispose of human waste within 200 ft. of any water. Treat all water for drinking with iodine tablets, backpacker's water filter, or boiling. Clear water you think is OK may be contaminated upstream by wildlife you cannot see.

may need to go away from established observation platforms to have success. Learn a bit about an animal's habits, where it hunts or sleeps, what time of day it moves about. Adjust your expectations to match the creature's behavior, and your chances of success will improve.

Photography: This section outlines good places or times to see certain species. If you have a zoom lens, use it. Sit still, be quiet, and hide yourself. Don't approach the wildlife; let it approach you. Never feed animals or pick growing plants

Hikes and walks: Here we list specific outings, with mileages and trailhead locations. Smooth trails and boardwalks, suitable for people with disabilities, are noted. On bigger refuges, there may be many trails. Ask for a local map. If you go bushwacking, first make sure this is permissible. Always carry a map and compass.

Seasonal events: National Wildlife Refuge Week, in October, is widely celebrated, with guided walks, lectures, demonstrations, and activities of special interest to children. Call your local refuge for particulars. At other times of the year there are fishing derbies, festivals celebrating the return of migrating birds, and other events linked to the natural world. Increasingly, refuges post event schedules on their web pages.

Publications: Many NWR brochures are free, such as bird and wildflower checklists. Some refuges have pamphlets and books for sale, describing local habitats and species.

Note: The categories of information above appear in A and B refuges in this book; on C-level refuges, options are fewer, and some of these headings may not appear.

—*David Emblidge*

Northern Midwest
A Regional Overview

In the great expanse of time that is earth's history, it may be said that the glaciers departed last night. It's early morning now in the Northern Midwest; the sun is up, the dew sparkling on prairie grasses and wildflowers. Most everywhere, it seems, there is water: five great lakes, each sprawling beyond the horizon; three great rivers, including the largest in the nation; ponds, wetlands, and lakes in every shape and size—kettle lakes, pothole lakes, tens of thousands of lakes.

The glaciers were generous. The natural world of the Northern Midwest—which in this guide includes the states of Ohio, Illinois, Michigan, Indiana, Iowa, Minnesota, Nebraska, and North and South Dakota—plays itself out over a tilled and chiseled terrain, with results as diverse as rolling plains and deeply shadowed forests of maple, oak, cedar and fir. Water, however, is seldom far away.

Of the 103 national wildlife refuges in the region, 43 are profiled here; most of the others are closed to the public to protect fragile habitats. The 103 refuges encompass well over a half-million acres, allowing naturalists and recreationists to experience a great many of the natural wonders here. On refuges in Iowa and Nebraska, bison graze the tallgrass and mixed-grass prairies; North Dakota which features the most refuges (64) of any state in the United States, is the nation's most prolific waterfowl breeding ground, where in spring and fall flocks of ducks and geese darken the skies. In the tangled spruce-fir forests of Minnesota and Michigan's Upper Peninsula, gray wolves stalk moose and deer. Bounded by four states in the region, the Mississippi River passes through a series of refuge lands, preserving lush bottomland forests, including rare stands of cypress and tupelo, the oldest living plants in the eastern United States.

Much has changed since presettlement days, and the pressures of growth and development continue; but a visit to any of the refuges described in this book will reveal that a good deal of our natural heritage endures, certainly enough to make the nation's public lands, including those in the national wildlife refuge system, the envy of the world.

ANCIENT PAST AND NATIVE PEOPLES

Evidence of the old people, the ancestors of America's Indian tribes, suggests a long and prosperous history in the Northern Midwest. At Lake Ilo National Wildlife Refuge, in North Dakota, excavation continues at a site first occupied 10,500 years ago. In areas of Wisconsin, people of the Old Copper Culture forged socketed spearheads; at 5,000 to 7,000 years old, they are among the earliest examples of metal-working in the world. Agrarian societies flourished throughout the Ohio and Upper Mississippi river valleys 2,000 years ago. Their sprawling burial mounds, in the shapes of animals and birds, may be seen today in Iowa and Ohio.

The descendants of ancient civilizations bear familiar names: the Cree, Miami, Ottawa, Ojibwa, Fox, Illinois, Iowa, Sioux, Pawnee, Hidatsa. They lived in villages and towns amidst the forests

Prairie white-fringed orchid

NORTHERN MIDWEST

ILLINOIS
1 Brussels District, Mark Twain NWR
2 Chatauqua NWR
3 Crab Orchard NWR
4 Cypress Creek NWR

INDIANA
5 Muscatatuck NWR

IOWA
6 DeSoto Bend NWR
7 Neal Smith NWR
8 Union Slough NWR

MICHIGAN
9 Kirtland's Warbler NWR
10 Seney NWR
11 Shiawassee NWR

MINNESOTA
12 Agassiz NWR
13 Big Stone NWR
14 Hamden Slough NWR
15 Minnesota Valley NWR
16 Rice Lake NWR
17 Sherburne NWR
18 Tamarac NWR
19 Upper Mississippi NW & FR

NEBRASKA
20 Crescent Lake NWR
21 Fort Niobrara NWR

NORTH DAKOTA
22 Arrowwood NWR
23 Audubon NWR
24 Des Lacs NWR
25 J. Clark Salyer NWR
26 Lake Ilo NWR
27 Long Lake NWR
28 Lostwood NWR
29 Sully's Hill NWR
30 Tewaukon NWR
31 Upper Souris NWR

OHIO
32 Ottawa NWR

Lake Superior

Marquette ● **10**

Marquette ●

Michigan

Lake Huron

Green Bay ●

38

con s in

37

Milwaukee ●

dison ★

ockford ●

Lake Michigan

Grand Rapids ●

Lansing ●

Detroit ●

Lake Erie

Cleveland ●

9

11 ★

32

avenport

Chicago ●

Gary ●

Fort Wayne ●

Ohio

Columbus ★

Illinois

2

Springfield ★

1

Indiana

Indianapolis ★

5

Cincinnati ●

3

4

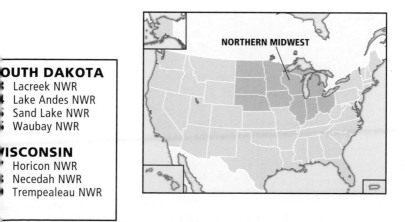

NORTHERN MIDWEST

OUTH DAKOTA
Lacreek NWR
Lake Andes NWR
Sand Lake NWR
Waubay NWR

ISCONSIN
Horicon NWR
Necedah NWR
Trempealeau NWR

of Michigan and Wisconsin, along the Missouri River in the Dakotas. In Ohio and Illinois they grew corn and other crops, harvested wild rice in what is now Minnesota, and hunted bison and elk on the prairies that would later become Iowa and Nebraska.

The Native Americans—their names, beliefs, preserved tools, and tipi rings—are an enduring presence at a great many of the region's wildlife refuges, where today's visitors can walk where others walked long before.

Prairie pothole country, Lostwood NWR, North Dakota

GEOLOGY

The Northern Midwest was inundated repeatedly over millions of years by a warm saltwater ocean, which came and left via the Gulf of Mexico. These periods were accompanied by a warm, humid climate; horsetail, bracken fern, and club moss—species still with us today—did well back then, the ferns reaching 40 feet in height, club mosses sprouting to 125 feet. Reminders of this ancient time are scattered throughout the region: Salt deposits 500 feet thick lie beneath the city of Detroit; the world's largest exposed coral reef is found at the Falls of the Ohio River; outcrops of sedimentary rock—the old sea floor—rise up here and there around the Great Lakes.

Today's landscape began to emerge about 60 million years ago, as the reign of the dinosaurs ended and the Rocky Mountains commenced their skyward movement. Mammals took center stage in the evolutionary drama. The Badlands region of South Dakota was once a richly forested plain, with shallow, meandering streams and lakes, inhabited by rhinos and sheeplike creatures called oreodonts. The birth of the Rockies would gradually bury this world beneath 2,000 feet of sediment, transforming the Badlands into one of the world's richest prehistoric burial grounds.

The Northern Midwest felt the full brunt of the Ice Age and its army of glaciers as it began nearly one million years ago. As the climate grew cooler and wetter, great fields of ice built up in the area of Hudson Bay. The Laurentide sheet, one of the first ice fields, moved southward like wet cement into the Mississippi Valley, at its peak burying 5 million square miles.

The cycle continued, successions of glaciers advancing and retreating, for another million years. The northward-flowing Missouri River, its course blocked by ice and debris, forged a new route to the east. On today's Minnesota–North Dakota border, the Red River faced a similar barricade; its impounded waters formed Lake Agassiz, a body of water 700 miles long and 250 miles wide. The silt-rich bottom of Agassiz would later become the fertile plains of western Minnesota, much of South Dakota, and eastern North Dakota, an area known today as the central lowlands.

Before the glaciers came, the basins of today's Great Lakes were thought to be river valleys. When the ice receded, the region featured a new lake, Superior, the largest in the world; along with the others—Michigan, Huron, Erie, Ontario—it held 20 percent of the planet's freshwater. The ice advanced to central Illinois and Indiana and very nearly to the Ohio River. South of here, the rolling prairies, with their deep, loamy soil, remained undisturbed.

Every physiographic feature of the Northern Midwest today, from the soils and topography to the great variety of lakes and streams, is in one way or another the work of glaciers—the last of which, the Wisconsin Glacier, lingered until about 6,000 years ago. If the predictions of experts mean anything, the ice will return at some future date to scour the region again.

CLIMATE AND PLANT LIFE

In the westernmost reaches of the region, the Rocky Mountains take the lion's share of moisture from eastbound Pacific air and deliver to the plains of North Dakota, Nebraska, and South Dakota dry, limitless wind. Between the 98th and 100th meridians—a north-south line passing through the western edge of Iowa—the air regains moisture, courtesy of the Gulf of Mexico and the Great Lakes.

Height is a perfect benchmark for the effects of moisture. Nearest the Rockies is short-grass prairie, where a plant that grows only 3 inches is considered tall. A few hundred miles to the east, with a bit more precipitation, the mid- or mixed-

Wild purple iris

grass prairie takes over. At the north-south line described above, the luxuriant tallgrass prairie appears, a landscape of grasses 6 feet high and more than 200 species of wildflowers. Not until the prairies reach the Mississippi Valley do the first stands of deciduous forests become dominant.

The Great Lakes are a major climatic force, cooling more slowly than surrounding lands in winter, warming more gradually in spring. The result, for Cleveland, Chicago, Traverse City, and other places immediately adjacent to the big lakes, is prolific snowfall. Across the fertile plains of Ohio, southern Michigan, and Indiana and Illinois, summers are hot and humid with plentiful rain. Throughout the region, summers grow appreciably shorter north of the 45th parallel, with long, often brutal winters marked by incursions of arctic air.

The Northern Midwest, then, is really the place where East meets West. Prior to settlement, its western portion encompassed a swath of grasslands stretching unbroken from Canada to the Mexican Highlands. Farther east, along the southern tier of the Great Lakes, was a mixture of deciduous forests and tallgrass prairie savanna, a parklike landscape of open grasslands with stands of burr and blackjack oak. Moving north, into the upper portions of Michigan, Wisconsin, and Minnesota, the hardwoods gave way first to unbroken forests of white pine, and finally, approaching the Canada border, the North Woods, or boreal forest—spruce, fir, birch, and hemlock—stretching all the way east to New England.

The almost endless variations of landscape wrought by the glaciers, combined with the effects of climate, created far more diverse and localized mosaics of natural communities. The Great Lakes' signature biome is the sand dune and interdunal wetlands. Near Sioux City, Iowa, the Loess Hills are high cliffs and scarps of rock dust hammered out by the glaciers, deposited by wind, and colonized by tallgrass prairie. Western Minnesota is a crossroads of prairie, pine and oak-hickory forest, aspen-birch and spruce-fir woodlands. Even in the semiarid reaches of west-central North Dakota, deciduous trees, such as hickory, ash, and oak, survive in cooler cuts and river bottoms.

Bog habitat, Seney NWR, Michigan

If there is one defining feature of the Northern Midwest, it is freshwater. Across northern Wisconsin, Michigan, Minnesota, and North Dakota, glacial lakes are spattered like paint flung off a brush; their associates are the peat bogs, cedar swamps, sedge meadows, shrub swamps, and, at Horicon NWR in Wisconsin, the largest cattail marsh on earth. Ottawa NWR, in Ohio, preserves original tracts of the Black Woods Swamp that once encircled western Lake Erie. Broad, lazy rivers and prairie wetlands blanket eastern South Dakota. The Missouri, Ohio, and Mississippi rivers traverse the region, the Mississippi originating as a trickle out of Minnesota's Lake Atabasca, and downstream forging a labyrinth of sloughs, oxbows, and islands, nourishing a floodplain forest of ash, alder, American elm, and silver maple.

WILDLIFE

The Midwest's climates and natural communities blend both East and West. Consider again the north-south meridian running along western Iowa up through the Dakotas. West of this line, mammals, such as the mule deer, the pronghorn, and the bighorn sheep, appear. The bison and elk, long-ago inhabitants of places farther east, reached their highest densities west of the meridian. The black-tailed and white-tailed prairie dog appear. East of this line, the white-tailed deer has no competition. The prairie dog is replaced by its cousins: the gray and fox squirrels and, farther north, by the red squirrel and northern flying squirrel. The jackrabbit of the western grasslands is replaced by the eastern cottontail rabbit of forest edges and open meadows.

Black-tailed prairie dog

A number of more adaptable or opportunistic mammals are found throughout the region: the red fox, raccoon, striped skunk, and coyote, as well as water-associated species including the muskrat, mink, northern river otter, and beaver. The raccoon fares better in the East; the beaver requires shrubs or trees in close proximity to water. The mink favors the muskrat as prey, and the muskrat lives most everywhere. The coyote, as usual, is a wild card. Seen more frequently in the open western areas of the region, it would hardly be a surprise if coyotes were discovered thriving in suburban Chicago. The red fox and skunk, too, have no qualms about making do inside city limits. The river otter demands high-quality water, be it river or lake, and holds a dim view of civilization.

The avian world follows suit with its own East-West variations: you're not likely to see the bobwhite quail west of the meridian, for example, or the sharp-tailed grouse east of it. And there's both an eastern and a western meadowlark. But because water is the defining feature of the Northern Midwest, its signature bird

Common loon, Seney NWR, Michigan

community is waterfowl and other water-dependent species. The Dakotas comprise the southern reaches of "The Duck Factory," the name given to a vast plains breeding ground that stretches into Canada and accounts for a significant percentage of all North America's varied duck population, among them blue-winged, green-winged, and cinnamon teal, canvasback, ruddy duck, scaup, wigeon, redhead, ring-necked, and others. They arrive in spring, when melting snow and rain recharge wetlands and pothole lakes.

Along the Mississippi and Missouri rivers are nesting colonies of great blue herons and great egrets; across Minnesota, Wisconsin, and Michigan are Canada geese, grebes, loons, cormorants, and still more ducks. Terns, gulls, and shorebirds ply the prairie marshes and Great Lakes. During spring and fall migrations, skeins of snow geese, tundra swans, and white-fronted geese stop in on their way to and from arctic nesting grounds. The Great Lakes area receives migratory birds traveling both the Mississippi and Atlantic flyways; to the west, Minnesota, Iowa, Nebraska, and the Dakotas see migrants following the Mississippi and Central flyways.

The wildlife refuges of the region provide critical nesting, feeding, and resting habitats for birds of the waters. Depending on the season, visitors can watch parent birds leading their fuzzy babies along the edge of a marsh, or marvel at the sight and sound of waterfowl in flight—some quarter million in number, pushed south by a sharp autumn wind.

THEN AND NOW

Settlement and civilization altered the landscape of the Northern Midwest as completely as the glaciers, and in far less time.

Early settlers wore out their horses and ruined their plows breaking the deep sod of the tallgrass prairie, but break it they did, aided greatly by the polished steel breaking plow, hammered out in 1837 by an Illinois blacksmith named John Deere. From Ohio to Nebraska and north into the Dakotas and Minnesota, loamy prairie soils are today the most productive agricultural land on earth. Native tallgrass prairie is the rarest North American biome; of some 142 million acres of prairielands, perhaps 10 percent remains in scattered fragments, including parcels on several wildlife refuges.

The market-driven slaughter of the plains bison is well known. As farming and cattle grazing boomed, a host of other species declined: the greater and lesser prairie chickens, long-billed curlew, trumpeter swan, and whooping crane. The prairie dog was declared a threat to grassland health; shot, trapped, and poisoned, its decline spelled disaster for two more species, the swift fox and the black-footed ferret. Today the swift fox is extremely rare, the ferret is the rarest mammal on earth, and the black-tailed prairie dog has been recommended for endangered-species listing.

The expansive white pine forests of Michigan, Wisconsin, and Minnesota were felled in fewer than four decades. Second-growth forests of jack pine, aspen, and birch have steadily reclaimed these areas; nearly one hundred years old now, the northern forests have again become home for increasing numbers of gray wolves and a scattering of reintroduced elk, along with moose, black bear, and a large herd of white-tailed deer.

For 60 years the Great Lakes endured a host of air- and water-borne contaminants from the region's thriving industrial centers in Detroit, Gary, Chicago, Milwaukee, and Cleveland. During the late 1960s, the toxic Cuyahoga River ignited in flames, and Lake Erie was declared "dead." The aquatic life of the lakes has been further altered by wave upon wave of nonnative species—such as the alewife, the parasitic sea lamprey, introduced Pacific salmon, the zebra mussel,

American bittern

and European perch. In recent years, Lake Erie has been revived and features a thriving sport fishery, but all of the lakes remain scarred. Residents are warned of health hazards associated with eating Great Lakes fish, as persistent toxins such as PCBs remain embedded in the food chain, running their course.

In a wet spring, across the sea of agricultural land that is present-day South Dakota, something unusual happens. The water table lies only a few feet below the ground in these lowlands, and the added moisture of rain and snowmelt is enough to cause hundreds of small glacial ponds and pools to reappear. In a state where nearly 80 percent of all prairie wetlands have been drained and filled, it is a powerful image: waterfowl feeding and resting, recovering from migration, just as their ancestors did for thousands of years. It is clear proof that the wetlands will never be eradicated, no matter how much people try. Anxious farmers can only wait for them to vanish again before spring planting begins.

REFUGES AND THE CHANGING LANDSCAPE

It's possible to see birds, animals, flowers, and trees on all manner of lands, public or private; yet the difference between a landscape serving human needs and one maintained solely for its natural diversity is often dramatic, immediately apparent even to the untrained eye. There is more of everything, and more kinds of everything.

Prescribed burning

This is one of the experiences to be had in visiting a wildlife refuge: the contrast between adjacent lands and refuge holdings is hard to miss. The difference between the two makes it easy to see the challenge and labor intensity involved in conserving plant and animal species. The word "management" may have negative connotations for some outdoor enthusiasts, but as wildlife habitat and biological diversity are lost elsewhere, human intervention is necessary to mimic or maintain natural systems, which tend to break down as habitats become fragmented. Notes and descriptions of management practices, and occasionally management dilemmas, are included for several of the refuges in this region.

Along with protecting intact plant and animal communities, refuges also have a mission of enhancing or restoring communities that have broken down or, in some cases, all but vanished. One of this region's most ambitious projects involves the restoration of native tallgrass prairie. The Neal Smith refuge in Iowa, and several Minnesota refuges—Sherburne, Hamden Slough, and Big Stone, among others—have made prairie restoration a priority.

In North Dakota, the Chase Lake Prairie Project (a Wildlife Management District) forges partnerships with landowners to develop farming and grazing methods compatible with the life-style of ground-nesting shorebirds and songbirds; the project encompasses a staggering 5.5 million acres in 11 counties, most of it privately owned.

Restoration of a Midwest trumpeter swan population is another regional effort. Lacreek NWR, in South Dakota, was the region's first reintroduction site in the 1960s; Indiana's Muscatatuck refuge began its reintroduction effort in 1998. As of this writing, several refuges in Minnesota were exploring the possibilities for trumpeter swans as well.

The devastating 1994 flood of the Mississippi and lower Missouri rivers prompted dialogue about the balance of human and natural communities in floodplain areas. DeSoto NWR, in Iowa, is overseeing the birth of a new refuge, Boyer Chute, on the Mississippi, with the goal of restoring bottomland hardwood forest in an area wiped clean by the flood.

GETTING UNDER WAY

The refuges in this book offer unparalleled opportunities for recreation, solitude, and natural splendor. There are marvelous rivers for canoeists, hiking trails and undeveloped footpaths for hikers, and highly accessible auto-tour routes where abundant wildlife and beautiful scenery are close at hand. A few refuges include designated Federal Wilderness Areas, where cross-country travel at certain times of year can lead to unexpected discoveries.

At a number of sites, visitors can participate in tours and educational programs. It's often the case that a refuge becomes more than a haven for wildlife— it becomes the focal point for a community, a place for people to meet and enjoy the outdoors or to volunteer their time on programs or conservation projects.

National wildlife refuge employees are downright passionate about the wildlife and ecology of their preserves, eager to assist visitors looking for specific wildflowers, bird species, and other points of interest. This is especially true at the wildest and least-visited refuges—the staff at these places know just how special and rare this land is, and want the public to realize it, too. Ask for their help, and enjoy the benefits.

Brussels District, Mark Twain NWR

Calhoun and Gilbert Divisions: Brussels, Illinois

Shorebirds and waterfowl at refuge wetland

Whether you're driving Great River Road, parked beside the Brussels Ferry, or resting on the flagstone veranda of the Pere Marquette State Park lodge, you will be front row and center for a spectacular air show. Every spring and fall migratory birds fill the skies over the Calhoun and Gilbert divisions of the Brussels District. Throngs of American white pelicans wheel and swoop over the refuge and the Illinois River. Canada geese stage flybys with the military precision of the Blue Angels; comic relief comes from a tattered gaggle of cormorants who lumber by in a disorderly V formation. High overhead, hawks and vultures circle slowly and search for updrafts, while at lower altitudes ducks barrel past in echelons of twos and threes. Walking through the wild, lonely shores of the district's wetlands, where a flock of pelicans glides over foam whipped up on the lake's opposite shore, it's hard to believe that downtown St. Louis is only 20 air miles away.

HISTORY

The history of the national wildlife refuges along the Mississippi River is interwoven with the history of the U.S. Army Corps of Engineers' work in flood control and navigation improvement on the great river. The Corps purchased the area within the present Brussels District in the 1930s during construction of a 9-foot navigation channel on the river. After completion of Lock and Dam 26 near Alton, Illinois, the U.S. Fish & Wildlife service assumed management responsibility for the wetlands, open water, and farmlands not needed for the navigation project. The 8,501-acre Brussels District of the Mark Twain NWR was established in 1958 and serves as an important nesting, feeding, and resting area for waterfowl and bald eagles traveling on the Mississippi Flyway.

The Calhoun and Gilbert Lake divisions face each other across the Illinois

River just upstream from where the Illinois empties into the Mississippi. They are the two southernmost divisions in the Brussels District, which is the southernmost district within the Mark Twain NWR. The entire district lies within the floodplain of the Mississippi.

GETTING THERE

Gilbert Lake is 17 mi. west of Alton on Great River Rd. The refuge's eastern boundary is just west of the Brussels Ferry; a parking lot on Great River Rd. marks the refuge's western end. To reach the Calhoun Division, cross the river on the Brussels Ferry and drive 4.5 mi. west on Illinois River Rd. and follow the signs to the Visitor Center.

- **SEASON:** Refuge, mid-Dec.–mid-Oct. Visitor Center open year-round.
- **HOURS:** Refuge, dawn to dusk. Visitor Center, 7:30 a.m.–4 p.m., Mon.–Fri.
- **FEES:** Free access.
- **ADDRESS:** Mark Twain NWR, Brussels District Office, Box 107, Brussels, IL 62013
- **TELEPHONE:** 618/883-2524

TOURING BRUSSELS

- **BY AUTOMOBILE:** Neither division has an auto tour. Except for the parking lot off Great River Road and the refuge overlook road adjacent to Highway 100, no cars are permitted on the Gilbert Lake Division, and the Calhoun Division contains barely a mile of gravel road open to the public. Pere Marquette State Park, directly north of Gilbert Lake on the Great River Road, boasts a paved, serpentine drive (open year-round) edging the high bluffs overlooking the Illinois River. Numerous scenic pulloffs tempt motorists to tarry and drink in the view.
- **BY FOOT:** Hiking and walking are permitted anywhere within the public areas of Brussels District. The only hiking trail within the refuge is a 5-mile-long service road in the Gilbert Lake Division, which hikers have adopted as their own. A number of fine hiking trails in the Pere Marquette State Park provide panoramic views of the refuge from bluffs overlooking the Illinois River. The trails vary in length, from a .5-mile trail to one that is more than 2 miles; all involve some climbing. Most begin at the park lodge across Great River Road from Gilbert Lake.
- **BY BICYCLE:** Bikes are permitted on Gilbert Lake Trail and on the gravel roads in the Calhoun District that are used by automobiles.
- **BY CANOE, KAYAK, OR BOAT:** Seven-mile-long, one-mile-wide Swan Lake, in the Calhoun Division, is open to boaters. Boats can be floated on Swan Lake from two launch ramps. The first is just north of the Visitor Center, the second is at Bloom's Landing on Bims Road north of the Visitor Center. Boat use is restricted to fishing and wildlife observation.

WHAT TO SEE

- **LANDSCAPE AND CLIMATE** Stand anywhere in the refuge and you get the feeling that you're at the bottom of a giant trough. Steep, high bluffs line the Illinois River, sharply contrasting with the bottomland. On the floodplain there seems to be no more than two feet of difference in elevation between the lakes, sloughs, ponds, and rivers and any place you can stand and not get your feet wet. Down in the bottom of the trough is water, muddy land, and land that will soon return to mud.

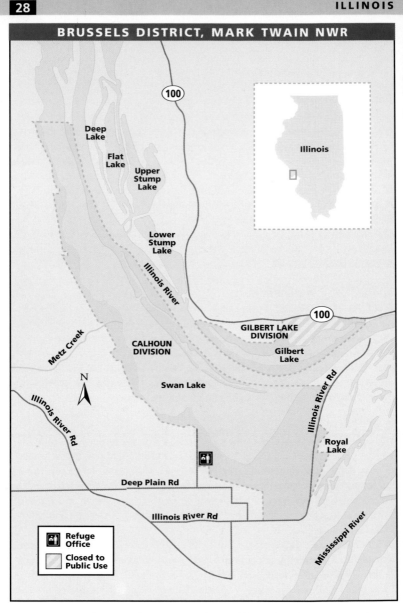

BRUSSELS DISTRICT, MARK TWAIN NWR

Summers in the Brussels District are hot and humid, and winters are often so mild that waterfowl stay on through the season rather than move farther south. A wet spring or fall can cause flooding on the Mississippi and Illinois rivers, inundating everything in the refuge except the Visitor Center.

■ **PLANT LIFE** The variety of habitats in the Brussels District is typical of river floodplains found throughout the Midwest and along the Mississippi. Bottomland forests, lakes, sloughs, cropland, marshes, and moist-soil units can be found in every division and district in the Mark Twain NWR. But both Calhoun and Gilbert Lake habitats exhibit individual personalities.

Wetlands The 2,400-acre Swan Lake, a backwater formed by the construction of Lock and Dam 26, dominates the Calhoun Division. The lake is the largest body of open water in the region and attracts large numbers of waterfowl. The division also contains several large moist-soil units important for feeding waterfowl. In summer the water level in the units is drawn down to encourage the growth of plant life. The water is then flooded in the fall to provide a food-rich waterfowl habitat.

Gilbert Lake Division stretches like a ribbon along the north shore of the Illinois River. The narrow 250-acre Gilbert Lake is an old channel of the river and runs nearly the entire length of the 736-acre division. Both Swan and Gilbert lakes are important feeding, resting, and nesting habitats for waterfowl. Marshes and shallow backwater sloughs dot the landscape. The green algaelike substance found floating on marshes and sloughs is duckweed, an important food source for waterfowl.

Bottomland forests Both divisions contain large stands of bottomland hardwoods. Eastern cottonwoods, black willow, elm, river birch, basswood, and pin oak vie for space and a place in the sun in bottomland forests. The line of hardwoods separating Gilbert Lake from the Illinois River includes some old trees of prodigious size. A brushy understory of poison ivy, river grape, and other creepers clings to the trees. In the Calhoun District, bottomland hardwoods still bear scars and suffer long-term effects from the Great Flood of 1993, which covered the Calhoun Division with 6 feet of water. High-water marks are still visible on the buildings and trees along the road from the Brussels Ferry to the Visitor Center. Many mature trees were weakened by the high water—they survived the flood only to succumb later to winter storms. On one notable stretch of road, a large stand of trees has been sheared off at a uniform 6 feet above the ground, with every downed tree trunk pointing in the same precise direction—as if a giant had parted his hair.

Cropland The division also holds small sections of cropland and a small meadowland of native grasses. Corn and soybeans are grown by local farmers, who leave a portion of the harvest as food for wildlife. Much of the cropland took a long time to recover from the 1993 flood. The 2,428-acre Batchtown Division of the Brussels District lies farther north and consists of cropland, sloughs, and moist-soil units.

■ **ANIMAL LIFE** The wide variety of wetlands and open water within the refuge makes for nearly ideal conditions for frogs, turtles, toads, salamanders, and other reptiles and amphibians. Many are prey for area birds and small mammals. Fish commonly found in the waters of the refuge include buffalo, freshwater drum, paddlefish, gar, carp, bluegill, and crappie. The three species of buffalo fish average about 30 inches at adulthood. Buffalo fish have large heads with a noticeable hump behind the head that resembles that of a bison. They are usually golden or reddish brown and eat plants, mollusks, crustaceans, and insect larvae. Buffalo fish are often thought of as trash fish because they take over lakes and streams from game and panfish.

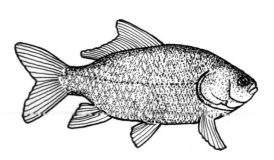
Buffalo fish

Birds The Brussels District lies within the Mississippi Flyway, one of the world's great bird migration routes. Every spring and fall upwards of 5 million ducks and 50,000 geese travel north and south along the river. Birds of prey also use the Mississippi as a highway on their semiannual migrations. The bluffs lining much of the Mississippi and Illinois rivers produce updrafts that soaring raptors use like elevators. These raptors gain altitude by hitching a ride on an updraft; when they near the top, they set their wings and soar off in search of another "up" elevator. During spring migration, the number of broad-winged hawks passing a given point on the river can exceed five figures in a 24-hour period.

The simplest way to comprehend the enormity of the district's birdlife is to follow the annual cycle at Calhoun and Lake Gilbert. January finds the entire area packed with bald eagles. As many as 600 overwinter in a 20-to-30-mile stretch of the Mississippi, with the refuge at the midpoint of the range. One of the largest winter populations of eagles in the lower 48 states has spawned a winter tourist industry. As many as 20,000 snow geese also spend the cold months in the area, joining Canada geese and a variety of ducks.

By March waterfowl are clogging the wetlands and both rivers as spring migration gets under way. Marsh birds are also arriving in large numbers, with

Bald eagle

many nesting here. Raptors join the northward wave in March and continue to move through the area into May. In late April and early May songbirds and warblers invade the refuge on their way to northern breeding grounds. By mid- to late July the flow of birds has reversed, with shorebirds leaving their nesting grounds near the Arctic Circle and heading south. Shorebirds move through in increasing numbers in September, with sandpipers, yellowlegs, plovers, and even local rarities such as American avocets and willets showing up. Songbirds move south in September, and waterfowl numbers rise as September turns to October. More than 20 species of ducks have been recorded at the refuge. As waterfowl peak in mid-October, the refuge hangs out the "Do Not Disturb" sign so that the birds can enjoy undisturbed rest.

A grand total of 245 species has been recorded in the refuge with 93 species nesting here. Several state endangered species, including great egret, little blue heron, and black-crowned night-heron, are found within the refuge.

Mammals Raccoon, opossum, and white-tailed deer are abundant and commonly seen. Red fox and mink prowl the refuge but are rarely spotted by the public. Coyotes are present in the Brussels District but are more often heard than seen. Coyotes are usually nocturnal; that is when their lonely howling is most often heard. Able to adapt to many different situations, coyotes make their homes in

Coyote

both remote habitats and urban areas. The average coyote rarely weighs more than 50 pounds; its diet consists of small mammals, birds, and even fruits and berries in the summer.

ACTIVITIES

■ **CAMPING:** Not permitted in the refuge. The Pere Marquette State Park campground (618/786-3323) is virtually across the road from Gilbert Lake.

■ **WILDLIFE OBSERVATION:** Birding is the top attraction at the refuge, and birders are encouraged to check at the Visitor Center for the latest sightings and tips. The Visitor Center observation deck overlooks two moist-soil units. A gravel road a quarter mile east of the Visitor Center leads north past several moist-soil units and a roadside canal that is often filled with ducks. The road ends at a pumping station a few steps from Swan Lake. In April and May, songbirds adorn the wooded edges of the lake, and the lake usually offers up a colorful smorgasbord of waterfowl. The service-road-turned-hiking-trail at the Gilbert Lake Division passes through prime songbird territory, while Gilbert Lake itself attracts waterfowl and marsh birds.

Hawk-watching is best done from atop the bluffs in Pere Marquette State Park. The most elegant way to watch birds is from the comfort of outdoor furniture on the park lodge's veranda overlooking the Illinois River and Gilbert Lake.

From mid-December through February some of the best eagle-watching in the country can be found on Great River Road from Alton, Illinois, to the state park. From Alton, motorists can look for eagles fishing in the Mississippi or perched in trees on the great bluffs bordering the river. The best spot in the entire area for eagle-watching may be from the Brussels Ferry to the park lodge. Eagles favor the trees close to the ferry; they swoop down and hook fish churned up by the ferry. In winter, hardwoods lining Gilbert Lake Trail often sport roosting eagles. From the comfort of the park lodge's fireplace-warmed great room, look for eagles flying along the river or perched in trees on the banks. It is not uncommon to see a hundred of the great birds in one day; a lucky few may spot a golden eagle among the bald eagles.

Birders should also check out Stump Lake, just west of the state park, for marsh birds, waterfowl, and, on occasion, large numbers of shorebirds. A paved park road .7 mile east of the Brussels Ferry climbs to the top of the bluffs along a narrow stream, providing great bird sightings. Warblers and songbirds occupy woods and brush along the road from late April through early June.

■ **PHOTOGRAPHY:** This is the place to photograph bald eagles. Better yet, fair close-ups can often be taken with telephoto lenses and 35mm cameras in the Brussels Ferry area.

■ **HIKES AND WALKS:** Gilbert Lake Trail is a six-mile round-trip on a level, well-maintained service road paralleling the Illinois River. While looking for birds and wildflowers, visitors may gather nuts, berries, and mushrooms (be sure to use a mushroom field guide or ask for expert advice before gathering mushrooms). Most of the Calhoun Division is open to hikers, except mid-October to mid-December, who can explore the rugged shore of Swan Lake or service roads and dikes bordering moist soil units.

> **HUNTING AND FISHING**
> Anglers are welcome mid-Dec.–mid-Oct.; state fishing regulations apply. **Catfish, carp, freshwater drum, paddlefish, bluegill, crappie, gar,** and **white perch** are taken.
>
> Hunting is not permitted on the refuge.

■ **SEASONAL EVENTS:** The Two Rivers Family Fishing Fair, held in early June in partnership with Pere Marquette State Park, features fishing workshops and hands-on demonstrations for children. Kids can catch trout from a stocked tank and watch fish from a 5,000-gallon aquarium filled with riverine species.

■ **PUBLICATIONS:** Refuge brochure with maps and a bird checklist.

Chautauqua NWR
Havana, Illinois

Handicapped-accessible trail, Chautauqua NWR

The circle remains unbroken at Chautauqua NWR. From prehistoric times the floodplain wetlands of the Illinois River have attracted immense numbers of waterfowl. The ruins of prehistoric villages and campsites within the refuge testify to the presence of ancient hunter-gatherers, who were drawn to the wetlands for its great wealth of animal life. Today's visitors are following in the footsteps of those first people who walked this land and marveled at its bountiful resources. If much has changed in a few thousand years, much has stayed the same. Waterfowl—still coming and going twice yearly—are nature's metronomes, counting cadence to the changing seasons through the centuries. That sure, steady beat links today's birds with those that awed the ancients, forming a circle that encompasses centuries.

HISTORY

One hundred years ago, the Illinois River wetlands were little more than a gathering spot for migrating waterfowl. In the 1920s, however, it was decided that the land should be put to better use. Thus, the wetlands were diked, drained, and converted to agricultural production. Unfortunately for the farmers, the river promptly flooded the fields, blanketed the cropland with silt, and reclaimed the land. The farms were wiped out by the flooding, but because the silt discouraged underwater plant growth, the area also proved unfit for waterfowl. In 1936 the ruined farmland was purchased by the federal government and became the Chautauqua NWR. Old river levees were rebuilt, and the wetlands were restored. The birds returned.

GETTING THERE

Drive northeast out of Havana on Manito Blacktop Rd. for 6 mi. to the refuge sign on the corner of County Rd. 1950E and Manito Blacktop Rd. Turn left on 1950E and drive 1 mi. to the refuge entrance.

■ **SEASON:** Refuge open year-round.
■ **HOURS:** Sunrise to sunset.
■ **FEES:** Free access.
■ **ADDRESS:** Chautauqua NWR, 19031 E. CR 2105N, Havana, IL 62644
■ **TELEPHONE:** 309/535-2290

TOURING CHAUTAUQUA

■ **BY AUTOMOBILE:** There is no auto tour, but the same public road recommended for bicycling makes an equally pleasant drive.

■ **BY FOOT:** The 0.5-mile-long Chautauqua Nature Trail makes a fine introduction to the refuge. The entire refuge and its dikes are open to hikers and nature lovers except from mid-Oct. to mid-Jan., when the general public is confined to the area immediately surrounding the nature trail.

■ **BY BICYCLE:** There are no formal bike trails within the refuge, but bicyclists may ride the refuge's extensive dike system. A lightly used public road bordering the east side of the refuge offers good peddling.

■ **BY CANOE, KAYAK, OR BOAT:** The waters of Lake Chautauqua are open to "no-wake" boating from mid-Jan. to mid-Oct.

WHAT TO SEE

■ **LANDSCAPE AND CLIMATE** Most of the refuge landscape is manipulated to mimic the "old time" backwater lakes that occurred naturally in the Illinois floodplain. Spillways, dikes, and other water-control structures are employed to re-create the age-old cycle of spring floods and late-summer drying up. Of the refuge's 4,488 total acres, impounded water covers 3,200 acres. About 900 acres of water and timbered bottomland are not impounded or controlled by humans, and this acreage may flood seasonally. The remaining acreage is dry land.

Great blue heron

The Illinois River, swamps, and sedge marshes mark the refuge's western side. The Kikunessa and Wasenza pools, which are shallow floodplain lakes, bookend Lake Chautauqua on the north and south, respectively. A steep bluff rising 70 feet above Lake Chautauqua guards the eastern border. Springs seep from the side of the oak-hickory crowned bluff, spilling water in the lake year-round. Summers are hot. Winters bring snow and ice to the refuge, but the hillside springs provide open water for waterfowl, even during the coldest of months.

■ **PLANT LIFE** The refuge's backwater lakes, bottomland forests, upland woods, and two patches of Illinois prairie sup-

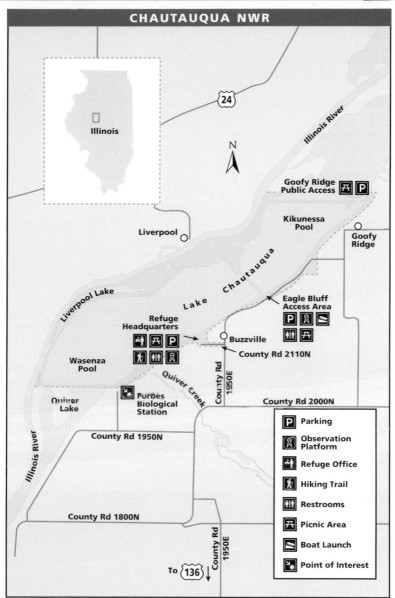

CHAUTAUQUA NWR

Illinois

24

N

Illinois River

Goofy Ridge
Public Access

Kikunessa
Pool

Goofy
Ridge

Liverpool

Lake   Chautauqua

Liverpool Lake

Eagle Bluff
Access Area

Refuge
Headquarters

Buzzville

County Rd 2110N

Wasenza
Pool

County Rd
1950E

Quiver Creek

Quiver
Lake

Forbes
Biological
Station

County Rd 2000N

Illinois River

County Rd 1950N

| P | Parking |
| Observation Platform |
| Refuge Office |
| Hiking Trail |
| Restrooms |
| Picnic Area |
| Boat Launch |
| Point of Interest |

County Rd 1800N

County Rd
1950E

To 136

port 404 plant species. Pin oak, silver maple, and willow predominate in the bottomland forests. The upland hickory and black oak produce nuts high in protein and are an important food source for wildlife. One of the refuge's more important plants is wild millet, which waterfowl depend on for food. Lowering the water level in the pools creates mudflats in which the plant thrives.

Chautauqua boasts a small patch of Illinois prairie near the parking lot and an even smaller sample in a wooded opening along the nature trail. Long ago, prairie covered 22 million acres in Illinois; today it has all but vanished. The prairie near the parking lot has the greatest diversity of plants, with Indian grass, big bluestem and little bluestem grasses, purple coneflowers, and prickly pear cactus numbered among the 36 species growing in the demonstration project. The prairie area on the nature trail contains 25 species of prairie plants.

■ ANIMAL LIFE

A wealth of animal life is sheltered within the refuge. A census of species found in the refuge includes 45 mammals, 102 fishes, 48 reptiles, and 254 birds.

Birds The bird life at Chautauqua borders on the incredible. The refuge's tally of bird species is impressive—but it is the sheer numbers that are difficult to believe, even when seen with the naked eye. In early winter when waterfowl numbers peak, the refuge hosts 100,000 ducks and 40,000 geese. In midsummer, shorebird concentrations can surpass 150,000. The refuge is designated as an "Important Bird Area" by the American Bird Conservancy and has been named "A Regionally Significant Site" by the Western Hemisphere Shorebird Network. Mallards compose the bulk of the duck population, but representatives of 20 other duck species are often present. Counted among the Canada geese every fall and winter are snow and blue geese and trumpeter swans.

Bald eagles overwinter at Chautauqua; as many as 80 have been tallied between Oct. and March. The largest number of eagles seen at one time is 35. Eagles are most often seen perched in the large trees bordering North Pool. Chautauqua is one of only five known nesting sites for eagles along the Illinois River.

Huge numbers of shorebirds arrive in the summer when low water exposes large mudflats. Many shorebirds begin fall migration in July, and it is not uncommon to find tens of thousands of yellowlegs, sandpipers, and plovers carpeting the mudflats and probing the ooze for food. The refuge also attracts numerous marsh birds. Bittern and sora are difficult to spot and more often heard than seen, while heron and egrets are ubiquitous. Finally, the refuge is inundated by waves of migrating songbirds from late April to early June.

Mammals The refuge is home to the usual assortment of midwestern mammals. Beaver, southern flying squirrels, and badgers are all common but seldom seen. Little brown, big brown, and hoary bats hunt summer skies for insects, while gray and red fox are most often spotted in the winter. A lonely call wafting across the lake is as close as anyone generally gets to a coyote.

Sora, a common rail

CHAUTAUQUA HUNTING AND FISHING SEASONS

Hunting
(Seasons may vary)

	Jan	Feb	Mar	Apr	May	Jun	Jul	Aug	Sep	Oct	Nov	Dec
geese	■	□	□	□	□	□	□	□	■	■	■	■
ducks	□	□	□	□	□	□	□	□	□	□	■	■

Fishing

	Jan	Feb	Mar	Apr	May	Jun	Jul	Aug	Sep	Oct	Nov	Dec
bluegill		□	□	■	■	■	■	■	■	■	□	□
crappie	■	■	■	■	■	■	■	■	■	■	■	■
catfish	■	■	■	■	■	■	■	■	■	■	■	■

Waterfowl hunting is permitted on the refuge as well as fishing in accordance with state and federal regulations. Geese can be hunted from Oct. 23–Jan. 21. Duck season is Oct. 23–Dec. 21. Fishing is permitted year-round except for the closure period from Oct. 15–Dec. 15. For more information on current hunting and fishing regulations for Chautauqua NWR, including license requirements and bag limits, consult refuge office.

ACTIVITIES

■ **CAMPING AND SWIMMING:** Camping and swimming are prohibited within the refuge. Eagle Bluff and Goofy Ridge access areas contain restrooms and picnic tables. The Sand Ridge State Forest Campground is 6 miles north of the refuge, and campgrounds are also available in Havana; for details call the Chamber of Commerce (309/543-3528).

■ **WILDLIFE OBSERVATION:** Chautauqua is one of the Midwest's great sites for birders: Birds are plentiful, and viewing takes little or no effort. The Eagle Bluff Access Area is an excellent vantage point from which to scope Lake Chautauqua and North Pool. The Goofy Ridge Public Access Area presents views of the northern end of North Pool. The refuge's nature trail leads to three observation platforms, equipped with spotting scopes, overlooking Lake Chautauqua and South Pool. Warblers, thrushes, and woodpeckers are active along the trail in May and June.

The viewing of waterfowl and eagles is best from Nov. through March. In April, birders can catch late-migrating waterfowl and early waves of songbirds. May is the best time for seeking the more than 30 warbler species that move through the refuge. July is the prime shorebirding month.

■ **PHOTOGRAPHY:** From close-ups of prairie grasses and wildflowers to panoramic views of Lake Chautauqua, this refuge has much to offer shutterbugs. The most photographer-friendly area in the refuge may be Chautauqua Nature Trail. Eagle Bluff Access Area holds out some hope for photographers wanting to shoot portrait studies of individual waterfowl, but the best way to frame a single bird in a viewfinder is with a telephoto lens.

■ **HIKES AND WALKS:** The refuge's only formal trail is the handicapped-accessible, 0.5-mile-long self-guided Chautauqua Nature Trail. The far reaches of the refuge are best explored by hiking the refuge's many dikes. Visitors are welcome to pick nuts, berries, and mushrooms along the trails.

■ **PUBLICATIONS:** Mammal and bird checklists, guides to the nature trail and demonstration prairie, and a general brochure with map.

Crab Orchard NWR
Marion, Illinois

Wintering Canada geese, Crab Orchard, NWR

Crab Orchard NWR has many faces. On the north side of the refuge, Crab Orchard Lake looks like a recreational boater's dream come true. Two busy marinas and five additional boat-launching ramps spread along the shoreline provide multiple access sites for speedboats, sailboats, and water skiers. Throw in two picnic areas, a swimming beach, fishing sites, and a campground (all on the lake's north shore), and you begin to understand how this refuge draws 1.2 million visitors a year. It is one of the region's top tourist attractions.

Drive the roads on the refuge's south side and you discover another, quieter Crab Orchard, filled with pristine lakes, nature trails leading to painted meadows and silver waterfalls, and a wilderness area barely touched since the Shawnee roamed the land. On the refuge's east side, great opportunities for birding are found along the edges of a sanctuary closed to the public except for the major manufacturing plants housed there.

HISTORY

The land destined to become a refuge once lay within the traditional hunting grounds of the Shawnee. The tribe was pushed off the land in the 1800s by a tide of homesteaders who planted cotton and tobacco. By the 1930s the soil was over-farmed and played out. The Resettlement Administration bought 32,000 acres to create three lakes for recreational use and to supply industry with a source of water. To that end Crab Orchard Lake was created in 1939, and by 1941, 3,000 acres had been planted with 3.5 million trees.

World War II interrupted these plans and changed the focus at Crab Orchard. The War Department built one of the country's largest ammunition plants, employing 10,000 workers, here among the newly planted trees. In 1947 the Crab Orchard NWR was created, but, in keeping with tradition, the 43,500-acre refuge still houses 20 firms, including a munitions plant, that employ a total of 700 people.

GETTING THERE

From the junction of I-57 and Rte. 13, drive 3 mi. west on Rte. 13 to Rte. 148. Turn south and drive 2.5 mi. to Visitor Center.

■ **SEASON:** Refuge open year-round; some areas closed Oct.–March for protection of waterfowl.

■ **HOURS:** Parts open 24 hours; Visitor Center 8 a.m.–4:30 p.m.

■ **FEES:** Boat or vehicle $15 annual; combination boat and vehicle $25 annual; vehicle $2 one-day; vehicle $5 five-day.

■ **ADDRESS:** Crab Orchard NWR, 8588 Rte. 148, Marion, IL 62959

■ **TELEPHONE:** 618/997-3344

TOURING CRAB ORCHARD

■ **BY AUTOMOBILE:** The only way to take in this sprawling refuge is by car. State and county highways total more than 30 miles within the refuge and provide access to all public attractions. Picturesque Devil's Kitchen Lake is paralleled on the east and west by two scenic roads, from which a series of loops lead motorists through forested land down to the lake's rocky shoreline.

■ **BY FOOT:** Four self-guided nature trails totaling 5.9 miles and several hiking trails etch the refuge's varied landscape. Visitor Center Trail is a 0.5-mile paved loop accessible by wheelchairs. Rocky Bluff Trail involves the most climbing of the three trails and completes a 1.4-mile loop near the north shore of Devil's Kitchen Lake. Wild Turkey Trail is a 3-mile mowed path through a young forest. The 1-mile Chamnesstown School Trail takes visitors through a variety of habitats. The refuge's wilderness area stretches south from the shores of Little Grassy and Devil's Kitchen lakes to the northern border of Shawnee National Forest. Birders, hunters, anglers, and hikers are welcome in the area. No camping, fires, or motor vehicles are allowed.

■ **BY BICYCLE:** No bikes are permitted on refuge foot trails, but there are miles of lightly traveled roads on the south side of the refuge and the adjoining Giant City State Park.

■ **BY CANOE, KAYAK, OR BOAT:** All three lakes within the refuge have full-service marinas. Crab Orchard Lake, the largest of the three, draws the powerboats and water skiers. The two other lakes are more oriented to fishing.

WHAT TO SEE

■ **LANDSCAPE AND CLIMATE** Crab Orchard lies on the northern edge of the rolling, wooded, unglaciated hills of the Shawnee National Forest. The three man-made lakes are the refuge's most dramatic physical features. Their rocky, timbered shores follow the contours of valleys and narrow ravines that were flooded with the creation of the lakes. On the two smaller lakes the ragged and convoluted shoreline makes a canoe trip an adventure, as narrow, twisting, almost fjordlike arms reveal new and scenic beaches around each bend. Devil's Kitchen Lake is so clear, clean, and cold that rainbow trout thrive in its depths. The dense woods carpeting large sections of the refuge are the result of the massive tree-planting programs in the 1930s. The refuge contains marshy wetlands and wet meadows that, along with the large expanse of open water, help attract huge numbers of waterfowl in the winter.

July and August are hot and humid. Fall at the refuge is often wet and cool but spectacularly beautiful. Winters are mild.

■ **PLANT LIFE**

Upland forest The Crab Orchard Wilderness Area, on the southern edge of

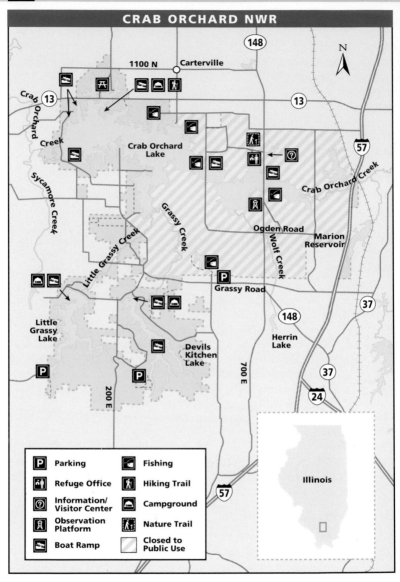

CRAB ORCHARD NWR

the refuge, contains the most interesting and impressive plant communities. The wilderness area was created by an act of Congress in 1976, which ensured that the 4,050 acres will be protected against any development by society. It includes steep terrain with sandstone cliffs, many small creeks, and faint foot trails. Hardwoods predominate, but 115 species of trees have been identified in the wilderness area, and an equally impressive number of shrubs make up a thick understory. Few places of comparable size in the Midwest have such a wide variety of plants, ranging from orchids to prickly pear cactus. Throughout the wilderness area and the entire refuge visitors will find a wealth of strikingly beautiful wildflowers, many with interesting stories. One, the wildflower star-of-Bethlehem, was also known in biblical times, but by a less poetic name—dove's dung. The plant's clump of small white flowers may have suggested its name. The Bible mentions that the plant was sold as food during the siege of Samaria. Present-day Muslims are familiar with it; a flour made from its dried bulbs is a traditional part of a pilgrim's diet on the journey to Mecca.

Spicebush is one of many shrubs found in the refuge. The spicebush has tiny yellow flowers that bloom March through April, which give it its nickname: the forsythia of the wilds. The plant's leaves and twigs were used as a substitute tea in the blockaded South during the Civil War. State endangered plants found here include black spleenwort, hairy synandra, and Bellow's beak sedge.

Prairie Small and large swatches of prairie and meadowlands are scattered throughout the refuge. By midsummer the prairies are alive with color, as black-eyed Susans, asters, purple coneflowers, wild petunia, tall blazing star, and other wildflowers bloom among the prairie grasses. Some 1,500 acres of grasslands are rented out for grazing in the summer. The grazing helps maintain the prairie by keeping shrubs and trees from encroaching on the grasslands. The cattle are removed in October when the geese begin to arrive.

Cropland Five thousand acres within the refuge are cultivated by local farmers under a sharecropping agreement. The farmers plant corn, sorghum, and soybeans and leave a quarter of the crop for the geese to eat.

■ **ANIMAL LIFE** The range and variety of animal life within the refuge is truly astounding. Prehistoric paddlefish (so-called because of their long paddle-shaped snout), copperhead rattlesnakes, Fowler's toad, cave salamanders, and northern fence lizards only begin to hint at the assortment of wildlife at Crab Orchard.

Birds In the winter, when it is too cold for water sports and the lake is empty of boats, 100,000 Canada geese and as many as 40,000 ducks take over Crab Orchard Lake and the other two lakes in the refuge as a major wintering ground. Waterfowl population reaches a peak from mid-December to mid-January. An adult Canada goose eats up to a half pound of food a day, and because the area does not produce much natural food, the geese depend on the corn, sorghum, and soybeans left by sharecropping farmers.

Fifteen species of ducks have been seen in the refuge, including such regional rarities as Barrow's goldeneye, royal tern, and surf scoter. Bald eagles and golden eagles also spend the winter here. When spring comes and the waterfowl head north, the local boaters return to the lakes.

The refuge checklist totals 245 species that, except for waterfowl, share the refuge with summer vacationers. The refuge has two active bald eagle nests and a large population of eastern bluebirds. Wild turkeys are so abundant that they are often trapped here for reintroduction to other areas. Other breeding birds include

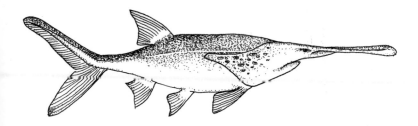

Paddlefish

the relatively rare Bell's vireo, black- and yellow-crowned night-herons, and both tanagers. The latter are two of nature's most striking birds. The male scarlet tanager is a bright scarlet-red except for tuxedo-black wings and tail. The male summer tanager is uniformly rose-red except for the wings and tail, which are a darker red. Crab Orchard lies in a relatively narrow geographic band where the nesting grounds of the two tanagers overlap. Good numbers and variety of warblers, woodpeckers, marsh birds, flycatchers, and birds of prey are all commonly seen.

Wild turkeys

Mammals Crab Orchard is one of the few regions in the state with a wilderness area large enough to accommodate bobcats. Both gray fox and red fox inhabit the refuge. The gray fox is easily distinguished from its cousin by a grayish coat and black stripe down the entire length of a bushy tail. In most of its range the red fox carries a bounty on its head, because it is mistakenly thought to compete with man for small game. It may take the occasional pheasant, but it also kills hundreds of mice and rats annually. Coyotes are occasionally spotted walking along the shoulder of a road—and are sometimes so nonchalant about strolling down a well-traveled road that motorists may mistake them for large dogs.

Five species of bats hang around the refuge every day and hunt by night. The eastern pipistrelle, the smallest eastern bat, often remains in vegetation during the day and appears in the sky before sundown. All eastern bats dine exclusively on insects captured in flight. Bats either grab the prey in their mouths or cup their tail membrane and scoop dinner out of midair. White-tailed deer, southern flying squirrels (which are nocturnal and therefore rarely seen), shrews, rabbits, and numerous other mammals also inhabit the refuge.

ACTIVITIES

Crab Orchard is a major summer playground. A marina on Crab Orchard even berths houseboats. But if the roar of outboard motors and the slap of skis on water can be heard throughout the summer on Crab Orchard Lake, there are plenty of quiet places where other outdoor activities and nature can be enjoyed.

■ **CAMPING:** The three campgrounds within the refuge, one on each lake, have a full range of camping sites and hookups. Crab Orchard Campground (618/985-4983) is on the north side of Crab Orchard Lake, near the refuge's only swimming beach. Devil's Kitchen Boat Dock & Marina (618/457-5004) has a bait shop, boat rental, and a campground that stretches along the lake's north shore. Little Grassy Boat Dock, Marina, & Campground (618/457-6655), on a peninsula on the lake's west side, offers bait, boat rentals, and a full-service campground.

■ **SWIMMING:** The refuge's designated swimming beach is located in the Crab Orchard Campground, on the north side of Crab Orchard Lake.

■ **WILDLIFE OBSERVATION:** Opportunities abound for birding and enjoying wildlife at Crab Orchard—even though it is one of the few national refuges where wildlife observation does not account for the majority of visitors. An observation tower rises from a meadow on the west side of Rte. 148 just south of the causeway that carries the road over the eastern end of Crab Orchard Lake. Ducks, geese, and a variety of other waterbirds can be seen on the lake from either the north or south approach to the causeway.

Waterfowl viewing is good from November through March from nearly any point on the three lakes. Birding from the paved trail behind the Visitor Center turns up plenty of warblers and other songbirds in late April and early May. Rangers lead bird walks down this trail, and personnel at the Visitor Center can direct visitors to the best place from which to view the nesting eagles. Eastern bluebirds are often seen in the open fields south of A-3 Road west of the Visitor Center. Wildlife observation is often best done by slowly driving the refuge's many roads.

■ **PHOTOGRAPHY:** The refuge's photo blind, built on the edge of a small wetland, is big enough to accommodate more than one photographer. A paved path to the blind makes it handicapped-accessible. The blind can be reached from the parking lot adjacent to the observation tower. Devil's Kitchen Lake is especially photogenic, and the many scenic auto loops edging the shoreline present a multitude of possible shots. Rocky Bluff Trail is the place to go for wildflower photography.

■ **HIKES AND WALKS:** The refuge's self-guided walking trails circle through diverse habitats and reveal the refuge's many scenic faces. The easy 1-mile Chamnesstown Trail cuts a large circle north of A-3 Road. In addition to stops

Waterfowl hunting

HUNTING AND FISHING There are 20,000 acres of legal hunting ground on the refuge, on which you can hunt **squirrel, deer, turkey, waterfowl, pheasant**, and **dove**. Only steel shot may be used; contact the refuge for more details including hunting seasons.

Crab Orchard NWR's three lakes offer an abundance of year-round fishing opportunities. Anglers most often go in search of **bluegill, crappie, catfish**, and **bass**.

along the trail that demonstrate wildlife-management practices, the trail passes a historic school. The 3-mile-long Wild Turkey Trail winds through pine plantations and a hardwood forest. The 1.4-mile Rocky Bluff Trail, the most scenic in the refuge, traverses meadows filled with wildflowers and leads to picturesque Grassy Creek, sandstone cliffs, and waterfalls. The paved trail behind the Visitor Center passes a quiet woodland pool and tunnels through a stand of hardwood trees and dense understory.

Several other foot trails wind through the farther reaches of the refuge, and the wilderness area on the southern edge of the refuge should not be overlooked by those who want to explore and experience a wildly beautiful area all but untouched by man. The area includes steep terrain with sandstone cliffs, numerous small creeks, 115 species of trees, and faint foot trails. Hikers are cautioned to be alert for poisonous copperhead snakes in rocky areas.

■ **SEASONAL EVENTS:** On Sundays in October from 1 p.m. to 4 p.m., the refuge presents the annual Auto Discovery Tours. With a self-guided brochure visitors can drive into areas normally closed to vehicles and the public—a rare opportunity for close-up views of area wildlife and fall foliage.

■ **PUBLICATIONS:** Bird, mammal, reptile and amphibians, and wildflower checklists and an introductory brochure with map.

Cypress Creek NWR
Ulin, Illinois

Waterfowl amid cypress and bottomland hardwoods, Cypress Creek NWR

The Cache River Wetlands envelops visitors in an enchanting watery landscape. A boardwalk leads to a quiet world of green. Floating vegetation blankets dark, still water, and where the emerald-green weeds part they frame the lacy reflection of overhanging trees. Even the occasional log floating in the water looks green on Heron Pond, in Cypress Creek NWR. The only contrasts are the brownish trunks of bald cypress and tupelo trees that rise from the water like tent poles keeping the leafy canopy taut and aloft. Cached away in this lushly saturated world are the oldest living things east of the Mississippi, plus an incredible diversity of plants and animals. Seven federally listed and 102 state-listed endangered or rare species live here.

HISTORY

A 19th-century U.S. Land Survey described the area as "a drowned land." When Europeans displaced Native Americans, the settlers began an assault on the wetlands. One of the Midwest's finest wetlands was partially drained, and when it was discovered that the land could not be farmed, it was logged. After more than a century of abuse, the area still contains 91 percent of Illinois's high-quality swamp and 42 percent of its shrub swamp. Recognizing the uniqueness of the area, the Illinois Department of Natural Resources (DNR), The Nature Conservancy, Ducks Unlimited, and the Citizens Committee to Save the Cache River began working to reverse wetland destruction. Cypress Creek NWR was established in 1990 and joined the DNR and the private organizations in protecting and restoring 60,000 acres of wetlands along a 50-mile corridor of the Cache River.

GETTING THERE

To reach refuge headquarters take Exit 18 on I-57 and drive east 6 mi. on Shawnee College Rd. to Shawnee College and Rustic Campus Dr. Points of access are on

Shawnee College Rd. and Perks Rd., between I-57 and IL 37 and Karnak-Belknap Rd. east of IL 37.
■ **SEASON:** Refuge open year-round.
■ **HOURS:** Office: 7 a.m.–4 p.m., Mon.–Fri.
■ **FEES:** Free access.
■ **ADDRESS:** Cypress Creek NWR, 137 Rustic Campus Dr., Ullin, IL 62992
■ **TELEPHONE:** 618/634-2231

TOURING CYPRESS CREEK

■ **BY AUTOMOBILE:** There is no auto tour, but a car is the only practical means of visiting the various points of interest.
■ **BY FOOT:** The Cache River Wetlands contains 20 miles of hiking trails ranging in length from 250 feet to a moderately difficult 5.5-miles. Several units without trails permit bushwhacking.
■ **BY BICYCLE:** Not permitted.
■ **BY CANOE, KAYAK, OR BOAT:** The lower Cache River is best appreciated from a canoe, and the Lower Cache River Canoe Trail's 3- and 6-mile routes take paddlers to a state champion bald cypress more than 1,000 years old and 34 feet in circumference. Except for the canoe trails, the upper Cache River is difficult if not impossible to canoe because of extensive logjams.

WHAT TO SEE

■ **LANDSCAPE AND CLIMATE** Scientists have identified six distinct regions within the continent based on soils, terrain, and plant and animal communities. The Cache River basin is only one of six places in the United States where four of these regions overlap. Whatever the region, there is a lushness about Cypress Creek that, in many places, reminds one of a rain forest. The land slopes from the hilly Shawnee National Forest on the north to the Ohio River to the south. As befits such a remarkable area, the Cache River basin holds an impressive number and variety of plants. Two National Natural Landmarks are found here, and UNESCO has included the Cache River basin in its list of 15 Wetlands of International Importance, placing it in select company with the Florida Everglades and Okefenokee Swamp.

River otter

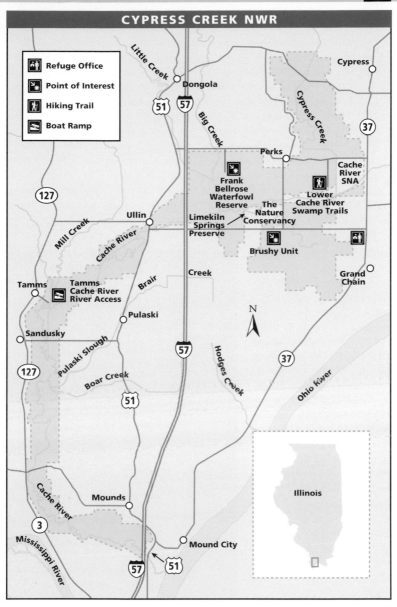

CYPRESS CREEK NWR

Legend:
- Refuge Office
- Point of Interest
- Hiking Trail
- Boat Ramp

Little Creek
Dongola
Cypress
51 57
Big Creek
Cypress Creek
37
Perks
Cache River SNA
Frank Bellrose Waterfowl Reserve
Lower Cache River Swamp Trails
The Nature Conservancy
Limekiln Springs Preserve
Ullin
Mill Creek
Cache River
Brushy Unit
127
Creek
Grand Chain
Brair
Tamms
Tamms Cache River River Access
Pulaski
N
Sandusky
127
Pulaski Slough
Boar Creek
57
51
Hodges Creek
37
Ohio River
Illinois
Cache River
Mounds
3
Mound City
57 51
Mississippi River

The area is farther south than Richmond, making the summers hot and humid. Winters are mild and wet, with 45 to 48 inches of rain in addition to 10 inches of snow.

■ PLANT COMMUNITIES

Wetlands More often than land, it is water—springs, ponds, sloughs, oxbow lakes, creeks, and the Cache River—that delineates the shrub swamps, upland forests, marshes, and nearly 20 other of the refuge's distinct natural communities. Wherever you turn, the land appears soaked to overflowing. No habitat is stranger or more fascinating than the area's true southern cypress and tupelo swamp. It is a

BALD CYPRESS There is something steadfast about the bald cypress. The tree rises from its swampy water habitat in an unequivocally straight line; its posture is perfect. As the tree ages, it broadens at the bottom—a lot like people in that respect—until the trunk ends in a massive buttress. When the tree reaches the age of 50 it develops knees. The tree's shallow roots project up out of the water and resemble someone lying on the floor with a foot on the ground and a knee in the air.

With its knees, buttress, and upright stance, the bald cypress has a firmly rooted presence. Even though it thrives in wet, unstable soil, the bald cypress is seldom blown down. It is not unusual for one to live more than a millennium—if it can escape the lumberman's ax. Even after being cut down, the tree maintains its steadfastness. Lumbermen call the heartwood of the bald cypress "the wood eternal" and prize it for its durability.

land of giants—the ancient trees are massive, the forest canopy reaches into the sky, and there is the understory is sparse. Many of the cypresses are more than a thousand years old and may be the oldest living things east of the Mississippi. Throughout the wetlands, pondweed, coontail, duckweed, and other floating plants add to the lushness. Buttonbush dominates the shrub swamps, and a variety of other special plants create their own ecosystem in the wetlands. Giant cane, a tall and slender plant with feathery leaves, is struggling to survive within the wetlands. If it disappears, in all probability so will the rare Swainson's warbler, which prefers to nest in the cane.

Hardwood forests The lowland hardwood forests of the Cache River basin often begin where the cypress swamps leave off. The country's largest water locust and

Bald cypress and Canada geese, Cypress Creek NWR

green hawthorn and 12 trees recognized as the largest of their species in Illinois can be found here. Even the names of many of the trees are remarkable: Drummond's red maple, pumpkin ash, cherrybark and willow oak, pignut hickory, and black haws. Farther north, where the land rises into the cliffs, bluffs, and hills of the Shawnee National Forest, the hardwoods share the forest floor with a thick understory of young trees and shrubs. Tulip trees and white, red, and black oak prefer the drier uplands—as does poison ivy, a common understory plant here.

Prairie Small patches of meadows and prairies cover some of the upland hillsides with little bluestem, side oats grama, big bluestem, Indian grass, and other grasses. In sharp contrast to the woodlands, prairie herbs and wildflowers paint the landscape in pastel colors.

■ **ANIMAL LIFE** The basin is home to a wonderful menagerie of birds, fish, and land-dwelling creatures. In addition to the wildlife that thrills visitors, there are others that most people would be happy to avoid: the copperhead, timber rattler, and cottonmouth snakes, all of which are venomous.

Birds John James Audubon enjoyed excellent birding in the Cache River area and noted thousands of "parroquets roosting in . . . giant sycamores." More than 250 species have been documented, and 128 species breed here. The area claims the highest density of breeding forest birds in Illinois. Marsh birds, waterfowl, and warblers are all plentiful, and the annual Christmas bird counts reveal the largest congregations of red-headed and pileated woodpeckers in the country.

Golden mouse

Mammals Two species found here signal the uniqueness of the Cache River basin. River otters have disappeared from the rest of Illinois, but because the basin meets their strict habitat requirements of pollution- and ice-free water, riverbank woods, and absence of people, otters thrive here. So does the bobcat, which needs an undisturbed 10-square-mile home range. The marsh rice rat and the golden mouse, along with raccoons, coyotes, rabbits, and some 40 other warm-blooded animals, call the basin home.

Invertebrates Bivalve mussels can be found on the lake and river bottoms almost anywhere in the United States. The warm, muddy waters of the Cache River basin are fertile ground for them. Whoever first started to name and categorize these creatures must have had a sense of humor—and was obviously influenced by each bivalve's shape and color. Among the mussels found here are the fat pocketbook, the pink muckett, and the incomparably named orangefoot pimpleback.

ACTIVITIES

■ **CAMPING AND SWIMMING:** Neither camping nor swimming is permitted within the refuge or adjoining conservation areas. Ferne Clytte State Park, within the northern edge of the river basin, contains 66 camping sites (618/995-2411).

■ **WILDLIFE OBSERVATION:** Wildlife observation accounts for the majority of visitors within the Cache River Wetlands. Wildlife watching can be enjoyed year-round and is best done from one of the many trails or aboard a watercraft.

Waterfowl viewing is good from fall through spring. Warblers and songbirds move through the area in April and May and nest here in big numbers. Bald eagles overwinter in the area, and the viewing of marsh birds is excellent from spring through fall.

■ **PHOTOGRAPHY:** Heron Pond, with its subtle shades of color, sharp contrasts between light and dark, large trees, and great beauty, is an especially challenging and alluring subject. The slow-moving lower Cache River presents photographers aboard canoes with unusual scenery, a variety of wildlife, and challenging technical problems.

■ **HIKES AND WALKS:** The most popular hike in the area follows the 1.5-mile Heron Pond Trail, with its board-walk traversing a cypress swamp. The 1-mile Lookout Point Trail edges a hill-side and presents a panoramic view of the Cache River area. The 1.5-mile Hickory Bottom Trail winds through 200 acres of old-growth lowland hard-woods. The area's shortest trail, the 250-foot Big Cypress Tree Access, leads to giant cypress and tupelo trees. The Linkage, Marshall Ridge, and Limekiln Springs Preserve trails all average about 2.5 miles in length, are easy walking, and take hikers to a variety of habitats and scenery. At 5.5 miles, Little Black Slough Trail is the longest and involves fording the Cache River and significant changes in elevation. Tamms Cache River Access and Brushy Unit have no trails, but visitors are welcome to wander through either area.

■ **SEASONAL EVENTS:** The refuge celebrates National Wildlife Refuge Week in October with special events.

■ **PUBLICATIONS:** Detailed brochure with map.

HUNTING AND FISHING The entire refuge is open to hunting for all species, except within the Bellrose Waterfowl Reserve—you may hunt only **goose** on the reserve. There are 21 species of waterfowl present on the refuge, including a large number of **mallard** and **wood ducks** and smaller numbers of **ring-necks, pintails,** and **diving ducks**. **Teal duck** season begins in early Sept., a youth hunt occurs the end of Oct., and the regular waterfowl season follows a week later. Contact the refuge for exact season dates and further details.

There is excellent **deer** hunting on the refuge, as well as good numbers of **squirrel, rabbit, quail,** and **upland game**. Upland game hunting is with steel shot only, and all hunters must have state and county licenses; contact the refuge for details.

Although Cypress Creek is generally a narrow waterway, good fishing can be found. Species include **crappie, catfish, bass, bluegill,** and **carp**. Contact the refuge for details.

Muscatatuck NWR
Seymour, Indiana

Wetland boardwalk, Muscatatuck NWR

A visit to Muscatatuck NWR is a sure-fire tonic for the blues. From spring through fall the refuge is home to nearly a thousand wood ducks. As the winter thaws, the brilliantly colored males and their delicately hued consorts drift across the refuge's open waters and glide through shadow-dappled stands of flooded hardwoods. Later in the year the attentive females shepherd their broods through these same woods. The sight of just one of these birds can raise a person's spirits; seeing hundreds of them can bestow a deep sense of serenity on any viewer. And wood ducks are only the most obvious curative at Muscatatuck, the only national wildlife refuge in the state of Indiana.

HISTORY

The refuge takes its name from the river marking its southern border. And that name came from the Plankeshaw Indians, who called the area Muscatatuck, or the "land of winding waters." The site of the future refuge embraced low and poorly drained land that was favored by waterfowl as a nesting area and a rest stop on their biannual migrations.

When Europeans arrived in the 19th century they attempted, with only limited success, to drain the wetlands and create productive farms. The refuge's fully restored Myer's Cabin and Barn, ca. 1900, recall the early efforts to farm the area. Beginning in 1966, money from the federal duck-stamp program was used to make initial purchases of what would become the 7,728-acre Muscatatuck NWR. The refuge was created to provide nesting, resting, and feeding habitats for migratory birds, provide biodiversity, and protect endangered and threatened species. It still attracts new species as the habitat continues to change, and the American Bird Conservancy has recognized Muscatatuck NWR as "continentally important" for birds.

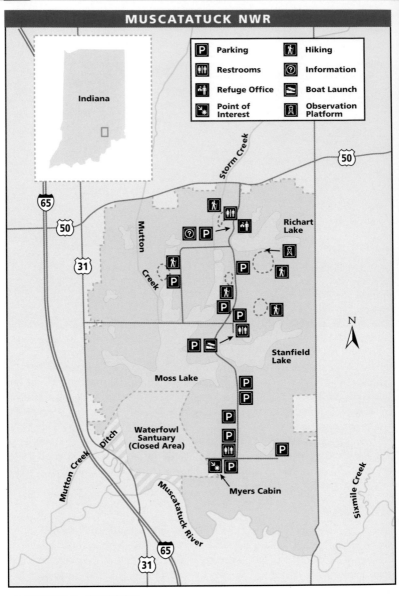

MUSCATATUCK NWR

GETTING THERE

The refuge entrance is on US 50, 3 mi. east of the junction of I-65 and US 50 and 5 mi. east of Seymour in southeastern Indiana.

■ **SEASON:** Refuge open year-round.

■ **HOURS:** Refuge and Visitor Center open daily, sunrise to sunset.

■ **FEES:** Free access.

■ **ADDRESS:** Muscatatuck NWR, 12985 East US Highway 50, Seymour, IN 47274

■ **TELEPHONE:** 812/522-4352

TOURING MUSCATATUCK

■ **BY AUTOMOBILE:** A 3-mile-long self-guided auto tour leads to many interesting sites. A pamphlet with numbered paragraphs corresponding to numbered stops on the auto tour is available at the Visitor Center. Part of the auto tour is on one-way roads. An additional 6 miles of good gravel roads are open to motorists.

■ **BY FOOT:** Eight well-marked hiking trails, varying in length from 0.4 to 3.9 miles, and one handicapped-accessible interpretive nature trail—beginning at the Visitor Center—web the refuge. All of the trails are relatively level and easily walked.

■ **BY BICYCLE:** Bikes are permitted on the refuge's 9 miles of well-maintained gravel roads. Bikes are not permitted on any hiking trails.

■ **BY CANOE, KAYAK, OR BOAT:** Hand-powered watercraft are permitted on Stanfield Lake and must be launched at the lake's designated launching ramp.

WHAT TO SEE

■ **LANDSCAPE AND CLIMATE** At Muscatatuck NWR water is the key to success in attracting and nurturing wildlife; everything that is not water is managed to benefit wildlife. The land is flat, well watered, and contains a variety of habitats. Summers at Muscatatuck can be hot and humid. Winters are mild with occasional light snow.

■ **PLANT LIFE**

Wetlands Only 1,300 acres of the refuge consist of permanent or seasonal wetlands. And much of that acreage is manipulated by man to enhance its attractiveness to waterfowl. In addition to the creeks, natural lakes, spring-fed ponds, and marshes, moist-soil units are flooded in the fall to provide feeding areas for migrating waterfowl. The units are drained in the late spring to promote plant growth that ducks will later feed on; the muddy, easily probed soil attracts shorebirds.

Woodlands Stands of bottomland hardwood forests—containing many trees with large cavities—have been encircled with dikes and are flooded each spring to provide wood ducks with nesting habitat. The oldest untouched acreage within the refuge is a stand of 100-year-old beech trees. The majestic, smooth-barked old-timers provide nesting cavities for wood ducks, while deer and turkey eat the nuts. Tulip, maple, and oak

Northern parula warbler

grow on the refuge's uplands while sweet gum, sycamore, river birch, and ash grow in the lowlands.

Cropland Sixty percent of the refuge was formerly farmland; today 800 acres remain under cultivation by local farmers who, in return for being allowed to work the land, leave a percentage of their crop in the fields for wildlife consump-

Wood duck

tion. Most of the old farm fields are being allowed to revert to forest and brushy areas favored by wild turkey, ruffed grouse, and woodcock. The refuge also contains grasslands and 3,000 forested acres. Clover and grasses are rotated with the soybeans, corn, and wheat in the cultivated fields. Old orchards, wild roses, irises, and other once-cultivated flowers dot the landscape and recall the land's former domestication. The most unusual botanical area in the refuge is a boggy wetlands containing "acid seep springs." These acidic springs support plants more commonly found in northern Canada than in southern Indiana. While rare to the region, to the untrained eye these plant communities look much like any other wetland.

■ **ANIMAL LIFE** Muscatatuck shelters a pleasing array of wildlife. Birds may be the most obvious, but attentive observers can be rewarded with singular sightings of a variety of animals. The refuge shelters several state and federal threatened or endangered species, including the bald eagle, peregrine falcon, Indiana bat, northern copperbelly water snake, river otter, and Henslow's sparrow.

Birds Birding is the number-one attraction at Muscatatuck NWR and accounts for the vast majority of its 185,000 annual visitors. The refuge's bird checklist tallies more than 250 species and identifies 70 that nest within the property. In spring and fall, upwards of 15,000 ducks and geese flock to the refuge. Nineteen species of ducks, plus Canada, white-fronted, and snow geese, turn up here every spring. If the fall population of ducks and geese does not quite measure up to the spring show, sandhill cranes, bald eagles, and osprey put in an occasional appearance when the leaves turn color, adding an extra air of anticipation to a fall birding trip.

Wood ducks are the signature bird at Muscatatuck, a traditional nesting site for the species. With the creation of the refuge, the ducks have returned to nest here in large numbers. They are Muscatatuck's most numerous species during the summer months.

The refuge also has a well-earned reputation for attracting large numbers and varieties of songbirds, especially in May. Thirty-four species of warblers and an

LEAP OF FAITH Considered North America's most beautiful native duck, the wood duck was near extinction in the early 1900s from overhunting and loss of habitat. The creation of refuges like Muscatatuck and the widespread program of building nest boxes for the ducks have literally saved the species.

True to its name, this duck not only perches in trees, it nests in tree cavities between 5 and 50 feet above the ground, preferring to nest near water. As with all ducks that leave the nest shortly after hatching, it is imperative that ducklings learn whom or what to follow. Most chicks visually imprint the first living thing they see—and follow it. But wood ducks cannot see their parent from their perch in the tree cavity. A wood duck mother begins calling her chicks even when they are still in the shell, and ducklings instinctively follow their parent's voice after hatching. Only one day old, the chicks claw their way to the nest opening and jump—regardless of height, or whether they are landing on terra firma or water—to where their mother is calling them from below. Every wood duck chick you see following its mother across a pond or lake is there because of a leap of faith.

impressive number of flycatchers have been spotted within the refuge. Nesting within the refuge are some of the most gorgeous warblers in North America. The azure-colored cerulean and black-throated blue warblers meet every expectation raised by their names. But the northern parula warbler outshines either one with its variety of subtle shades, including a blue-gray back and head and a yellow throat and breast highlighted with a band of black and rufous. The nattily feathered bird tops off his splendor with a white eye-ring and two white wing bars.

Mammals While not as common or numerous as birds, a wide range of mammals call the refuge home. White-tailed deer are often seen, and foxes are plentiful. Beavers inhabit the refuge but lead a reclusive life. If seldom seen, their handiwork is usually evident along Storm Creek. Coyotes roam the refuge but are seen by only a very lucky few.

Playful, inquisitive river otters are active within the refuge but only occasionally observed. The sleek 3- to 4-foot-long furbearers were reintroduced by the Indiana Department of Natural Resources in 1995 and 1996. The animals had been eliminated in the state by the 1940s because of overtrapping and destruction of habitat. Muscatatuck is one of two sites in Indiana where transplanted Louisiana otters were released and now thrive.

Reptiles Among the usual population of frogs, toads, and other reptiles is a large remnant population of the nationally endangered northern copperbelly water snake. These snakes live in swamps, ponds, and marshes, where they dine on frogs, tadpoles, crayfish, and small fish. The refuge is home to a fair number of nonpoisonous snakes, including eastern ribbon, midland brown, northern water, black rat, rough green, southern black racer, black king, Kirtland's, and Midwest worm snake. Poisonous snakes have not been found within the refuge.

ACTIVITIES

■ **CAMPING AND SWIMMING:** Neither camping nor swimming is permitted within the refuge. Public camping is available east of the refuge at Muscatatuck County Park near North Vernon (812/346-2953). The nearest private campground is a few miles north on I-65 at Columbus, Indiana, at Woods-N-Waters Kampground (800/799-3928).

■ **WILDLIFE OBSERVATION:** Muscatatuck offers numerous opportunities to enjoy wildlife without ever leaving your car. The refuge's roads, including the self-guided auto tour, border numerous marshes, timbered swamps, small ponds, and two lakes. The car serves as an excellent movable wildlife blind, allowing visitors to get close-up views of waterfowl, marsh birds, and shorebirds. March, late October, and early November find the most impressive concentrations of waterfowl, but wildlife observation is rewarding and interesting year-round. Warblers and other songbirds push through the refuge in late April and early May on the way to their northern nesting grounds. Even the winter months can make for enjoyable wildlife viewing, when a wide variety of ducks overwinter in the refuge—and are sometimes joined by tundra swans and bald eagles.

■ **PHOTOGRAPHY:** Wildlife photographers could not ask for a better subject than the refuge's ever-present wood ducks. The chance to capture these beauties on film—and the variety of backgrounds to choose from—can eat up several rolls of film. Catching herons and egrets on film is equally addictive, and, for those with the patience and the equipment, warblers and other songbirds can lead photographers on a merry chase along the refuge's wooded trails. Myer's Cabin and Barn are not only interesting but offer photographers a change of focus from the abundant natural vistas and wildlife.

Myer's Cabin, restored farmhouse, Muscatatuck NWR

■ **HIKES AND WALKS:** If waterfowl and shorebird watching can sometimes be more rewarding from the comfort of a car, spotting songbirds, woodpeckers, and other small birds is usually best done on foot along one of the refuge's nine trails. The trails also lure nature lovers with plenty of opportunities for both exercise and close-up examination of Muscatatuck's habitats and micro-ecosystems. A portion of Chestnut Ridge Interpretive Trail is the refuge's only handicapped-accessible trail. At the end of that portion of the trail, stairs lead to a boardwalk bordering a natural spring wetland. Deer are plentiful in this area, as are tree frogs.

The 1.1-mile Turkey Trail penetrates a hardwood forest, a flooded timberland popular with waterfowl, and fields and woods known to attract wild turkeys. The half-mile misnamed Wood Duck Trail does not pay off with wood duck sightings, but turkeys are often seen. The 0.7-mile Bird Trail fully lives up to its name during spring migration, when songbirds often pack trailside vegetation. The 0.9-mile Richart Lake Trail may be the best all-around birding trail in the refuge. It weaves through open fields and woodlands before arriving at a grand overlook of Richart Lake. The overlook is a great vantage point from which to watch waterfowl on the lake, while the dense shrubs and brush bordering the lake are often busy with songbirds. Endicott Trail is the refuge's newest and leads to a new observation platform overlooking North Endicott Marsh.

HUNTING AND FISHING Fishing is permitted May 15–Oct. 15 for **crappie**, **largemouth bass**, **catfish**, and **panfish**. Because fishing is permitted at various sites at different dates, it is best to write for the refuge's brochure on fishing regulations. There are concurrent muzzle-loader and archery **deer** permit hunts, followed by an open archery deer hunt, and special seasons for **rabbit** and **quail**. Ask for the refuge hunting brochure, which gives specific information concerning hunting seasons, no-hunting areas, limits, and regulations unique to the Muscatatuck NWR.

Another enjoyable thing to do while walking or hiking at Muscatatuck is the gathering of wild edibles. Gathering nuts and picking berries and mushrooms is permitted. A stand of persimmon trees is a particular favorite among many wild-food epicureans.

The two longest trails, East and West River trails, crease the southern edge of the refuge, offering hikers a 2.8- and a 3.9-mile walk, respectively. As the names imply, both trails border the river before looping back to the trailhead.

■ **SEASONAL EVENTS:** National Wildlife Refuge Week is celebrated in mid-October, with nature walks and programs, a once-a-year walk through the refuge's "closed area," a 5k run walk, and a Log Cabin Day celebration at Myer's Cabin. This includes wagon rides, "old-time" craft demonstrations, and a dinner of ham and beans.

■ **PUBLICATIONS:** Hunting rules and regulations, a bird checklist, and a guide with map. *Duck Tales* is an attractive, information-rich, quarterly newsletter on doings at the refuge.

DeSoto Bend NWR
Missouri Valley, Iowa

Snow geese (white and blue phase), DeSoto Bend NWR

On a road map, the Missouri River appears as little more than a serpentine blue line tracing the Nebraska-Iowa border. Within the 7,823-acre DeSoto NWR., every meander of the nation's longest river contains its own, discreet world. Bounding the great expanse of open water and its dense, black-green fringe of forest are shimmering grasslands, smooth as a tabletop. Throughout, the Missouri pulses along, pushing its murky reddish-tan water on to another bend in the landscape.

The river the natives called "Big Muddy" has held powerful sway over those who traveled its waters. It was on a summer day in August 1904, the air redolent of river water and damp earth, that Meriwether Lewis and William Clark first made camp on these riverbanks. More than 50 years later, rain and snowmelt caused by an early spring honed the Missouri's already-potent current to a fine edge; it was three o'clock in the afternoon on April Fool's Day 1865, when the steamboat *Bertrand*, plowing upstream, rammed a snag here and sank. A hundred years later, the fickle Missouri changed its course, tossing the *Bertrand* into a newly exposed field, entombed beneath 30 feet of silt. The steamboat's hull was subsequently salvaged, and modern-day visitors to the refuge can see the display of some 200,000 artifacts excavated from the *Bertrand*.

These days, much of the river is swollen with boat traffic. Hydropower dams are steadily choking the life from the floodplain forests. Threatened habitats hold endangered species and an overabundance of snow geese. DeSoto NWR works as equal parts wildlife refuge and shrine to the Missouri and to its influence on America's human and natural history. One leaves the refuge with a greater appreciation for what this magnificent river once was and with renewed interest in helping determine the fate of others like it.

HISTORY

Long before it was a refuge, this was DeSoto Bend, a U-shaped meander of the

Missouri some 7 miles in length. Through the latter half of the 19th century, for the paddle-wheeling steamboats ferrying settlers, miners, and merchandise to frontier towns as far West as Montana, DeSoto was one more hazardous stretch of a wild, unpredictable river. Cyclical spring floods, during which the Missouri powered across its massive floodplain—scouring out new channels and washing away towns, forests, roads and cropfields—were viewed as a hindrance to economic development.

Spurred on by such interests as agriculture and river transport, Congress in the 1950s developed the Pick-Sloan Plan. Named for Major General Lewis A. Pick, head of the Army Corps of Engineers, and William Glenn Sloan, leader of the Bureau of Reclamation, the Pick-Sloan Plan was a blueprint for remaking the Missouri to serve the needs of commerce: irrigation, transportation, flood control, and hydroelectricity. From Montana downstream to Missouri, multimillion-dollar projects—channelization, dams, dikes, dredging—radically altered the river's character and ecology.

One such project in 1959-60 involved DeSoto Bend. Dikes were built at its upper and lower ends, severing the meander from the river. A newer, shorter channel was constructed in its place; DeSoto Bend became DeSoto Lake, and DeSoto NWR was established in 1959.

GETTING THERE

From Council Bluffs, Iowa, or Omaha, Nebraska: travel north on I-29 for 22 miles and take Exit 75 at US Hwy 30; continue west for 5 miles to the refuge and Visitor Center.

■ **SEASON:** Visitor Center, steamboat *Bertrand* excavation site, and adjacent trails open year-round; other public-use areas closed to visitation Oct. 15–April 14.

■ **HOURS:** Visitor Center open daily, 9a.m.–4:30 p.m.

■ **FEES:** $3.00 per vehicle.

■ **ADDRESS:** 1434 316th Lane, Missouri Valley, IA 51555

■ **TELEPHONE:** 712/642-4121

TOURING DESOTO

■ **BY AUTOMOBILE:** The 12-mile auto-tour route is open daylight hours, with nine interpreted stops traversing most refuge habitats and the steamboat *Bertrand* excavation site.

■ **BY FOOT:** Many options here: Bertrand Trail; Cottonwood Trail; Wood Duck Pond Trail; Missouri Meander Trail, a loop which is partially paved and wheelchair-accessible.

■ **BY BICYCLE:** Bicycles permitted on refuge roads.

■ **BY CANOE, KAYAK, OR BOAT:** Boating on DeSoto Lake mid-April–mid-Oct; motorized boats are limited to no-wake speeds.

WHAT TO SEE

■ **THE STEAMBOAT *BERTRAND*** DeSoto features outstanding exhibits interpreting the region's natural and human history. One of the most fascinating and well-developed is the displayed cargo of the steamboat *Bertrand*, which sank on its maiden voyage up the Missouri in 1865. The boat, with a vast array of cargo, was excavated in 1968. Elsewhere, a viewing area overlooks the 178-foot hull of the *Bertrand*, with wayside exhibits nearby.

■ **LANDSCAPE AND CLIMATE** DeSoto lies in the lower Missouri River

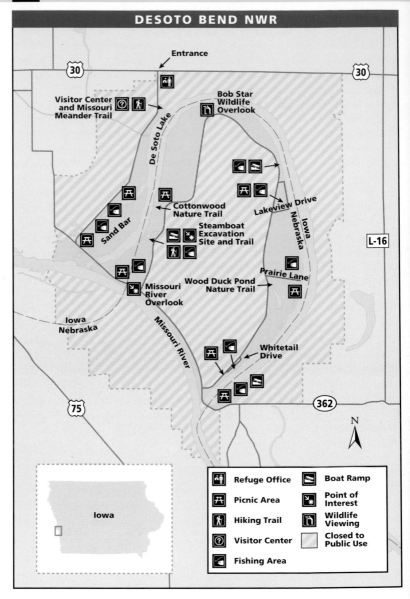

DESOTO BEND NWR

Entrance

30

30

Visitor Center and Missouri Meander Trail

Bob Star Wildlife Overlook

De Soto Lake

Cottonwood Nature Trail

Lakeview Drive

Iowa Nebraska

Sand Bar

Steamboat Excavation Site and Trail

Prairie Lane

Missouri River Overlook

Wood Duck Pond Nature Trail

L-16

Iowa Nebraska

Missouri River

Whitetail Drive

75

362

N

Iowa

Refuge Office		Boat Ramp	
Picnic Area		Point of Interest	
Hiking Trail		Wildlife Viewing	
Visitor Center		Closed to Public Use	
Fishing Area			

Basin, the nation's second-largest watershed. From its origins in Three Forks, Montana, to its meeting with the Mississippi in Saint Louis, the "Mo" covers a territory of 2,565 miles. During late summer, the river supplies as much as 60 percent of the Mississippi's flow. Through its lower reaches, including DeSoto, the floodplain spans 10 to 15 miles; in its presettlement state, the heavily braided and meandering river shifted course yearly by as much as a mile, carving out new channels, islands, sandbars, and oxbow lakes. Spring floods regenerated a dense floodplain forest, with open areas colonized by tallgrass species.

Today's harnessed Missouri is an altogether different river from the Big Muddy of old. Adjacent to DeSoto, agriculture occupies much of the floodplain, with productive fields of corn and soybeans bordering the river channel just 6 to

8 feet below. Situated entirely within the floodplain, most refuge lands are secured from flooding (which still occurs) by a system of dikes.

This region of Iowa is heavily influenced in summer by warm, humid air masses from the Gulf of Mexico, which generate lengthy spells of hot, humid weather and significant rainfall. Winters, with subzero temperatures lasting for a week or so at a stretch, are the work of arctic air descending from the north. Annual precipitation here totals 31 inches.

■ PLANT LIFE

Floodplain forest Though it appears lush and hardy, DeSoto's forest, like others up and down the Missouri, is on its last legs. Without annual floods to till the soil and disperse seeds and nutrients, the native cottonwood and river willow cannot reproduce naturally. Some very impressive cottonwoods on the refuge, with trunks 6 to 8 feet in diameter—invaluable as perches and nest sites for bald eagles and other river-associated birds—are still here but steadily dying out. Roughleaf dogwood, a shrub better adapted to the absence of flooding, has taken over the

SNOWED UNDER Conservation groups and wildlife-management agencies in the United States and Canada say the midcontinent population of snow geese and Ross' geese has greatly exceeded the carrying capacity of the birds' arctic nesting grounds.

In La Perouse Bay, near Churchill, Manitoba, scientists have watched the breeding population rise from fewer than 2,000 pairs in 1968 to 225,000 pairs in 1998. Estimates of the midcontinent population—the flocks nesting in Hudson Bay, James Bay and the Queen Maud Gulf and wintering along the U.S. Gulf Coast—have increased from some 800,000 geese in the 1960s to more than 3 million today; some biologists say the actual total may be closer to 10 million.

On their nesting grounds, snow geese feed by grubbing, or pulling up the roots of plants with their serrated bills. Under normal conditions, their feeding stimulates growth of some species. With record populations, however, cordgrasses, sedges, and other tundra plants have been unable to regenerate rapidly enough; stripped of vegetation, soil temperatures rise, evaporation increases, and natural salts in the ground are pulled to the surface, rendering the soil too saline for anything to grow in it.

Along a 1,200-mile coastline of Hudson Bay, government officials estimate 35 percent of tundra habitat has been converted to barren, cracked earth, with another 30 percent severely damaged. The disruption has affected other species dependent upon tundra for nesting, such as the parasitic jaeger, yellow rail, stilt sandpiper, oldsquaw, and Lapland longspur.

In searching for means to control the snow goose population, the U.S. Fish & Wildlife Service, supported by conservation groups including the National Audubon Society, has urged state and provincial governments to liberalize laws regulating the hunting of snow geese. But because the species is notoriously wary and difficult to hunt, the F&WS goal of a 50 percent population reduction over four years may be achieved only through a combination of efforts.

understory and invaded grassland areas throughout the floodplain. The most widespread ground cover in the forest is poison ivy—an important food source for more than 400 wildlife species—which climbs the trunks of many trees to a height of 60 feet and offers surprisingly beautiful colors in autumn. Scouring rush and stinging nettle are also well represented on the damp forest floor, as are a variety of mushrooms, including the delectable morel mushroom.

Open water DeSoto Lake is most accurately described as a man-made oxbow lake. It covers nearly 700 acres and reaches a depth of 24 feet. Most of its shores are forested with willow and cottonwood. A thriving fishery includes flathead and channel catfish, crappie, walleye, and white bass. Fishing is extremely popular and productive. A few years ago the refuge introduced 800 paddlefish, which is a prehistoric oddity with a long, fleshy snout and nary a bone in its body. Native to the Missouri, the paddlers are growing: A 60-pound specimen was landed recently.

The Missouri River in its engineered channel sweeps through the southern reaches of the refuge. Through this region the gradient is gentle, the river descending about one foot per mile. Its sediment-rich waters led Native Americans to call it the "Big Muddy," a feature that hasn't changed. Straightening and narrowing of its channel, however, along with conversion of floodplain areas to cropfields, have eliminated most of the seasonal sloughs and ponds attractive to waterfowl and shorebirds. River survivors include the gizzard shad, a population of channel and flathead catfish, and the endangered pallid sturgeon.

Grasslands About 1,800 acres of former croplands on DeSoto have been reseeded to native grasses, including sideoats grama, switchgrass, and big and little bluestem, among others. Some 2,000 acres continue to serve for crop production, primarily alfalfa, as a food source for wildlife.

■ **ANIMAL LIFE** Snow geese blanket DeSoto in unimaginably large numbers—numbers equalled only by the thousands of people who jam the auto tour and Visitor Center to view them. Spring and fall flocks of a quarter million were

typical through the early 1990s; in recent years, the numbers have grown—from 500,000 and 600,000 to a staggering concentration of 800,000 birds in 1996. Snow geese are now overabundant throughout their range and have denuded their tundra nesting grounds in Canada, to the detriment of many other bird species.

DeSoto's other big annual wildlife attraction is bald eagles. Birds from the northern United States and Canada wend their way south along the Missouri, following flocks of migrating waterfowl and shorebirds. They arrive on the refuge during the winter holidays and remain through early

Red-headed woodpecker

Yellow-headed blackbird in grasslands

spring. Bald eagles can be spied perching in large cottonwoods around DeSoto Lake and along the Missouri River, watching for gizzard shad, their favorite meal. A refuge-record 145 eagles were counted in 1999; the Visitor Center offers prime viewing.

The woodlands support a broad range of species. Mammals include coyote, raccoon, Virginia opossum, white-tailed deer, and eastern fox squirrels, including a melanistic, or darkly pigmented, group colored jet black. Wild turkey and bobwhite quail walk the forest and grassland edges. Both red-headed and red-bellied woodpeckers are common, though the latter is more secretive. Notable songbirds include the veery, wood thrush, yellow-billed cuckoo, orchard oriole, northern cardinal, and rose-breasted grosbeak. Colorful flocks of migrating monarch butterflies pass through the refuge in autumn. On summer evenings, barred owls chant "*Who cooks for you? Who cooks for you all?*"

Wood ducks are the only waterfowl species nesting here in significant numbers. Several nesting houses can be seen along Wood Duck Pond. Muskrat, along with an occasional great blue heron and yellow-headed blackbird, may be spotted in this area as well. In grassland areas, the dickcissel is a common and beautiful sight; the grasshopper, lark, and Henslow's sparrows all nest on site in limited numbers.

Along the shore of DeSoto Lake and in the Missouri River, beaver are abundant; also seen here occasionally is the northern river otter. The endangered least tern nests on-site; the refuge works to enhance sandbar nesting sites for the tern and another rare species, the piping plover. A successful reintroduction of Canada geese has taken place, and parents with broods are now a fairly common sight.

Songbird diversity reaches its peak here during spring migration. Waterfowl are most diverse and abundant during spring and fall migrations, as are several species of terns and gulls.

ACTIVITIES

■ **CAMPING:** Camping is not permitted on the refuge, but both primitive and developed camping facilities are available at the Wilson Island State Recreation Area, adjacent to the refuge.

■ **SWIMMING:** Swimming is not permitted.

■ **WILDLIFE OBSERVATION:** One of the great things about DeSoto is the relative ease with which such species as bald eagles, white-tailed deer, coyotes, and Canada geese may be observed. A favorite pastime at the Visitor Center is watching a coyote stalk family groups of snow geese; fish are seen cruising the lakeshore, and white-tailed deer are visible as well. Visitation is heavy during the snow goose migration in Nov.; on weekends expect a full-to-overflowing Visitor Center and long lines on the auto tour.

HUNTING AND FISHING You may fish in the refuge waters from April 15–Oct. 14; there is also ice fishing, when the lake has frozen deeply enough, in Jan. and Feb. **Crappie, carp, bullfish, northern walleyes**, and **catfish** are all present.

There are separate archery and muzzle-loading **deer** hunting seasons on the refuge, on a small, isolated area of the refuge apart from the visitation area. Because the refuge spans two states, there are two different seasons—contact the refuge for exact dates.

For prime viewing keep in mind this schedule: the geese depart the refuge at sunup to forage in surrounding fields, and may return again in mid-day.

■ **PHOTOGRAPHY:** From late fall through early spring, DeSoto is a prime site for bald eagle photography. The Bob Star Overlook and the Visitor Center are the two best viewing sites. The other attraction has to be the fall migratory flocks of snow geese. A telephoto lens is important; even in large numbers, a flock of geese shot with a standard or fixed lens will resemble little more than windblown scraps of white paper.

■ **HIKES AND WALKS:** Adjacent to the Visitor Center, DeSoto's Missouri Meander Trail allows exploration of the site's rich bottomland forest, including some of its largest cottonwood trees. The other must is the *Bertrand* excavation site, where a short trail leads to the exposed hull of the 1800s-era steamboat.

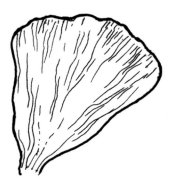

Oyster mushroom

■ **SEASONAL EVENTS:** Hundreds of people visit DeSoto each spring to gather fresh mushrooms. Two varieties, the morel and oyster mushroom, are the focus of this popular event. Oyster mushrooms, firm and with a sweet taste not unlike that of almonds, are excellent in soups and stews.

■ **PUBLICATIONS:** Auto Tour Guide; bird checklist; general visitor brochure; steamboat *Bertrand* brochure; snow goose migration brochure; Wood Duck Nature Trail guide; events schedule; booklet, "Living on the Edge: Endangered Species in Iowa."

Neal Smith NWR and Prairie Learning Center

Prairie City, Iowa

American bison

If it is true that place plays a major part in shaping one's identity, what exactly do the people of a region lose when a natural landscape—the defining landscape of a region, even, celebrated by the likes of Willa Cather, Walt Whitman, and Carl Sandburg—disappears altogether? Does America's heartland lose its heart?

The answer may be found at Neal Smith NWR, where the restoration of a once-dominant landscape is under way. In an extraordinary effort, a native ecosystem is being remade more or less from scratch. The challenge is to revert 8,000 acres of well-used Iowa farmland to a thriving, self-sustaining landscape of native tallgrass prairie, wet meadows, and oak savanna. An ecological restoration effort like this has never been attempted before, and it is expected that its impact will be felt not only ecologically but socially.

Tallgrass prairie is an old thing, an ancient thing, and no one alive today in central Iowa really knows what life within a prairie landscape was like. Neal Smith, therefore, is a "process" refuge, working to reconnect people to their local and regional history and make them a part of its future. In that sense, Neal Smith may be a prototype for the next era of American conservation.

HISTORY

The idea of reestablishing a viable, self-sustaining prairie ecosystem began in 1991, when the U.S. Fish & Wildlife Service acquired 3,600 acres of farmland originally intended for a nuclear-power generator. Unlike most would-be refuge lands, there was little to "preserve." The area was largely old farm ground, with scattered bits of native plant communities in a highly degraded state. The site was ideal for the many questions the F&WS sought to explore: What was here? What is here? What are the processes and opportunities—scientific, social, ecological—

Western meadowlark

associated with remaking an ecosystem from scratch?

It may be no exaggeration to say that the most recent generations of Iowans, and midwesterners as a whole, pass into and out of their formative years without an answer to the first question. Less than one-tenth of Iowa's original 35 million acres of tallgrass prairie remains; in Illinois, Indiana, and Ohio, the total is certainly no larger. Even in rural communities today, most residents grow up understanding that their midwestern soil is as rich as any on earth, but with little understanding of what made it that way. In determining their mission, refuge planners looked for a wide array of educational opportunities, realizing that prairie restoration would serve only limited ends if it remained separated from the daily lives of people. From beginning to completion, it was decided that the entire refuge would serve as an outdoor classroom.

On a cold, windy day in May 1992, refuge staff and volunteers celebrated the birth of a prairie. The first batch of local seeds—wildflowers and grasses—were planted; an old-time band played, and participants, holding hands, "danced" the seeds into four acres of earth. In doing so, a new tradition began: "Sow Your Wild Oats Day," now held each year in spring.

At its inception the refuge bore the name of Walnut Creek; in 1998 the name was changed to Neal Smith NWR, to recognize the efforts of the former Iowa congressman who helped make the project a reality. Land acquisition continues to this day; the goal of 8,654 acres is now two-thirds completed. In 1996, one of the most celebrated and long-absent members of the prairie community—a herd of bison—arrived at its new home. Already the refuge has been taken into the lives of many Iowans, volunteers, and visitors. Things, as they say, are blooming.

GETTING THERE

From Des Moines, travel east on US 163 for 20 mi. to refuge entrance and Visitor Center.

■ **SEASON:** Refuge open year-round.

■ **HOURS:** Refuge administrative office is open Mon.–Fri., 8 a.m.–4:30 p.m.; headquarters, Visitor Center, and Prairie Learning Center are open Tues.–Sat., 9 a.m.–4 p.m.; Sun., 12 p.m.–5 p.m..

■ **FEES:** Free access.

■ **ADDRESS:** P.O. Box 399, 9981 Pacific Street, Prairie City, IA 50228

■ **TELEPHONE:** 515/994-3400

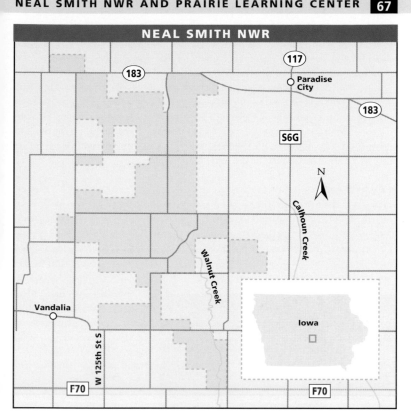

TOURING NEAL SMITH

■ **BY AUTOMOBILE:** The 4-mile entry road to the refuge Visitor Center features interpretive signs and viewing points. The 8-mile auto tour, open year-round and with interpretive stops and scenic overlooks, takes visitors through the prairie home of bison and elk herds.

■ **BY FOOT:** Tallgrass Trail (a hard-surfaced trail) meanders about 2 miles. The unsurfaced Oak Savanna Trail, 0.75 mile, explores savanna restoration. The unsurfaced Basswood Trail, 0.5 mile, features 15 interpreted points of interest.

■ **BY BICYCLE:** No bicycles permitted on refuge trails or off-trail. Bicycles are permitted on the country and refuge roads.

■ **BY CANOE, KAYAK, OR BOAT:** No boating permitted on refuge; just south of the refuge is Lake Red Rock, an impoundment on the Des Moines River.

WHAT TO SEE

■ **LANDSCAPE AND CLIMATE** Neal Smith's historic natural communities evolved as part of the Southern Iowa Drift Plain. Formed by glacial "drift," deposits of soil and rock, the region over many years accumulated an extensive covering of wind blown soils and rock dust called loess, another glacial by product. Wind, rain, and time then set to work, carving the porous loess soils into the present-day topography of low, rolling hills, gulches, and valleys.

More than a hundred years ago this landscape was a matrix of tallgrass prairie, oak savanna, wet meadows, and wetlands. General Land Office survey notes and other historical texts from the 1800s indicate that no trees were present in the northern reaches of the refuge. To the south, sources indicate a mixture of open prairie with stands of bur oak and other deciduous trees. These savanna sites probably served as nursery colonies for the Indiana bat, an endangered species that today survives on the refuge.

Climatic conditions fluctuate greatly and tend to defy generalities. Summers are hot and very humid, with a monthly average of 5 or so inches of precipitation and temperatures into the 90s through July and August. From January through March, conditions often swing between subzero days to readings into the 50s and above. Cool, wet springs, with abundant rainfall, are typical. Frosts may arrive as early as Labor Day or as late as the first days of October.

■ PLANT LIFE

Tallgrass prairie Each year the size, vitality, and species diversity of Neal Smith's prairiescape grows. It is a slow and highly labor-intensive process, rife with challenges, setbacks, and surprises. Among other things, the effort illustrates the difficulty of reviving a complex natural system that was allowed to become highly fragmented. As interest in native prairie spreads among area residents, landowners view old patches of untilled ground or ditches of "weeds" with new eyes. As a result,

a number of rare local species—turtlehead, Riddell's goldenrod, wood betony and sedges—have been discovered, and seeds have been donated to the refuge. Scouring the countryside, volunteer teams of "seed seekers" bring in some 150 species each year, in quantities ranging from a gunnysack to a thimble. The tenacity of nature, its ability to endure at a near-invisible level, is another lesson. Surviving prairie remnants on the refuge are often disguised as woodlots of elm and locust trees; look closely, poke around, and there, hanging on for dear life, are three species of native orchid: Dutchman's-breeches, bloodroot, and compass plant. Hardly a week goes by at Neal Smith without a new discovery, a cause for opimism.

Prairie white-fringed orchid

For staff, volunteers, and many visitors, this refuge is a hands-on experience. Many Iowans have fallen in love with the place, and Iowans don't shy from hard work. Visiting dignitaries are occasionally enlisted to roll up their sleeves and pull nonnative sweet clover and other plants. Preparing for the first prescribed burn of refuge woodlands in 1999, high school and college students cut down trees and

OF ANTS AND EARTHWORMS The remaking of a natural landscape at Neal Smith has provided a rare opportunity for the scientific community. Just about every living thing on the site allows one or another specialist a chance to inventory, monitor, and study its progress over a sustained period. The process extends to some less-glamorous species, including ants and earthworms.

An expert in the ant realm has identified 29 species here. A mound-building variety occupying the southern portion of the refuge is responsible for a single mound measuring 10 feet in diameter. Another species, adapted to the prairie, appears to thrive in the presence of fire and has not been documented anywhere else. Still other ants restrict themselves to the savanna areas.

Even more unusual here is the earthworm community. The worms seen by most Americans are imported species from Europe or China and are not native species. Dr. Sam James, an earthworm ecologist from Fairfield, Iowa, in a single day identified six native species, none of which occur anywhere else in northern Iowa. All were found only in areas where native prairie plants survived. James speculates that these species are a remnant population at the northern extent of their range, in central Iowa. Relatively recent glaciation in northern Iowa may have caused the demise of these species in the north.

---

cleared brush on 60 acres by hand. Hidden in the overgrowth, prairie wildflowers responded quickly to the fire; the increased air circulation through the woodlands will also help native bur oak in reestablishing natural savanna conditions.

To date, some 2,300 acres of native grasses and wildflowers, sown by hand or machinery, are staging a colorful revival. A number of remnant prairie sites have now been freed of nonnative competition. The eastern and western fringed prairie orchids, both endangered, are about to be reintroduced. As part of ongoing work involving the habitat needs of the regal fritillary, a rare prairie butterfly, prairie violets have been reestablished; the bird-foot violet, another flower important to the fritillary, may be introduced as well.

Open waters Walnut Creek is a typical Iowa stream, which is to say it has been ravaged to serve the needs of agriculture. Straightened in several areas, a receptacle for runoff from crop fields, the creek carries a heavy load of sediments, as well as a stout mix of nitrates, herbicides, pesticides, and effluent from livestock. Its banks are currently subject to steady collapsing, which only adds to the turbidity problem. A state-of-the-art water-monitoring system is now in place. Researchers have learned that in areas owned by the refuge and planted to prairie, water is becoming considerably cleaner. Refuge staff is trying to prioritize rehabilitation efforts and has received cooperation from adjacent landowners in its efforts to reduce erosion and stabilize the stream.

Woodlands Though it once ranged from Ohio to Minnesota, oak savanna was so thoroughly eliminated early in the settlement era that the ecology of this woodland type is not well understood today. Thus the process of restoring savanna on Neal Smith presents an equally rare opportunity for increasing knowledge. Drawing from historic records, on-site detective work, and extrapolations from remaining sites, refuge biologists are piecing together the mysteries of oak savanna as they revive remnant stands and make plans for establishing new ones.

To date, some very interesting things have been deduced. Oak savanna is a highly dynamic and localized plant community. The mix of oak species, grasses, and wildflowers can vary greatly within an area of just 10 miles. Fluctuations in climate probably caused a never-ending cycle of expansion and contraction, the woodlands ranging farther afield during some periods, and shrinking back during others. Historically, savannas were rich in legumes such as violet bush clover, which provided excellent browse for elk. A rich assortment of berries and nuts, from such species as wild rose, mayapple, raspberry, and Solomon's seal, were also part of the mix. Other unique wildflowers in the savanna understory would include creamy gentian, purple milkweed, and leatherflower, a tiny vine with soft, bell-shaped blooms of blue. All of these varieties appear to have been part of the mix at Neal Smith and will be reestablished, though some are already present in existing savannas. The surviving variety of oaks on site—red, white, bur, and a few black—suggest this was an especially diverse savanna, and one that benefited from a number of springs and "seeps" where groundwater percolates out of the hillsides. Bur oak, however, is by far the most characteristic oak species.

■ ANIMAL LIFE

Birds Grassland birds appear in greater numbers and diversity each year. At this early stage, species such as grasshopper sparrows, eastern bluebirds, eastern and western meadowlarks, a few bobolinks, and upland sandpipers have moved in. Northern harriers and short-eared owls have returned as well and are nesting on site. In 1999, Henslow's sparrows were sighted on the refuge. Future plans call for

bringing back the greater prairie chicken. In the woodlands are a number of species adapted to the unnaturally dense growth—Bell's vireo, scarlet tanager, orchard oriole—which may or may not persist when savanna conditions return. Indigo buntings, too, are a question mark: will they stay or will they go? refuge staff is interested to see what will happen.

Mammals Through a combination of reintroduction and natural recolonization, prairie and savanna wildlife is making a comeback. A herd of 10 elk was established with animals from the National Bison Range in Montana, and the first calf was born on the refuge in 1999. The reintroduced bison herd of 38 has produced 16 calves to date,

Grasshopper sparrow, singing

with more sure to follow. Both herds roam a 750-acre enclosure that also includes a good number of white-tailed deer. Grazing machines all, the elk in particular are mowing down nonnative Kentucky bluegrass, doing their part to eliminate the stuff and make room for native prairie. As herd numbers grow, the enclosure will expand; at carrying capacity for the prairie, it will encompass about 2,000 acres.

American bison and calf

Mink and short-tailed weasels are seen prowling the area again, along with the opportunists—striped skunks, raccoons, and red fox. Refuge staff believe it is only a matter of time until a northern river otter or two takes up residence; they have been successfully reintroduced in the Des Moines River, of which Walnut Creek is a tributary.

ACTIVITIES

■ **PRAIRIE LEARNING CENTER:** The Prairie Learning Center (PLC) encompasses multimedia exhibits, lectures and programs, research labs, and a greenhouse/seed nursery, and it utilizes the entire refuge as a living textbook. An outdoor amphitheater brings student groups and visitors into direct contact with topics presented at the PLC. For information on PLC scheduled programs and related opportunities, contact the refuge headquarters at 515/994-3400.

■ **CAMPING AND SWIMMING:** Camping is not permitted on the refuge, and the nearest campground is some 40 miles away.

■ **WILDLIFE OBSERVATION:** A major attraction in spring are the aerial courtship displays of the American woodcock. Songbird diversity during spring and fall migration continues to grow; bison and elk calves are typically born from April through July. Elk calves totter about on long, spindly legs, tawny-colored with large white spots; bison young are fleecy, buckskin-colored, and love to run.

■ **PHOTOGRAPHY:** Of course there are many possibilities for "before" and "during" and "after" photographs here, as the landscape changes from farmland to prairie. Elk and bison, including their offspring, may be photographed along the auto-tour route; wildflowers are the prime attraction, with spectacular bloomers like blazing star flowering between May and October. More plant species are observed each year on the refuge, as the prairie plantings mature.

■ **HIKES AND WALKS:** Along Tallgrass Trail, visitors gain an appreciation for the scope of the work. The trail passes along reconstructed prairie lands in various stages of recovery, as well as surviving areas now being restored. It also traverses some of the woodland and savanna areas, most of which are in their prerestoration state, and passes along the southern reaches of the bison and elk pasture.

HUNTING AND FISHING There is no fishing allowed in the refuge waters. You may, however, hunt for **upland game** and **white-tailed deer** within the prescribed state seasons. State of Iowa regulations apply; contact the refuge for details.

■ **SEASONAL EVENTS:** Sow Your Wild Oats Day, a springtime celebration and ceremonial planting of prairie seeds, takes place in May. Buffalo Day takes place in July, and National Wildlife Refuge Week is celebrated in October with special events. Contact www.tallgrass.com for more information.

■ **PUBLICATIONS:** Bird checklist; refuge map; additional interpretive brochures and materials are in development.

■ **VOLUNTEER OPPORTUNITIES:** This dynamic refuge is a labor of love for volunteers of all ages and backgrounds. Seed Collecting Teams harvest, inventory, dry, and clean native grass and wildflower seeds for planting; bird surveys take place; computer jocks assist with databases and mapping of restoration areas. Other volunteer opportunities include maintenance, administration, work in the book store, environmental education, and assisting with special events activities. The refuge has attracted a good deal of interest from the scientific community, and opportunities exist for volunteers to assist with research projects supervised by professionals.

Union Slough NWR
Titonka, Iowa

Union Slough NWR

A 3,405-acre prairie oasis of wind-ruffled water framed by low, sweeping hills of native grass, Union Slough preserves a bit of Iowa's past in a landscape that today is dominated by agriculture. Beneath a great dome of sky are flourishing marshlands and a fine annual display of native wildflowers.

HISTORY

The deep, loamy soils here attracted settlers, who between 1906 and 1920 converted more than 90 percent of Iowa wetlands to farmland by draining Union Slough and converting it to pasture. Despite these efforts, some wetlands persisted, encouraging local conservationists to restore 2,500 acres of the original slough when the refuge was established in 1937.

GETTING THERE

From US 169 at Bancroft, drive 6 mi. east on County A-42 to refuge headquarters.
■ **SEASON:** Refuge open year-round.
■ **HOURS:** Open daylight hours; refuge headquarters is open weekdays, 7:30 a.m.–4 p.m.
■ **FEES:** Free access.
■ **ADDRESS:** 1710 360th Street, Titonka, IA 50480
■ **TELEPHONE:** 515/928-2523

TOURING UNION SLOUGH

■ **BY AUTOMOBILE:** A 4.5-mile tour route is open seasonally, paralleling refuge wetlands; county roads provide access to parking areas on the north end of the refuge and to the boat launch to the south, near Buffalo Creek Bottoms.
■ **BY FOOT:** The refuge offers gentle walks in season along the mowed Deer Meadow Nature Trail and in the Vanishing Prairie Grassland Area.

■ **BY BICYCLE:** Bicycles are not permitted on refuge.

■ **BY CANOE, KAYAK, OR BOAT:** Canoeing is allowed on Buffalo Creek only. Spring and fall, when the creek becomes a marsh, are prime seasons for an easy scenic paddle; the creek narrows in summer, although it remains navigable.

WHAT TO SEE

On the eastern edge of the tallgrass prairie, Union Slough is a shallow preglacial riverbed, a "union" of the Blue Earth River and the East Fork of the Des Moines River. So level is this riverbed that in presettlement days the wind determined the direction in which the water flowed.

Buffalo Creek qualifies as open water, deep enough on the south end of the refuge to support walleye, catfish, and northern pike on Tienan's Dam. Six impoundments on the slough allow for manipulation of water levels; the goal, however, is to mimic natural, presettlement cycles.

Winters are typically cold and windy, with moderate amounts of snow; in summer, stretches of heat and humidity give way to cooler, drier air. September and October are beautiful here. Annual precipitation exceeds 40 inches.

Hemi-marsh is the term given to the mosaic of beautiful wetlands here.

Goldenrod

Some are seasonal, filling and drying over the first weeks of spring; others retain some water year-round and feature thickets of emergent vegetation, including cattails, sedges, and bulrush.

Remnants of native tallgrass prairie occur in several areas, with showy stands of big bluestem grasses and an excellent display of wildflowers—butterfly milkweed, leadplant, blazing star, asters, goldenrods, coneflowers, and wild sunflowers, among many others. Restoration of former croplands to native prairie species is an ongoing priority.

The southern reaches of the refuge feature a second-growth bottomland hardwood forest of green ash, willow, scattered cottonwood, oak, and maple.

A mixture of species common to prairie, forest, and marshland exist in close proximity here. Water-associated mammals—beaver, muskrat, mink, and raccoon—are regularly seen. A thriving community of shorebirds, ducks, and other marshland birds occurs, from the elusive king rail to the great egret, least bittern, green-backed heron, stilt sandpiper, blue-winged teal, lesser yellowlegs, and black tern. American white pelicans are often seen in mid- to late summer. Some 2,500 wood ducks are born here each year; the refuge maintains one of the largest wood duck nesting-box efforts in the United States.

Union Slough's woodlands feature a different mix. Along with white-tailed deer and red fox on the edges, the forest is home to the eastern screech owl, black-billed cuckoo, and red-headed woodpecker; few warblers nest here, though a great many species are seen during spring migration. Numerous songbirds favor the prairie: the bobolink, dickcissel, brown thrasher, willow flycatcher, and eastern kingbird are all commonly seen.

ACTIVITIES

■ **CAMPING:** Camping is not permitted on the refuge. Camping facilities are available at nearby Smith Lake and Crystal Lake.

■ **WILDLIFE OBSERVATION:** Spring and fall migrations bring large numbers of waterfowl—ducks, horned and eared grebes, greater white-fronted geese, snow geese, and occasionally tundra swans. A number of raptors, including bald eagles, make their appearances at these times as well. Canoeing Buffalo Creek in spring or fall is a treat, with abundant birdsong, old oxbow sloughs, and some lovely stands of forest. There is excellent shorebird diversity from mid-August to mid-September, when conditions are right.

■ **PHOTOGRAPHY:** A very good site for wildflower photography. July through early September are the prime months, and the Deer Meadow and Vanishing Prairie are the best areas. Wading birds are readily encountered along the auto-tour route.

■ **HIKES AND WALKS:** Deer Meadow Trail traverses Buffalo Creek on the south end of the refuge, through a tallgrass prairie with a first-rate wildflower display in midsummer. This area offers the best woodland birding on the refuge. American white pelicans and brown thrashers are seen along the creek in summer. Walk the Vanishing Prairie area to ascend a small series of bluffs with views of the marsh complex and views of wetland species.

HUNTING AND FISH-ING Portions of the refuge are open to hunting for **small game**, **upland birds**, **water-fowl**, and **white-tailed deer** in accordance with state seasons; contact the refuge for details. There is a limited fishing season for **northern pike**.

■ **SEASONAL EVENTS:** Guided canoe tours of the marshland complex during National Wildlife Refuge Week in October are popular. In May, an auto tour opens the International Migratory Bird Day, which includes other activities. Call for details.

Kirtland's Warbler NWR
Grayling, Michigan

Brown-headed cowbird

The guided nature tour to Kirtland's Warbler NWR looks less than promising at first. The tour originates from a Holiday Inn situated in a typical "Up North" Michigan tourist town. The destination? A scraggly, sterile-looking stand of one of nature's least imposing trees, the jack pine. What makes this tour exceptional— exciting, even—is the very good opportunity of spotting one of the rarest birds in the world.

HISTORY

Kirtland's Warbler NWR is a refuge unique to the Great Lakes—indeed, to the entire national refuge system. It consists of 119 tracts totaling 6,684 acres of land scattered through eight counties in Michigan's Lower Peninsula. The sole purpose of the refuge is to provide critically needed nesting habitat for Kirtland's warblers. To that end the public is barred from entering the refuge except for guided tours during the warbler's breeding season. Because Kirtland's warbler is such a rare species—the total population was recorded at roughly 1,600 in 1998—people come from all over the world for a glimpse. In 1998, 773 people from 41 states took the warbler tour from Grayling. Among them were visitors from nine countries including Australia, Sweden, Russia, Ireland, and India.

GETTING THERE

Kirtland's warbler tours begin at either Grayling or Mio, Michigan. No dogs or taped birdcalls are permitted. The U.S. Fish & Wildlife Service conducts the Grayling tours from mid-May through July 4, starting at the Holiday Inn on the south I-75 Business Loop. Tours begin at 7 a.m. and 11 a.m. daily and take about 90 minutes. The tours from Grayling are free. Call the Holiday Inn (517/348-7611) for tour reservations.

The U.S. Forest Service conducts tours mid-May through July 2 from Mio and charges $5 per person. The tours depart the Mio Ranger District Office on the corner of 4th and MI 33 in Mio at 7 a.m. Wed. through Fri. and at 7 and 11 a.m. on weekends. Because Mio tours are subject to change, call ahead for details (517/826-3252). Visitors planning to enter the refuge on their own—permitted outside the breeding season only—should consult with one of the government agencies first.

KIRTLAND'S WARBLER Kirtland's warblers owe their scarcity, in part, to their extreme fussiness over nesting habitat. They will nest only near the base of young jack pines that are between 5 and 16 feet tall, and thus they are able to raise a family in only eight counties in Michigan's Lower Peninsula.

That's not the only thing limiting the warbler's nesting habitat. Jack pine cones open and release their seeds only after being burned. Unaware of the consequences to the warbler, the official policy of the state Department of Natural Resources was to prevent—and, if started, stop—forest fires. That approach to forest management was pushing the little bird, which winters in the Bahamas, to the brink of extinction. Today the birds' nesting habitat is managed by controlled burns and by the planting of jack pine seedlings.

Brown-headed cowbirds also threaten the warbler's existence. The cowbird lays its eggs in a host nest; when the larger cowbird chick is born, it out-competes the nest's rightful chicks for food, and the cowbird becomes the only fledgling to leave the nest alive. Cowbirds were making serious inroads in the warbler population before a program of trapping and destroying the parasites was inaugurated.

ACTIVITIES

A Kirtland's warbler tour starts with an introductory slide show detailing the bird's natural history and the efforts being made to ensure its survival. After the slide show a motorcade of cars follows the ranger to an unimpressive and out-of-the-way stand of jack pines alongside a country road. (The term "in the sticks" comes to mind.) The ranger parks on the shoulder of the road and leads the eager group into the trees in a search for a singing male. The bird is distinguished by a blue-gray back and lemon-yellow belly. Spotting a Kirtland's warbler is an undeniable thrill for dedicated birders, not to mention anyone who has traveled halfway around the world and spent thousands of dollars hoping to catch a glimpse of the bird.

Seney NWR
Seney, Michigan

Great Manistique Swamp, Seney NWR

It offers grand vistas and a wide, expansive horizon, yet the 153-square-mile Seney National Wildlife Refuge reveals its soul in small increments. The eloquence of Seney shines through in the delicate, almost ethereal beauty of a starflower, in the tiny speck in the tree that, upon closer inspection, is revealed as a fledgling bald eagle, and in a pair of long-billed snipes probing the muddy fringes of a marsh pool. Dozens of these and other distinctive sights and sounds make Seney unforgettable for each of its 100,000 annual visitors.

HISTORY

Lying within the Great Manistique Swamp in Michigan's Upper Peninsula (UP), the area that is now refuge land escaped the first swipe of the lumberman's ax simply because its trees were considered less valuable than the area pines. But after the UP's white and red pine fell, hungry sawmills dined on Seney's hardwoods and conifers. Fueled by brush and kindling left by the lumbermen, fires roared across the clear-cut barrens and even burned the humus in the soil. Speculators bought and drained the played-out land and, with extravagant claims of fertility, sold parcels to would-be farmers. Doomed to failure, the farms reverted back to the state, as dreams went bust and taxes couldn't be paid. In 1935, at the urging of Michigan's Conservation Department, Congress established Seney as a refuge and breeding ground for migrating birds. Today, Seney is among the eastern UP's major tourist attractions.

GETTING THERE

The headquarters, Visitor Center, and main entrance are located on MI 77, 2 mi. north of Germfask. Coming from the north, the entrance is 5 mi. south of the intersection of MI 28 and MI 77 in Seney.

■ **SEASON:** Open year-round.

■ **HOURS:** Refuge open from dawn to dusk, daily. Visitor Center, 9 a.m.–5 p.m., from May 15–Sept. 30. Refuge office, 8 a.m.–4 p.m., Mon.–Fri. all year.
■ **FEES:** No charge.
■ **ADDRESS:** Seney NWR, HCR 2, Box 1, Seney, MI 49883
■ **TELEPHONE:** 906/586-9851

TOURING SENEY

■ **BY AUTOMOBILE:** The paved entrance road serves as a scenic teaser for the refuge's most popular feature, a 7-mile-long, one-way, self-guided auto tour, passing several large ponds and meandering through numerous habitats.

■ **BY FOOT:** In addition to a 1.5-mile nature trail, visitors are welcome to hike most of the refuge. Inside the refuge are 80 miles of gravel roads closed to motorized traffic. Areas not open to the public are so posted.

■ **BY BICYCLE:** Bikes may well offer the best chance of seeing the largest slice of the refuge in a single day of exploring, because camping is not allowed anywhere on the property and visitors are expected to leave by sundown. Bikes are permitted on the self-guided auto tour and on the refuge's gravel roads. The cross-country ski trails and the nature trail are closed to bikes. Areas closed to bikes are so posted.

■ **BY CANOE, KAYAK, OR BOAT:** The Manistique River flows through the southern part of the refuge and makes for fine canoeing. Headquarters can supply a list of local canoe rental companies. Canoeing is not recommended on the Driggs River because of its many snags and shallow water. Watercraft are not allowed on the refuge's pools.

■ **CROSS-COUNTRY SKIING:** Nordic skiing is allowed anywhere on the refuge, but most skiers are drawn to the groomed trails in the Northern Hardwoods Cross-country Ski Area. The area has seven loops totaling 8.5 miles of trail. Snowshoeing is allowed everywhere except the ski trails.

WHAT TO SEE

■ **LANDSCAPE AND CLIMATE** The refuge is a patchwork of second-growth forests, open pools, bog, marsh and meadows. Nearly two-thirds of the 95,455-acre refuge is wetlands. Most of the open water fills 21 man-made pools totaling 7,000 acres. The pools, built by the Civilian Conservation Corps in the 1930s, dominate the landscape adjacent to the Visitor Center and along the auto tour. If the CCC transformed much of what was wasteland by reseeding forests and rebuilding wetlands, there is a 25,000-acre wilderness area within the refuge that remains untouched since the logging era. The unique Strangmoor Bog, lying within the wilderness area, has been designated a National Natural Landmark. The bog's peculiar topography was formed when low sand dunes left by retreating glaciers were combed by the wind into long, thin parallel ridges. Crowned by brush and trees, the ridges run like parallel islands through the wilderness area.

Summers at Seney usually feature daytime temperatures in the low 70s. Winters here are surprisingly mild due to the lake effect from lakes Michigan and Superior. The lakes may warm passing winds in the winter, but those winds pick up moisture and drop it in the form of snow, lots of snow.

■ **PLANT LIFE** The fires that swept across the Seney area in the wake of the lumber clear-cutting in the 1870s were so devastating that many areas within the refuge have still not recovered. Second-growth forests of spruce, fir, tamarack, pine, and hardwoods are reclaiming some barren lands; other areas have reverted to meadows. A mature stand of sugar maple, beech, and yellow birch silently waits to impress hikers and cross-country skiers in the Northern Hardwoods Cross-Country Ski Area. Aspen are also common throughout the refuge and in the fall paint the refuge with golden brushstrokes.

Cattails and other common marsh plants prosper in Seney's extensive wetlands. Several species of clover and numerous sun-loving wildflowers populate the many treeless meadows. The nature trail passes through various habitats, revealing iris, wild rose, turtle's head, and a pleasing bouquet of other wildflowers.

For those who like to harvest and dine on nature's bounty, the refuge allows the gathering of wild foods and fruits. Morel mushrooms, blueberries, and strawberries are among the more popular edibles flourishing here.

■ **ANIMAL LIFE** Seney is a veritable Noah's Ark for northwoods wildlife.
Birds From spring through fall birdsong fills the air at Seney. More than 200 species have been recorded in the refuge, in all seasons. Waterfowl make themselves conspicuous from the moment a car pulls into the Visitor Center parking lot. The refuge's unofficial greeters—a gaggle of Canada geese, both adults and goslings—waddle over to examine the newcomers. These geese are descended

Mosquito

from a captive band released at Seney the year it became a national wildlife refuge. The goslings from that first nesting season were allowed to migrate, and when they returned to Seney in the spring of 1936, it was the first time in decades migrating geese had come to Seney.

Hooded mergansers, mallards, American black ducks, wood ducks, and ring-necked ducks all nest in the

BUZZ, SWAT, ITCH, SCRATCH Some of the wildlife at Seney doesn't wait to be discovered. It comes looking for visitors like heat-seeking missiles. Other regions boast of the ferocity of their biting insects, but final judgment should be reserved until the blackflies, deerflies, mosquitoes, and wood ticks of Michigan's Upper Peninsula and Seney NWR have been sampled. The British literary traveler Anna Brownell Jameson was moved to recall a man who claimed mosquitoes made of brass and the size of beetles resided in hell, when she passed through the UP in 1839. She wrote, "he was an ignoramus and a bungler; you may credit me, that the brass is quite an unnecessary improvement, and the increase of size equally superfluous. Mosquitoes as they exist in this upper world are as pretty and perfect a plague as the most ingenious amateur sinner-tormentor ever devised." Jerry Dennis, in his book *A Place on the Water*, testifies that spraying a cloud of mosquitoes on the Fox River, just up the road from Seney, "hardly altered their flight. They absorbed the poison and developed genetic immunity right before my eyes." Mosquitoes and blackflies are at their worst in June and seem to thin out as summer progresses. The good news is, if you're a cross-country skier, you won't need bug repellent. For visitors to Seney at all other times, bug spray is a must.

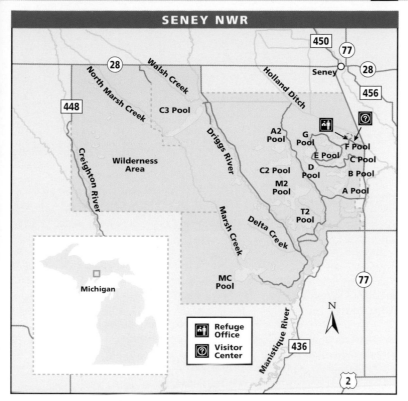

SENEY NWR

refuge and are joined by numerous other waterfowl species in the spring and fall. Seney boasts the highest density of nesting common loons in Michigan pools; the soft yodeling wail of a loon is a signature sound at Seney. It's not unusual to spy newborn loon chicks riding their mother piggyback on one of the refuge's many pools.

One of Seney's success stories is the reintroduction of trumpeter swans. By 1933, the species numbered a mere 66 birds in the lower 48 states. The magnificent bird—weighing more than 30 pounds and with an 8-foot wingspan and a call rivaling an air horn—was nearly hunted to extinction for food and feathers. In 1991 and 1992 hand-raised swans were released here at Seney, and the birds immediately took to the excellent habitat and food sources. The released birds migrated the first winter and successfully returned in the spring. Today, this great bird, the world's largest waterfowl, is regularly seen at Seney.

Ruffed grouse also nest in the refuge and perform their extravagant courtship rituals each spring, with males raising their crests, fanning their tails, and beating their wings so rapidly they sound like muffled drums. Other common nesters include black-billed cuckoos, great horned owls, a half-dozen warbler species, and both sharp-tailed and spruce grouse. Some sandhill cranes nest here, and many more of these 4-feet-tall birds funnel into the refuge each fall for a rest before heading south for the winter.

Eagles are most commonly seen here in the summer, but there are always one or two active eagle nests at Seney. The rare black-backed woodpecker has occasionally been spotted. Seney also gets its fair share of rare birds wandering far from their familiar haunts. A few years ago an American white pelican spent part of the summer at Seney instead of its normal summer grounds in the Dakotas.

Spruce grouse, Seney NWR

Winter species—such as redpolls, pine siskins, and groups of pine and evening grosbeaks—can add interest to any cross-country-ski or snowshoe trek. In the cold season, look for large flocks of snow buntings.

Mammals Sharp eyes, patience, and a little luck are needed to spot many of Seney's usually shy mammals. White-tailed deer, porcupines, and beaver are not shy, however, and are plentiful. Visitors will probably hear the plaintive howl of coyotes rather than see them. It's a cry that will raise the hair on the back of the neck. The refuge is within the boundaries of two different timber wolf packs, but they are rarely seen—finding wolf scat is as close as most visitors will ever get to viewing one. When moose are sighted, it's usually along MI 28 in the north-west corner of the refuge, where they feed in the wetlands. Sleek and inquisitive river otter and the reclusive bobcat, with its trademark tufted ears and bobbed tail, are glimpsed by only a lucky few.

Reptiles and amphibians Frogs and snapping and painted turtles are the most frequently observed amphibians.

ACTIVITIES

■ **CAMPING AND SWIMMING:** Neither swimming nor camping is allowed at Seney, but there are many private and public campgrounds within a few miles of the refuge; call headquarters. Campers can choose from secluded, rustic state forest campgrounds overlooking the Manistique River or private campgrounds with amenities.

■ **WILDLIFE OBSERVATION:** The refuge auto tour is the favored way to observe wildlife. Three observation decks, equipped with spotting scopes, along the drive invite visitors to leave their cars and probe the wetlands, meadows, and woods for wildlife. Motorists are welcome to stop anywhere on the tour there is room to pull off the drive. The one place where everyone seems to stop is the spot from which an active eagle's nest can be observed. After the long winter, geese are the first birds to return to the refuge, in mid-April, with sandhill cranes and red-winged blackbirds following close behind. Songbirds arrive on the crest of spring migration in May and are best seen along the refuge's nature trail. The number of waterfowl on the refuge peaks in late September to mid-October just before the birds head south for the winter.

■ **PHOTOGRAPHY:** Because the car makes a natural photo blind, the auto tour

SENEY HUNTING AND FISHING SEASONS

Hunting
(Seasons may vary)

white-tailed deer (using following hunting methods)

	Jan	Feb	Mar	Apr	May	Jun	Jul	Aug	Sep	Oct	Nov	Dec
bow	■									■	■	■
firearm											■	
muzzle-loader	■											■
bear									■	■		
varying hare	■	■	■						■	■	■	■
ruffed grouse									■	■	■	
woodcock										■	■	

Fishing

	Jan	Feb	Mar	Apr	May	Jun	Jul	Aug	Sep	Oct	Nov	Dec
northern pike	■	■			■	■	■	■	■	■	■	■
yellow perch	■	■	■	■	■	■	■	■	■	■	■	■
brown bullhead	■	■	■	■	■	■	■	■	■	■	■	■
sunfish	■	■	■	■	■	■	■	■	■	■	■	■
walleye	■	■			■	■	■	■	■	■	■	■
bass						■	■	■	■	■	■	■
brook trout	■	■	■	■	■	■	■	■	■	■	■	■
brown trout	■	■	■	■	■	■	■	■	■	■	■	■

Portions of the refuge are open to upland bird, big- and small-game hunting, as well as fishing in accordance with state and federal regulations. Ruffed grouse season is Sept. 15–Nov. 14; woodcock season is Sept. 25–Nov. 8; and varying hare is Sept. 15–March 31. Bow-hunting white-tailed deer season is Oct. 1–Nov. 14 and Dec. 1–Jan. 2. White-tailed deer can also be hunted with a firearm Nov. 15–30 and with a muzzle-loader Dec. 3–12 and Dec. 18–Jan. 2. A drawing is held for the distribution of bear-hunting licenses—hunters must apply with the state for the special permit. For more information on the current hunting and fishing regulations for Seney NWR, including license requirements, seasons, and bag limits, consult refuge office.

often presents opportunities for fairly close-up wildlife portraits. Those with telephoto lenses may wish to spend more than a single day along the auto tour. Canada geese frequenting the Visitor Center are among the most photographed birds in Michigan. Visit the refuge in mid-September at the peak of fall foliage, when photo possibilities increase exponentially. The nature trail is the place to capture wildflowers on film.

■ **HIKES AND WALKS:** A well-marked, pleasant, and easily walked nature trail departs and returns to the Visitor Center. It passes through a variety of habitats rich in fauna and flora. The entire refuge is open to hikers.

■ **PUBLICATIONS:** Refuge brochure with maps, wildflower and bird checklist, and a guide to the auto tour.

Shiawassee NWR
Saginaw, Michigan

Snow geese (adult and immature)

"Wildlife comes first" is the number-one tenet of the National Wildlife Refuge system, and nowhere is this more evident than at Shiawassee. Everything at the refuge—the marshlands, open pools, extensive bottomland hardwoods, grasslands, and cropland—is managed to benefit native wildlife and to maintain habitat crucial for its survival. A spring walk along the dikes in Shiawassee NWR lets the visitor reap the rewards of such careful management. A herd of white-tailed deer moves with incredible grace through the flooded woodland. Where the dikes border meadows, a delicate fawn stands mute and still. Suddenly, thousands of ducks and geese fill acres of sky, ringing in their arrival in a cacophonous symphony.

HISTORY

Ten thousand years ago, the land that is now a refuge lay at the bottom of a vast glacial lake. The old lake bottom was nearly dead-level flat. Today the dikes are the highest elevation within the refuge; at most, they are 5 feet higher than the former lakebed. Not surprisingly, the area has been known as "The Flats" since the logging era. Archaeological evidence suggests that hunter-gatherers camped and hunted here 5,000 years ago. Down through the ages, this corner of the Saginaw Valley was rich in food plants (including wild rice), waterfowl, moose, deer, elk, and bear. Native Americans lived off the land until they were removed, by treaty, in 1819. The area was heavily lumbered during the last half of the 1800s, and in 1903 farmers began draining the land and raising crops on the flats. By the 1950s, pumps, drainage tile, ditches, and dikes permitted extensive farming. The refuge was established in 1953 with the mission to restore the wetlands for migratory waterfowl.

GETTING THERE

To reach Ferguson Bayou Trail and the refuge headquarters, drive 5 mi. south of Saginaw on MI 13 to Curtis Rd. Turn west and drive 0.5 mi. to the headquarters and another 3.5 mi. to the trailhead. Access Woodland Trail by driving west on MI 46 from where the highway crosses the Saginaw River for about 2.5 mi. to Center Rd. Turn south for 1.5 mi. to Stroebel Rd. Turn east and drive to the parking lot and trailhead. To get to Green Point Environmental Learning Center drive 3 blocks west of the river on MI 46 and turn south on South Michigan Ave. Drive 1.5 mi. to Maple St., turn south and drive .5 mi. to the entrance.

- **SEASON:** Refuge open year-round.
- **HOURS:** Office hours: 7:30 a.m.–4 p.m. Mon.–Fri. Refuge open for public use Sun.–Sat., from dawn to dusk.
- **FEES:** Free access.
- **ADDRESS:** Shiawassee NWR, 6975 Mower Rd., Saginaw, MI 48601
- **TELEPHONE:** 517/777-5930

TOURING SHIAWASSEE

- **BY AUTOMOBILE:** Cars are not permitted on refuge roads except on the second Saturday in September.
- **BY FOOT:** Woodland Trail, on the north side of the refuge, makes a 3.5-mile circuit through bottomland forest. A cutoff shortens the trail to a 1.5-mile walk. Ferguson Bayou Trail winds along the tops of levees on a 4.5-mile loop, or a 1.5-mile shortcut, through a variety of habitats. From Oct. through Dec., trail closures vary annually to accommodate hunting seasons. Trails are often closed on alternate days during deer season and for parts of days during goose season. No pets are permitted in the refuge, and trails are open only during daylight hours. Cross-country skiing and snowshoeing are permitted in the winter. Trails are not groomed. The Green Point Environmental Learning Center contains 2.5 miles of undemanding trails divided into easily managed short hikes. All the trails lie within the floodplain of the Tittabawassee River. During hours when the headquarters office is closed, visitors can pick up trail brochures from an outdoor kiosk.
- **BY BICYCLE:** Bikes may be ridden on trails, but bicyclists should be aware that in early spring the trails (even the ones along the tops of dikes) are often muddy and impassable on wheeled vehicles. If the goal of a visit is watching geese and ducks from the observation tower at the end of Ferguson Bayou Trail, bikes provide the quickest and easiest mode of conveyance.
- **BY CANOE, KAYAK, OR BOAT:** Boating is not permitted on the refuge pools. Although the refuge has no boat ramps, boaters, canoeists, and anglers are free to travel the rivers traversing the refuge. The nearest boat ramps are at Wickes Park in Saginaw and on the Cass River where it crosses MI 13 about 3 miles north of Curtis Rd.

WHAT TO SEE

- **LANDSCAPE AND CLIMATE** The refuge is the bull's eye where four major rivers and several small creeks meet to form the Saginaw River. Most of the refuge is billiard-table flat, and elevation changes very little from the point where the Saginaw River is born to where it empties into Saginaw Bay, 25 miles to the north. Add to the above equation the fact that the Saginaw River system drains 3.5 million acres, and the result is almost annual flooding in the refuge. During unusually wet springs, just about everything but the dikes is underwater

Summers are warm and humid. July temperatures average in the 70s. From Sept. through early Nov. the air is cool and crisp, a sharp contrast to the warm, even hot, colors of the fall foliage. Winters are cold, with January temperatures averaging in the low twenties. With an average annual snowfall of 46 inches, it is the rare winter that does not provide enough snow for cross-country skiing.

■ **PLANT LIFE** The refuge contains a wide variety of grasses, wildflowers, hardwood trees common to bottomland forests, and shrubs one would expect to find in the upper Midwest. But the most important plants are also among the most common—smartweed and wild millet. Migrating waterfowl rely heavily on both for food. Smartweed acquired its name because it made the skin smart when touched by the plant. A Virginia farmer in 1687 described Indians chewing the plant and applying the masticated mess to wounds and infections. It was also once used to kill fleas, and horsemen believed that sticking the plant under a saddle kept a horse from tiring on a long journey.

Croplands Croplands cover 1,430 acres and are sharecropped by local farmers who leave one-third of their crop for wildlife. Corn, soybeans, barley, and winter wheat grown on the refuge make a significant contribution to the diets of ducks and geese. It is common to see seagulls following boats, looking for possible handouts, but it is quite a different matter watching them follow behind a tractor plowing refuge fields. The gulls are there to snap up worms and grubs turned over by the plowing.

Bottomland forest Shiawassee's bottomland forest is dense with eastern cottonwoods, oak, hickory, and willow. A large, flooded woodland borders parts of Ferguson Bayou Trail. From the trail, some vines and creepers can be seen clinging to the mature trees, but because of the frequent floodings and thick canopy of leaves there is little understory here. A huge nesting colony of 1,500 great blue herons packs dozens of nests in each of the refuge's big water-tolerant hardwoods.

■ **ANIMAL LIFE** Visitors must sometimes stop and remind themselves that Shiawassee is more than a refuge for birds. Turtles, frogs, snakes, and other reptiles and amphibians can be spotted with patience and keen eyes. The refuge shelters the state-threatened eastern fox snake and least shrew.

Birds It is generally acknowledged that Shiawassee is one of the great birding spots in Michigan and the nation. The refuge bird checklist totals 246 species. But

Least bittern in swamp grass

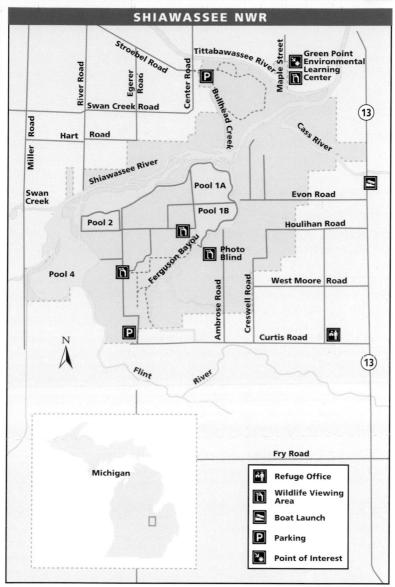

SHIAWASSEE NWR

Stroebel Road
Tittabawassee River
Maple Street
Green Point Environmental Learning Center
River Road
Egerer Road
Center Road
Bullhead Creek
Swan Creek Road
Cass River
13
Hart Road
Miller Road
Shiawassee River
Pool 1A
Evon Road
Swan Creek
Pool 1B
Pool 2
Houlihan Road
Ferguson Bayou
Photo Blind
Pool 4
West Moore Road
Ambrose Road
Creswell Road
N
Curtis Road
13
Flint River
Fry Road
Michigan

👥	**Refuge Office**
🔭	**Wildlife Viewing Area**
⛴	**Boat Launch**
P	**Parking**
✳	**Point of Interest**

the attraction is not just the variety; it is also the jaw-dropping number of birds within a species that shows up here. The refuge supports a nesting colony of 1,500 great blue herons. In the early spring, upwards of 5,000 tundra swans stop over for some R&R on their way to breeding grounds in northern Canada. Eighteen species of ducks have been noted in the refuge, and each fall 4,000 black ducks call at Shiawassee, as do thousands of other ducks and geese. Most of the Canada geese using the refuge as a rest stop nest in the far north along the shores of James Bay, and many of the mallards flying into the refuge also hail from the same area. Duck hunters will tell you that long-flight mallards are remarkably bigger than the mallards that nest locally. During peak migration periods in spring and fall, 25,000 geese and 40,000 ducks pack themselves into the refuge.

Birds on state threatened and endangered lists found here include king rail, short-eared owl, osprey, and Caspian tern. Large numbers and varieties of marsh birds nest here, and warbler-watching can be feverish. More than 100 songbird species have been counted on the property.

Mammals White-tailed deer will be seen on nearly any visit. During the summer hikers often find themselves sharing the top of a dike with groundhogs. These woodchucks, seen anywhere in their range, look fat, lazy, and—no matter what time of year—as if they have just been woken up for Groundhog Day and can't get the sleep out of their eyes. The woodchucks at Shiawassee look exceptionally out of shape and barely have the energy to get off the trail when overtaken by even the slowest hiker. Beavers are present but seldom seen. Muskrats are much less shy and are commonly spotted swimming in ponds, pools, or flooded areas. In the spring, fox pups can sometimes be spied playing on distant dikes.

ACTIVITIES

■ **CAMPING AND SWIMMING:** Neither is permitted within the refuge. The closest public campground is in Bay City State Park (517/684-3020), about 20 miles to the north on Saginaw Bay.

■ **WILDLIFE OBSERVATION:** With more than 10 miles of trails and two observation towers, wildlife observation at Shiawassee can be an aerobic exercise. An observation deck at the Curtis Road parking lot for Ferguson Bayou Trailhead affords a good view of a small wetland depression that habitually attracts ducks and a good assortment of shorebirds. There are two observation towers on the trail, with the most memorable views coming from the tower at the farthest point of the trail. The tower has a spotting scope through which hikers can scan two large pools and an equally large farm unit—that, from mid- to late March, may be carpeted with as many as 16,000 geese and 6,000 ducks. Among the thousands of Canada geese are tundra swans and snow geese. During the first two weeks of November, the number of geese doubles and 25,000 ducks are temporarily in attendance.

Spring is a great time for spotting fawns in the grassy edges of Ferguson Bayou Trail and picking wildflowers scattered on the forest floor. The shrub-edged drainage ditches often hold rails, sora, and other marsh birds. The grassy meadows at the beginning of Ferguson Bayou Trail frequently shelter an assortment of sparrows. For warblers and other songbirds, birders will want to hit Woodland Trail and the short nature trails at the Green Point Environmental Learning Center.

Shiawassee is one of the rare birding areas that make for good watching year-round. The large numbers of nesting birds keep things lively through the summer. Wading birds, such as bitterns, egrets, and herons, and birds of prey can be found from spring through fall. Even a winter birding trip can pay good dividends, with bald eagles, rough-legged hawks, snow buntings,

HUNTING AND FISHING White-tailed deer can be hunted using a bow, shotgun or muzzleloader during two- or three-day hunts within the scheduled seasons—contact the refuge for specific dates. Bow hunting is from mid-Oct. through Dec. 31; shotgun season is November; Muzzleloader season is mid-Dec. **Geese** can also be hunted from Oct. 9–31.

Fishing is permitted year-round from boats only. Anglers can bring in **catfish**, **walleye**, **white bass**, **suckers**, and **pike**.

horned larks, snowy owls, northern shrikes, and even an occasional golden eagle turning up.

Northern shrikes are an especially interesting winter species. The shrike family has the world's only predatory songbirds, and they possess unique table manners. The 10-inch-long northern shrike has a gray body with a black tail and a Lone Ranger mask. The bird hunts insects, small birds, mice, and snakes. It has a beak like a falcon but does not have talons. In order to hold its prey while eating, the shrike impales the mouse or bird on a thorn or barbed wire, or wedges it into a small fork of a branch. In the summer the shrike has been observed catching insects and hanging them on a sharp branch or thorn to eat later. The northern shrike is a bird of the far north and is seen in the United States in the winter.

Northern shrike

■ **PHOTOGRAPHY:** Ferguson Bayou Trail has the refuge's only photography blind. Opportunities for a variety of wildlife photos are best along this trail, and there may not be a better spot in Michigan for panoramic shots of large flocks of ducks and geese on the wing than from the trail's two observation towers.

■ **HIKES AND WALKS:** Woodland Trail, on the refuge's northern border, is a great place to find migrating songbirds in May, but a walk anytime of the year is likely to include an encounter with resident wildlife. The trail edges a marsh, skirts brushy openings in the bottomland forest, and for a part of its length follows an old railroad grade. This trail can be wet in the spring and thick with mosquitoes. Insect repellent is standard equipment when visiting any part of the refuge.

Ferguson Bayou Trail, the refuge's most popular trail, was designated as a National Recreation Trail by the secretary of the interior in 1981. Except for one foray into a forested area, where a cutoff allows hikers to opt for a shorter hike, the pathway sits atop dikes that pass cropland, moist-soil units, forested wetlands, and extensive pools. This is the trail to take for waterfowl in either spring or fall.

The Green Point Environmental Learning Center contains six short trails totaling 2.5 miles. The entire trail system lies within the floodplain of the Tittabawassee River, and at some point in the early spring it is not uncommon to find all trails underwater. The various trails brush the Tittabawassee River, circle wetlands, cross open meadows, tunnel through woods, and border two ponds.

■ **SEASONAL EVENTS:** On the second Saturday in September the public is invited to explore the refuge by car on a self-guided auto tour.

■ **PUBLICATIONS:** Bird checklist, general introductory brochure to refuge, map.

Agassiz NWR
Middle River, Minnesota

Marsh, Agassiz NWR

Wild enough for wolves, 61,500-acre Agassiz NWR features a level of natural diversity found in few other places. Shading into one another across this distant northwest corner of Minnesota are landscapes of prairie and northern hardwood forest and the southern fringe of the great spruce-fir forest. Birds, gray wolves, and beasts of several natural worlds are at home here; people, by and large, are merely visitors.

HISTORY

A series of ill-fated and wildly expensive wetland drainage projects in the early 1900s caused Mud Lake and surrounding lands to revert to public ownership. The state of Minnesota found the area too expensive to manage even for conservation purposes, and in 1937 turned the land over to the Bureau of Biological Survey (today the U.S. Fish & Wildlife Service). Massive restoration of wetlands followed. Originally named Mud Lake Migratory Waterfowl Refuge, the site was renamed in 1961 at the request of area residents, who felt the name a disservice to the region's natural beauty. In 1976, 4,000 acres within the north-central area of the refuge received wilderness designation.

GETTING THERE

From the city of Thief River Falls, travel east on MN Hwy 1 for 3 mi., turning north onto Pennington County Road 20, which becomes Marshall County Road 12. Continue 12 mi. to Marshall County Road 7 and turn east; continue 7 mi. to refuge headquarters.
- **SEASON:** Refuge open year-round.
- **HOURS:** Daylight hours; headquarters open weekdays, 7:30 a.m.–4 p.m.
- **FEES:** Free access.
- **ADDRESS:** RR 1, Box 74, Middle River, MN 56737
- **TELEPHONE:** 218/449-4115

TOURING AGASSIZ

■ **BY AUTOMOBILE:** Lost Bay Habitat Drive is a 4-mile self-guided tour open year-round as weather permits. All-season gravel roads offer vehicular access to much of the site; a network of seasonal roads allows further access to a few areas, including the Mud River, during summer months.

■ **BY FOOT:** Some 100 miles of trails, most of them undeveloped, await visitors. Two self-guided trails include a 0.25-mile Lost Bay Habitat Trail along the auto tour, and a 0.5-mile trail near refuge headquarters. Winters are long and snow plentiful, and cross-country skiing and snowshoeing are permitted on all trails and refuge roads. Agassiz Wilderness Area is open to cross-country foot travel, skiing, and snowshoeing year-round.

■ **BY BICYCLE:** Permitted along the auto-tour route and main refuge roads. Terrain is level and very accommodating for bikes; wildlife, however, are actually less bothered by vehicles.

■ **BY CANOE, KAYAK, OR BOAT:** Boating is not permitted.

WHAT TO SEE

■ **LANDSCAPE AND CLIMATE** The glacial Lake Agassiz receded 10,000 years ago, leaving a vast plain. With elevations varying less than 2 feet per mile, water has always taken its time leaving the region. Over thousands of years, organic materials have accumulated into deep deposits of peat, upon which a great diversity of specialized plant communities—most notably bogs—have evolved.

The refuge sees 115 frost-free days per year. Annual snowfall averages 37 inches, and arctic temperatures, with extremes of -47 degrees, are always a possibility in winter. Summers are short, with periods of intense heat and moderate humidity.

■ **PLANT LIFE**

Wetlands Agassiz is 40,000 acres rich in wetlands. Cattail marsh, with reed grass, spikerush, and water millfoil, is the predominant variety. The refuge wilderness area features a black spruce-tamarack bog, the most westerly example of this unique forest/wetland community in the state. The 40-foot-high conifers occupy a continuous, undulating mat of sphagnum mosses, with an understory of cinnamon fern, carnivorous pitcher plants, and wild orchids. Another important wetland is the shrub swamp, a midsuccessional

Cattail

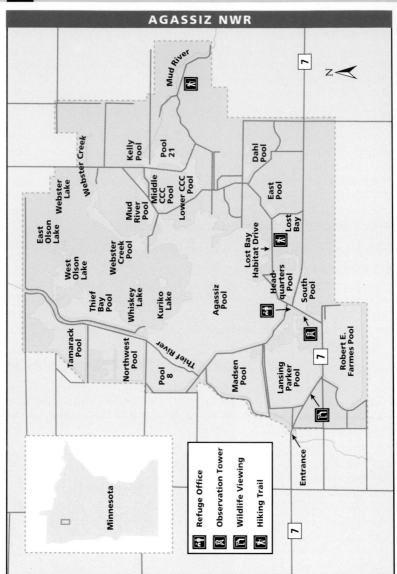

AGASSIZ NWR

Mud River

Webster Creek

Kelly Pool

Pool 21

Dahl Pool

Webster Lake

East Olson Lake

Webster Lake

Middle CCC Pool

Mud River Pool

Lower CCC Pool

East Pool

West Olson Lake

Webster Creek Pool

Lost Bay

Thief Bay Pool

Whiskey Lake

Kuriko Lake

Agassiz Pool

Lost Bay Habitat Drive

Head-quarters

South Pool

Tamarack Pool

Northwest Pool

Thief River

Pool 8

Madsen Pool

Lansing Parker Pool

Robert E. Farmes Pool

Entrance

Minnesota

Refuge Office

Observation Tower

Wildlife Viewing

Hiking Trail

community vital to the refuge moose population; tall clumps of willow, with some alder or bog birch, rise above an understory of sedges such as blue joint or northern marsh fern. The prairie pothole wetland is represented as well; temporary and seasonal potholes are the most common.

Forests Aspen woodlands are the dominant forest type here, a transition zone between the mixed-grass prairie to the west and coniferous forest to the north and east. Encompassing 7,000 acres, the forest features quaking aspen, with bur oak, green ash, and elm above a dense understory of shrubs—including dogwoods, Bebb's willow, and meadowsweet.

Grasslands Native tallgrass prairie occurs in a mosaic across some 4,200 acres, in an uneasy alliance with aspen woodlands, which forever attempt to convert grasslands into forested "parklands." Big bluestem, Indian grass, and prairie dropseed are dominant grasses, with leadplant, false indigo, and several goldenrod species among a handsome display of wildflowers.

■ ANIMAL LIFE

Mammals The presence of the eastern gray wolf makes Agassiz a special place. The two resident packs, heard more often than seen, number between 8 and 12 members each. Through the long winters they roam the entire 100-square-mile refuge; during the balance of the year they prefer the grasslands and forested areas to the east and south. All Minnesota gray wolves are thought to be of the Great Plains wolf subspecies. Do not expect to see them, but do keep in mind the story of the Agassiz refuge worker—sitting on a tractor in an open field, he watched as one entire pack trotted up to sit in a semicircle before him, gazing at his noisy machine.

The wolves live here for a number of reasons—among them, moose and white-tailed deer. The Agassiz moose herd has averaged about 265 animals; in the late 1990s, due in part to several bad winters, moose numbers were at their lowest level in 30 years, with about 70 on site. At the same time, the deer herd also reached a 25-year low.

The northern flying squirrel is the most abundant squirrel on the refuge; other notable mammals include the river otter, often seen in marshes and ditches along roads, along with the mink, red fox, and muskrat. Elk live on adjacent state lands and are seen here occasionally.

Birds Agassiz does not lack for birds, with 280 species recorded. Highlights include four nesting pairs of bald eagles, an immense rookery of black-crowned night-herons, and 70 nesting pairs of sandhill cranes. The refuge supports one of the largest nesting colonies of Franklin's gulls in North America. The Nashville, chestnut-sided, and Blackburnian warblers nest on site, as does the northern goshawk and 13 duck species. A rich assortment of songbirds and waterfowl are present during migration.

Reptiles and amphibians A fair diversity of frogs includes the boreal chorus frog, mink frog, and eastern gray treefrog, along with the Jefferson and eastern

Gray wolves

tiger salamanders. Snakes are the most abundant reptile, with as many as eight species on site, the northern red-bellied and western hognose snakes among them.

ACTIVITIES

■ **CAMPING AND SWIMMING:** Camping and swimming are not permitted. Primitive camping is available on state lands adjacent to the refuge; Old Mill and Hayes State parks offer developed sites close by.

Dunlin

■ **WILDLIFE OBSERVATION:** It is difficult not to encounter something memorable at Agassiz throughout the year, though fall is an excellent time to visit. Moose are seen most often at this time of year, browsing the willow thickets; waterfowl, including tundra swans, large numbers of ducks, and less-common species such as the white-winged scoter, are migrating through, as are many shorebirds—the Baird's and pectoral sandpipers, dunlin, stilt sandpiper, and long-billed dowitcher, among others.

■ **PHOTOGRAPHY:** An observation tower just south of refuge headquarters offers a sweeping view of the South Pool wetland unit; in the southwest end of the refuge, a viewing deck on Lansing Parker Pool is another good choice for scenic images and water-associated wildlife.

■ **HIKES AND WALKS:** Intrepid visitors will want to inquire with refuge staff about gaining permission for a walk into the wilderness area to explore Whiskey or Kurko lakes. Walk the unimproved road into the Mud River area for a good sampling of the Agassiz prairie, and watch for wolf scat or tracks in wet areas along the road and in openings.

■ **SEASONAL EVENTS:** International Migratory Bird Day is celebrated in May; waterfowl banding takes place in Sept.; National Wildlife Refuge Week is observed in Sept. or Oct.

■ **PUBLICATIONS:** Bird checklist; mammal checklist; introductory brochure; hunting and fishing regulations.

HUNTING AND FISHING
There is no fishing on the refuge. A one-week **white-tailed deer** hunt is held in early Nov.; rifles or bows may be used during this season, as there is no separate bow-hunting season.

Big Stone NWR
Odessa, Minnesota

Granite outcropping and wetland, Big Stone NWR

Big Stone lies off the beaten path in a landscape of hushed beauty, With 11,500 acres and scantily traveled roads, the refuge offers ample opportunities for solitude. The terrain includes tall grass prairie and bluffs of granite outcrops supporting populations of cacti more commonly found in the landscapes of the Southwest. Two rivers cloaked in bottomland forests meander through the refuge. Grab a canoe, follow one of the designated river routes, and roll along to the gentle, almost noiseless rippling of water against paddle.

HISTORY

Located along the South Dakota–Minnesota line, the region that is Big Stone was once the territory of the Dakota, or Sioux, Indians. Settlers colonized this valley around 1877, purchasing land for about $1.25 an acre; a stone foundation along Rock Outcrop Hiking Trail is all that remains of a modest cabin built during that settlement. Farms occupied the valley until 1971, when the Army Corps of Engineers constructed a dam downstream, flooding about 3,500 acres. Big Stone was created to provide wildlife habitat and an area for public recreation. A lively schedule of seasonal events brings refuge visitors into contact with the area's thriving agricultural communities.

GETTING THERE

From Watertown, SD: travel north on I-29 for 31 mi. to US 12; exit east and continue 32 mi. to Ortonville, MN; drive south on US 75 for 5 mi, to refuge headquarters. From the town of Willmar, MN: travel west on US 12 for 77 mi. to Ortonville; drive south on US 75 for 1 mi. to refuge entrance.
- **SEASON:** Refuge open year-round.
- **HOURS:** Daylight hours.
- **FEES:** Free access.

■ **ADDRESS:** Refuge headquarters: 5 miles southeast of Ortonville, MN, off Hwy 75. Mailing Address: RR 1, Box 25, Odessa, MN 56276

■ **TELEPHONE:** 320/273-2191

TOURING BIG STONE

■ **BY AUTOMOBILE:** Big Stone's 5-mile tour route is a deluxe affair—a paved loop, highly scenic, with turnouts and interpretive stops.

■ **BY FOOT:** The interpreted 1-mile-long Rock Outcrop Trail is open year-round; walking conditions are of moderate difficulty. Snowshoeing and cross-country skiing are terrific in winter; park outside refuge entrance and proceed anywhere (refuge roads are favored by beginners). All interior roads are open to foot travel year-round.

■ **BY BICYCLE:** Permitted along auto-tour route and main refuge roads. Terrain is level and very accommodating.

■ **BY CANOE, KAYAK, OR BOAT:** Canoes are the only watercraft allowed in refuge waters. Good thing, because Big Stone is a highly recommended canoeing experience. Follow a marked canoe trail on the Minnesota River, with half-day or full-day trips possible through the refuge. Spring through midsummer is the optimal period; in fall, low water levels often require some portaging. Call refuge headquarters for an update on water conditions prior to visiting. There are two places on the auto-tour route to launch canoes. Boaters must stay in the channel.

WHAT TO SEE

■ **LANDSCAPE AND CLIMATE** When glacial Lake Agassiz receded 10,000 years ago, it left behind a plain believed to be larger than today's five great lakes combined. Its outlet, the glacial River Warren, was a raging torrent 2 to 8 miles across. The broad valley carved by that ancient river is traversed today by the Minnesota River—no River Warren, by any means, although it still leaves its banks periodically in spring. Repeated scouring by glaciers exposed the fins and outcrops of the reddish-colored granite that gave this refuge its name.

The Mississippi River Valley to the east, a pipeline of warm, humid air, is a par-

Raccoon

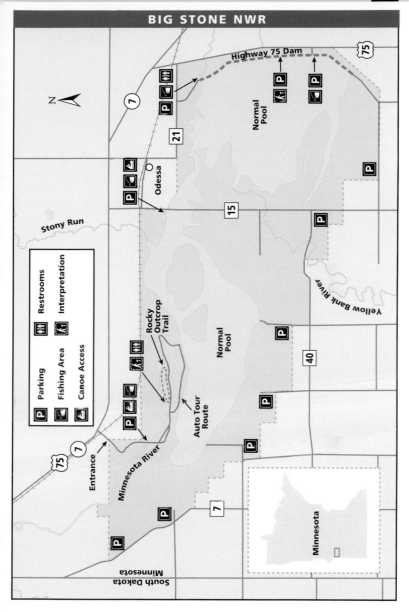

tial influence on Big Stone's summer climate, which features temperatures in the 70s to 90s and occasional extremes of 100 degrees. Winters are the product of cold, dry air blowing in from the Plains or Canada; extremes may reach well below zero, with moderate temperatures in the 20s. Annual precipitation averages 24.2 inches.

■ **PLANT LIFE** Notably, the refuge supports a large population of ball cactus, which is unusual to find this far north (generally a southwestern species); this rare habitat and the granite outcroppings it grows on are unique to Minnesota.

Open water The Minnesota and Yellowbank rivers meander through Big

Stone. Both are shallow, at 8 or so feet, though subject to spring flooding, which recharges the adjacent floodplain forest. A diverse native fishery includes walleye, bullhead, northern pike, yellow perch, and black crappie. Runoff from surrounding croplands has had a significant negative impact on water quality; the issue is a concern for refuge management and local residents alike, who are working cooperatively on mitigation efforts.

Wetlands Big Stone features three major wetland types, beginning with some 1,500 acres of submergent open water. This is a sprawling, open pool created by the dam on the Minnesota River. Vegetation such as milfoil, sago pondweed, and coontail nutsedge provide a rich food source for waterfowl. An additional 2,000 acres are classic cattail-bulrush marsh; both narrowleaf and broadleaf cattail are present, along with hardstem bulrush. On the margins of these areas and slightly upslope are about 1,200 acres of sedge meadows, along with wet prairie sites. These areas remain saturated through much of the year.

THE ALL-AMERICAN CHICKEN In the summer of 1999, Big Stone began a long-term effort aimed at reintroducing the greater prairie chicken to its tallgrass prairie home. Once widespread through the tallgrass prairie region and points west, prairie chickens exist only as isolated remnant populations today. Most Americans have never seen this most American of upland birds. With vivid orange throat sacs and gaudy headdresses of upraised feathers, male prairie chickens perform elaborate courtship displays each spring. Big Stone will release 15 to 30 birds each year over the next four years.

Floodplain forest Big Stone features 700 acres of lovely floodplain forest along the Minnesota and Yellowbank rivers and Stony Run Creek. Silver maple and green ash, along with sandbar and peachleaf willows, are dominant native trees; a number of cottonwoods were planted during the agricultural years—now inundated by a managed water regime, the cottonwoods have died and support a sizable nesting colony of great blue herons, double-crested cormorants, and great egrets. As the snag trees dwindle, the colony size shrinks accordingly.

Upland deciduous forest Encompassing about 250 acres, this mixture of trees—box elder, green ash, and sugar maple, along with such understory species as currant, chokecherry, wild rose, and western snowberry—has encroached upon areas of native prairie. In the years to come it will be thinned or removed altogether to allow grasslands to recolonize; for the moment, however, it supports an array of shrub- and sapling-associated songbirds.

Native tallgrass prairie About 1,700 acres of Big Stone's tallgrass prairie has never been touched by a plow. At least 15 species of grass and 60 wildflower species have been documented. Big bluestem, a plant that epitomizes the meaning of "tallgrass," reaches 7 to 8 feet high here. June grass and Indian grass are also present. Flowering plants include meadow rue, several coneflowers, leadplant, common milkweed, prairie smoke, and wood lilies. The Dakota skipper, an endangered butterfly species and an indicator of prairie health, survives here; skipper surveys continue on-site. Work on returning more of the refuge to natural prairie continues; in 1999, for example, about 200 acres were reseeded to native species, turning back the clock on former farmland. Another prairie native, the greater prairie chicken, is being reintroduced beginning in the summer of 1999 (see sidebar, above).

Greater prairie chicken

Granite outcrops A small but vital element of this refuge is its assortment of granite bluffs and outcrops. These areas support the state's largest remaining population of ball cactus, a tiny plant that sends up a very showy, bright pink flower, and a population of prickly pear cactus—both plants that are unique to the area and more commonly found in southwestern landscapes. The cactus lives exclusively in granite outcrops, an increasingly rare commodity in the region because of a thriving granite quarrying trade.

■ **ANIMAL LIFE** An intermingling of eastern and western wildlife species makes Big Stone an interesting place to study animals.

Birds The common yellowthroat is an oft-seen bird that nests locally; the American white pelican, a majestic and quintessentially western sight, is common spring through fall. A large pelican nesting colony inhabits Lac Qui Parle Wildlife Management Area, a state-managed property located east of the refuge.

Big Stone takes in a great diversity of birds—waterfowl, shorebirds, and songbirds—during spring and fall migrations. Songbirds such as the ruby-crowned kinglet, Nashville and Orange-crowned warblers, and white-throated and American tree sparrows have become common sights; rarities include the palm and blackpoll warblers, and the LeConte's and fox sparrows. Shorebirds are equally diverse: the stilt, Baird's, and least sandpipers pass through, as do the black-bellied, American golden, and semipalmated plovers; none are commonly seen, though all remain a seasonal possibility. The array of ducks spans 17 species, with increased numbers during migration of the many varieties that nest here—American wigeon, blue-winged teal, northern pintail, wood duck, and canvasback. Secretive marsh birds include the sora, Virginia rail, and American bittern.

Prairie songbirds nesting on site include the grasshopper and savannah sparrows, bobolink, eastern bluebird, and eastern kingbird; the upland and spotted sandpipers, and northern harrier. Look for six nesting species of swallow, including purple martins.

Mammals Though white-tailed deer are by far the most common, their western cousin, the mule deer, makes an occasional appearance at Big Stone. The woodlands are home to the eastern gray and eastern fox squirrels, found as far east as New England; on the prairie, their burrowing cousins, the Richardson's and Franklin's ground squirrels, thrive as far west as Montana and Wyoming. The eastern cottontail and white-tailed jackrabbit are both present. The floodplain forest and adjacent wetlands are the year-round haunts of beaver, muskrat, mink, and raccoon.

Reptiles and amphibians The rare spiny softshell turtle, swampy tree frog, prairie redbelly snake, and northern leopard frog can be found here.

ACTIVITIES

■ **CAMPING AND SWIMMING:** No camping or swimming is allowed on the refuge; Big Stone Lake, upriver, offers public and private campgrounds and has a popular summer swimming area.

■ **WILDLIFE OBSERVATION:** Big Stone features an active bald eagle nest, with parents arriving in early spring and fledging from one to three eaglets each year. More than 1,000 white-tailed deer winter on the refuge and may be observed at close range along the auto tour. Patient visitors will see an occasional river otter along the Minnesota or Yellowbank. A sizable breeding population of hooded mergansers is present; the striking parents, with young, appear in late May. An impressive flock of Canada geese—some 20,000 strong—remains through the winter.

■ **PHOTOGRAPHY:** Prairie wildflower colors are best in June and July, though many species bloom throughout the growing season and into fall. Images of refuge wildlife and scenic views of the area are plentiful along the auto-tour route; rock formations

HUNTING AND FISHING Big Stone NWR has both bow and muzzleloader season for **white-tailed deer** hunting in the fall months, in accordance with state seasons. Maps showing which areas of the refuge are open to hunting are available at the refuge office.

You may fish in refuge waters in the late spring and summer. Fishing by nonmotorized boat is permitted in the Minnesota River channel. Also popular is bank fishing along the East Pool adjacent to the Hwy. 75 dam. Anglers find **northern pike, walleye, largemouth bass, crappie, sunfish, perch, bluegill, rock bass, catfish, bullhead**, and **carp**. Contact the refuge for dates and details.

here make for splendid landscape imagery—the developed hiking trail offers the best access.

■ **HIKES AND WALKS:** Along Rock Outcrop Trail visitors can explore several major features of Big Stone—its granite outcrops, a thriving segment of tallgrass prairie; and nearby meanders of the Minnesota River.

■ **SEASONAL EVENTS:** Spring bird festival in May; Youth Fishing Day in June; Wildflower Field Day in late June or early July. A "Prairie Days" festival, with workshops, seed collecting, bird identification walks, and talks on Native American regional history, is in the planning stage; in August, during the city or Ortonville's annual Corn Festival, Big Stone hosts 5K and 10K runs along the auto tour; along public lands bordering the Minnesota River, including the refuge, the annual "Run, Ride and Row" event is loads of fun. The refuge celebrates National Wildlife Refuge Week in October with special events.

Hamden Slough NWR
Audubon, Minnesota

Hooded mergansers with brood, Hamden Slough NWR

Hamden Slough is a waterfowl factory in the making. When you visit the refuge and watch thousands of ducks crowd into 70-acre Homestead Lake or spot a marbled godwit (a crow-sized shorebird dressed in rich-brown feathers and sporting a beak even Jimmy Durante would envy), you get more than just an inkling of this refuge's bright future.

HISTORY

The federal Migratory Bird Conservation Commission authorized the creation of the 5,944-acre refuge in 1989 for the purpose of increasing waterfowl production and to restore a badly damaged prairie wetland ecosystem. Plans for the young refuge are visionary and ambitious. Within 15 to 20 years Hamden Slough is expected to produce 10,000 waterfowl annually. The cost of water-control structures, buildings, impoundments, and equipment will total $10 million. The cost for these improvements is not being borne by taxpayers alone. Ducks Unlimited, the Izaak Walton League, and the Minnesota Waterfowl Association have made major financial contributions for wetlands restoration, and their generosity is expected to continue.

GETTING THERE

To reach the refuge's headquarters, drive 1.5 mi. east of Audubon, Minnesota, on County Road 104, following signs to the refuge.
■ **SEASON:** Refuge open year-round.
■ **HOURS:** Dawn to dusk. Headquarters office hours vary, depending on whether staff is in the field.
■ **FEES:** Free access.
■ **ADDRESS:** Hamden Slough NWR, 21212 210th St., Audubon, MN 56511
■ **TELEPHONE:** 218/439-6319

WHAT TO SEE

■ **PLANT LIFE** Hamden Slough lies within a unique area where three major regional habitats meet. The refuge marks the transition zone between the western tallgrass prairie, the eastern hardwood forest, and the Great Lakes pinelands. The eastern edge of the tallgrass prairie begins at the bottom of a long glacial outwash. As you head east, away from the prairie, climbing the long, gentle slope, plant species and communities begin to change until you reach the top, where hardwood forests and pinelands stretch to the northeast and east. This intermingling of large regional plant communities and a landscape that is peppered with large and small wetlands—or former wetlands that have been drained—made the area one of the best waterfowl nurseries in western Minnesota.

It would be more accurate to say that the tallgrass prairie once reached its easternmost point here. But most of the prairie disappeared under the plow decades ago. Restoration of the prairie and the wetlands is an ongoing commitment. The North Star 2000 project is the first of many programs aimed at restoring the refuge's ecosystem to its pre-sodbuster days. When completed, the program will have restored 220 individual wetlands and 965 acres of upland prairie. Restoring the prairie includes plowing, reseeding, and controlled burns.

The single biggest wetland restoration undertaking is returning Bisson Lake's currently dry lakebed to its former glory. Occasionally in the spring, when the lake's drainage ditches are blocked by ice, the lake briefly fills and attracts tens of thousands of shorebirds, waterfowl, and marsh birds. With the drains mechanically plugged, Bisson Lake would cover 100 acres to a depth of about 18 inches. The restoration of this huge "wading pool" of a lake will be a major step toward meeting the refuge's stated goals.

■ **ANIMAL LIFE**

Birds The refuge bird checklist currently stands at 209 species, but numbers are expected to rise, and the status of birds on the list will continue to change. In 1998 alone, 10 new species were added to the list of birds that nest in the refuge, and three of the species—ruddy duck, redhead, and Brewer's blackbird—were the first

Peregrine falcon

confirmed nesting by their species in Becker County. As the wetlands and grass-lands are further restored, the refuge will become one of the great birding sites in the state.

Presently, 25 waterfowl species have been seen here, including tundra and trumpeter swans, snow geese, and all three merganser species. All five grebes common to North America call at the refuge, and American white pelicans are occasional visitors. Raptor viewing is very good, with bald eagles becoming a common—but never dull—sight. Peregrine falcons, the fastest birds in the world, make rare appearances. The falcon dives on its victims from a great altitude, often reaching 180 miles an hour before striking its prey in an explosion of feathers. Watching a peregrine plummet toward the earth is an unforgettable and often once-in-a-lifetime experience.

ACTIVITIES

Although there are no established trails or observation decks, visitors are wel-come to roam the refuge, but wildlife viewing is often equally rewarding from the County Roads 12, 13, 14, and 106 that border or bisect the refuge. Neither swimming nor camping is allowed.

■ **PUBLICATIONS:** The headquarters has refuge maps and a bird checklist.

HUNTING AND FISHING
There is neither hunting nor fishing allowed on the refuge.

Minnesota Valley NWR
Bloomington, Minnesota

Refuge overlook, Visitor Center, Minnesota Valley NWR

Minnesotans make no secret of their love for all things wild. The state consistently ranks among the highest nationwide in public support for conservation. In Minnesota, wildlife observation and outdoor recreation are community affairs. Even city dwellers can't get enough of the natural world. Nowhere is this more evident than in Minnesota Valley NWR, a lush, 34-mile greenbelt along the Minnesota River right in the heart of the bustling Twin Cities metropolitan area. In this handsome refuge—to which land is still being added and restored—people are the attraction, and their enthusiasm for the place, for wildlife and the natural world, makes Minnesota Valley a unique place to visit.

Visitors will discover a bonus when visiting the refuge: the Visitor Center is a stunning work of architecture and includes four levels of interactive exhibits, an auditorium, library, and bookstore. It's also a natural gathering place. The Visitor Center calendar of events—slide shows, storytelling, guided hikes, all manner of winter outings—is chockful year-round. A large fieldstone fireplace houses a fire in the winter, warming visitors back from an expedition, whether a winter wildflower walk, a snowshoe stomp, or a visit to the great blue heron rookery—while above a daily squadron of jets rumbles in and out of nearby Minneapolis–Saint Paul International Airport.

HISTORY

Minnesota Valley is one of four urban wildlife refuges in the United States; its neighbors are freeways, the Mall of America, and more than 2 million people. The refuge is an example of the power of grassroots activism. In the early 1970s a small group of citizens began an odyssey aimed at gaining widespread local support for protection of all that was left of the Minnesota River Valley. The Lower Minnesota Valley Citizens' Committee saw their efforts realized in 1976, when the refuge was formally established. The group continues today as the Friends of

Minnesota Valley—and the refuge is still expanding. Plans call for the 12,500-acre refuge to acquire more land parcels as they become available and to link the refuge to area parks through a network of hiking and biking trails.

GETTING THERE

In Minneapolis–Saint Paul, MN: The refuge Visitor Center is at 3815 E. 80th St., across from the Airport Hilton Hotel in downtown Bloomington, MN. From I-494, exit onto 34th Ave. south. Turn left at the Holiday Inn and continue about 0.25 mi. to Visitor Center entrance on right.

■ **SEASON:** Refuge open year-round.

■ **HOURS:** The Visitor Center open Tues. through Sun., 9 a.m.–5 p.m. year-round and at other times for refuge events (check with staff).

■ **FEES:** Free access.

■ **ADDRESS:** 3815 E. 80th St., Bloomington, MN 55425-1600

■ **TELEPHONE:** For Visitor Center staff, 612/335-2323; for recorded information, 612/335-2299.

TOURING MINNESOTA VALLEY

■ **BY AUTOMOBILE:** Beyond parking areas at all major trailheads, there are no developed refuge routes.

■ **BY FOOT:** More than 20 miles of developed trails—utilized by hikers year-round and by cross-country skiers in winter—traverse five separate refuge areas: Bass Ponds Environmental Study Area, Long Meadow Lake, Black Dog Preserve, Louisville Swamp, and Wilkie. Three more refuge areas—Bloomington Ferry, Upgrala, and Chaska Lake—are open to exploration but have no designated routes.

■ **BY BICYCLE:** The 2,400-acre Louisville Swamp area features 13 miles of trails, some of which are open to bicycles and horseback riders; all are open to hikers and skiers.

■ **BY CANOE, KAYAK, OR BOAT:** Boating is not permitted on the refuge.

WHAT TO SEE

■ **LANDSCAPE AND CLIMATE** The Minnesota River Valley took shape in the wake of the Ice Age, when an immense prehistoric river, the glacial River Warren, formed as an outlet for the equally vast inland sea called Lake Agassiz, which covered much of what is today western Minnesota. The watercourse cut by this river lies as much as 200 feet below adjoining lands and in places stretches 5 miles wide. Today it is occupied by the Minnesota River, which drains one-third of the state. The river has always been subject to seasonal

Spring peeper

floods, which recharged its wetlands and floodplain forests. Ongoing urbanization of its watershed has increased runoff and triggered more severe flooding in the

MINNESOTA VALLEY NWR

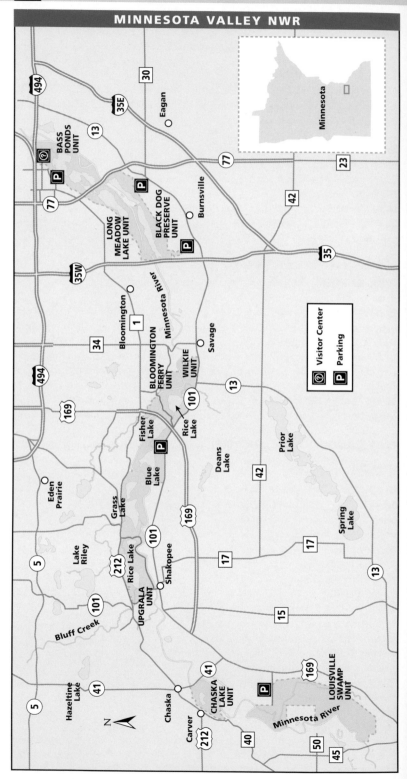

Great horned owls

1990s. Downstream from the refuge, the Minnesota delivers itself to the Mississippi River, which bisects the Twin Cities.

The presettlement landscape included a mixture of deciduous woodlands interspersed with tallgrass prairie and oak savanna. While civilization would alter almost every facet of the immediate area, the Minnesota River Valley eluded more irreversible forms of development, serving primarily as agricultural land before the birth of the refuge.

A visitor here is never far from water, with the Minnesota River a dominant presence. Though the refuge does not play a role in managing its aquatic life, the river is responsible for the refuge's many wetlands and often has final say in how they are managed. Its waters are significantly polluted with storm sewer and sewage discharges, not to mention agricultural and industrial contaminants. Even so, a large number of native fish survive—northern pike, crappie, catfish, and large numbers of carp—though health advisories are in effect for anglers who might want them as table fare.

The Bass Ponds are a series of man-made pools fed by spring creeks. Constructed in the late 1920s by the Izaak Walton League for the raising of large-mouth bass and other gamefish, a few of the ponds still support bass and panfish today, while the water levels in other pools are drawn down to stimulate emergent vegetation for waterfowl.

The warm, humid summers here are in part a result of Gulf of Mexico air pushing up the Mississippi River Valley. The process reverses in winter, with cold, dry arctic air encroaching from the north. Precipitation averages 28.4 inches per year, with about 56 inches of snow annually.

■ PLANT LIFE

Riverine marsh Minnesota Valley features a rich assortment of riverine marshes, most of which are known as "lakes," though they freeze solid in winter. Long Meadow Lake, Black Dog Lake, and Chaska Lake—all separate units on the refuge—are long, shallow basins paralleling the river, inundated each year by flooding. They are fed by springs and feature an array of emergent plants, including arrowhead, cattail, and water lily. The refuge is constructing a series of dikes and ditches in several units to better control water levels for maximum benefit to emergent plants and wildlife.

Swamp Louisville Swamp is a 2,400-acre mosaic of cattails and bulrush, arrowhead, and such bottomland hardwoods as silver maple, willow, and basswood. Sand Creek meanders through the swamp en route to its meeting with the Minnesota. Seasonal flooding has been excessive here, due largely to upriver draining and filling of wet-

SAVANNA REDUX Mosaics of oak savanna, a transition zone between open grasslands and deciduous forests, once spread across much of the tallgrass prairie region. Minnesota Valley inherited many acres of badly degraded savanna around Louisville Swamp. Without wildfires to clear out competing vegetation, river grape, sumac, and buckthorn moved in, along with non-native trees planted by long-ago farmers.

Now, things are looking up for the savanna. An ambitious restoration project is under way on a 15-acre parcel within the Louisville unit. Nonnative trees and shrubs will be cut or otherwise removed, after which the area will be burned to clear out invasive plant species. Biologists hope that native grass and wildflower seeds remain dormant in the soil, and that, with time—at least 10 to 20 years—the savanna can re-establish itself.

lands; a water-control structure on Sand Creek, built by Ducks Unlimited, allows for some manipulation.

Fen Scattered throughout the refuge are a number of fens. Cold, often calcium-rich groundwater has formed these unique oases, which harbor plants associated with more northerly climates: uncommon sedges and grasses, along with some lovely wildflowers, such as orchids, gentians, and asters.

Grasslands Minnesota Valley's tallgrass prairie encompass 2,010 acres, 210 of which is original, with another 1,800 acres of restored native species. Big bluestem, Indian grass, and sideoats grama are dominant grasses; a rich selection of wildflowers includes leadplant, pasqueflower, yellow prairie coneflower, white lady slippers, blazing star, prairie phlox. puccoon—in all more than 250 species.

Lowland deciduous forest This is the floodplain forest of silver maple, swamp oak, cottonwood and elm, with dogwood and smaller willows along the margins. Nettles and some riverbank grape occupy the understory. Most every section of the refuge features some amount of this forest type.

Wooded blufflands It is about a 100-foot climb from the floodplain to the bluffs, which are the ancient shoreline of the Glacial River Warren. These hillsides are cloaked in maple, ash, basswood, and several oak species. Chokecherry and dogwood are among the understory plants.

Scattered remnants of oak savanna are found adjacent to the Louisville Marsh. Bur oak, with its ridged, corky bark, is the marquee species of this plant community, which is rarer even than tallgrass prairie across its historic range. The refuge is gearing up an ambitious restoration effort.

■ **ANIMAL LIFE** All around Minnesota Valley, the human world of free enterprise beeps and clatters and—every time a plane arrives or departs Minneapolis–Saint Paul International Airport—thunders overhead. Down along the

Setting a prescribed burn

river, the natural world carries on its own ancient commerce, accompanied by twitters, quacks, and croaks. Amazingly, the two worlds manage to coexist rather well.

Birds The lush floodplain forests are a focal point for birdlife. A sizable great blue heron rookery is on-site, with treetop nests of double-crested cormorants and snowy egrets tucked into many of the same stands. Dead standing trees, often overrun with insects, are the haunts of seven woodpecker species, including the red-bellied, hairy, and the beautiful pileated woodpecker, a large, timid bird not easily encountered. Sharp-shinned and Cooper's hawks are present, as are the eastern screech owl and great horned owl. Songbirds are diverse: the Swainson's thrush, cedar waxwing, northern cardinal, American redstart, and rose-breasted grosbeak are common or abundant, as are the willow flycatcher and eastern phoebe; rare or uncommon species during summer include the prothonotary warbler, great crested flycatcher, scarlet tanager, blue-gray gnatcatcher, ovenbird, and cerulean warbler. A limited variety of ducks and shorebirds nest on refuge grasslands or marshes, the most typical being the wood duck, mallard, and blue-winged teal, and for shorebirds the common snipe and killdeer. During spring and fall migration, however, species diversity climbs appreciably. Tundra swans appear in spring, along with American wigeon and ring-necked ducks; migrant shorebirds include the black-bellied plover, greater and lesser yellowlegs, least sandpiper, and willet. The Virginia rail and sora, both secretive birds, are nonetheless abundant; marsh-dependent songbirds include the common yellowthroat, marsh wren, and red-winged and yellow-headed blackbirds. Refuge grasslands and savanna feature songbirds such as the indigo bunting, dickcissel, Savannah, and chipping sparrows; the LeConte's, fox, white-throated, and Lincoln's sparrows are commonly seen during spring and fall migrations.

Mammals Red, gray, and fox squirrels chatter away in the floodplain forests.

Though uncommon, the southern flying squirrel also resides here. The eastern cottontail rabbit, woodchuck, eastern chipmunk, and red fox are typical upland mammals seen in the grasslands and the savannah. White-tailed deer, the most commonly seen mammal on the refuge, may appear almost anywhere, at any time.

Reptiles and amphibians Living along damp areas of the forest floor are Blanding's and painted turtles, the northern water snake, fox snake, and plains garter snake, and several frog species—spring peeper, gray-striped chorus frog, wood frog, and gray treefrog. Look for a number of turtles in the marshes, including the painted, soft-shell, spiny soft-shell, false map, and snapping turtle.

ACTIVITIES

■ **CAMPING:** Camping is not permitted on the refuge. Options nearby include Minnesota Valley Trail State Park, toward the southern end of the refuge near Jordan, MN; and Lebanon Hills Regional Park, located 15 miles south of the refuge Visitor Center in Apple Valley, MN.

■ **WILDLIFE OBSERVATION:** Minnesota Valley's exceptional network of hiking trails provides a wonderful first-hand experience of all major natural habitats and the wildlife that resides there. The refuge is user-friendly in other ways. Community members volunteer their expertise, leading walks to view birds, reptiles, and other species. The volunteers' knowledge of both natural history and wildlife observation, often geared to different age groups, enriches any visit here. At the Visitor Center, ask for the Bird Trek Pack, which includes an audiocassette identifying several bird species and their calls.

> **HUNTING AND FISHING** Fishing is permitted on all refuge waters in accordance with state regulations; **panfish** and **largemouth bass** are the principal species. Hunting for **white-tailed deer**, **waterfowl**, and **small game** is allowed in various units subject to Minnesota State regulations; contact refuge for details and a brochure.

■ **PHOTOGRAPHY:** Those who appreciate nature photography will want to keep up with exhibits at the Visitor Center art gallery. In addition to paintings and sculpture, the gallery features the works of local and regional photographers from time to time. Workshops on nature photography are also held here; check with refuge staff for details on attending, or leading, a workshop.

■ **HIKES AND WALKS:** Of the many hikes or walks possible, Black Dog Preserve offers the chance to experience several distinct natural habitats—tallgrass prairie, one of the refuge's unique fens and its associated rare plants, as well as the marshlands of Black Dog Lake, a favored waterfowl resting area. The 2-mile-long trail crosses the prairie en route to the fen at the base of the bluffs.

■ **SEASONAL EVENTS:** The art gallery, Friends Association, and refuge staff offer an almost unending succession of imaginative programs and special events throughout the year. Many take place on weekends and are free of charge, with no reservations required. To keep up with them all, call the refuge's recorded information number, or subscribe to *The Minnesota Valley News*, the quarterly publication of the Friends of the Minnesota Valley. Call refuge for details or to receive a calendar of events. The refuge celebrates National Wildlife Refuge Week in October with special events.

■ **PUBLICATIONS:** *The Minnesota Valley News*, published quarterly by the Friends of the Minnesota Valley; visitor guides (brochures) for most major units of the refuge; mammal, bird, and reptile/amphibian checklists; calendar of events.

Rice Lake NWR
McGregor, Minnesota

Rice Lake wetlands, Rice Lake NWR

Rice Lake NWR is wild and beautiful, a feast for the eyes and a delight for the soul. Every last blade of grass, kernel of wild rice, and tree with a knothole is there because of the work of the refuge staff. The 18,000-acre refuge is intensely managed to enhance its ability to support large concentrations of migrating waterfowl. It's a bed-and-breakfast for ducks and geese, operated with loving care by the U.S. Fish & Wildlife Service.

HISTORY

As its name implies, Rice Lake has extensive wild rice beds, plus large beds of wild celery—both favored foods of waterfowl. People, too, have been drawn to the bounty of Rice Lake. Potsherds and burial mounds found within the refuge indicate that humans camped along the shores of the lake as far back as 1000 B.C. Until railroads opened the area for settlement, American Indians came here regularly to gather wild rice and hunt game. An old railroad bed today serves as a refuge road.

The refuge was established in 1935 as a refuge and breeding ground for migrating waterfowl.

GETTING THERE

Rice Lake is 5 mi. south of McGregor, MN, on MN 65.
■ **HOURS:** The refuge is open to the public year-round, dawn to dusk; headquarters office hours are 8 a.m.–4:30 p.m., Mon.–Fri.
■ **FEES:** Admission is free.
■ **ADDRESS:** Rice Lake NWR, Route 2, Box 67, McGregor, MN 55760
■ **TELEPHONE:** 218/768-2402

TOURING RICE LAKE

■ **BY AUTOMOBILE:** Eleven miles of roads crisscross the refuge, including a 9.5-mile auto tour that is open from May to mid-Nov.

■ **BY FOOT:** Five trails ranging from three-quarters of a mile to 2.5 miles lead to a variety of habitats and scenery.

■ **BY BICYCLE:** Bicycling is permitted on all refuge roads.

■ **BY CANOE, KAYAK, OR BOAT:** Boats without motors or with electric motors are allowed on Rice River. Mandy Lake, and Twin Lakes.

WHAT TO SEE

■ **LANDSCAPE AND CLIMATE** When the last glaciers withdrew from Minnesota, they left a band of moraines, or glacial ridges, in the Rice Lake area, which blocked the natural drainage to the south. As groundwater flowed toward the moraines, a wetland area formed. The wetlands filled with sediment and a spongy mass of floating vegetation. The dense, floating mat of vegetation became a seedbed for other plants, and slowly the floating bog expanded to cover any open water. Another set of moraines formed the 4,500-acre Rice Lake.

■ **PLANT LIFE** In addition to the bogs and open waters of Rice Lake and other smaller bodies of

Black bear

water, the refuge contains grasslands, cropland, and forested areas. All habitats are managed to improve the refuge's ability to shelter and protect waterfowl and other wildlife. The grasslands next to the lakes are maintained for nesting sites. Trees prone to developing cavities are preserved within the forests for wood duck nests and other wildlife that raise their young in tree cavities. Even the water level of Rice Lake is maintained at the optimum level for best wild rice production.

Wild rice is not really rice. It is a tall grass that grows in shallow lakes and marshes. The plant produces seeds each fall and dies with the coming of winter. The seeds lie at the bottom of the lake all winter, and, if conditions are just right in the spring, the seeds will germinate and a new crop will emerge. Wild rice has long been a staple of American Indians in the northern Great Lakes. The Chippewa still harvest rice at Rice Lake in the traditional way. A canoe is poled into a ricebed by one man. A second man sits in the canoe and with a ricing stick carefully bends rice stalks over the canoe and gently taps the stalks with another stick. The ripe grain falls into the canoe and is taken ashore for processing and storage.

■ **ANIMAL LIFE** White-tailed deer, black bear, and timber wolves all ca[ll the] refuge home, and Rice Lake is a natural spawning ground for northern pike. B[ut it] is birds that get top billing here. The refuge bird checklist totals 227 species, w[ith] waterfowl accounting for the greatest numbers. Every spring and fall ducks an[d] geese move through the refuge like commuters at rush hour. As many as 70,000 ring-necked ducks alone call at the refuge home. September through October and April through May are the peak periods for water-fowl concentration. Mallards, blue-winged teal, wigeon, and wood ducks nest here. Two dozen different raptors have been seen at the refuge, and a wide variety of songbirds, shorebirds, and marsh birds make for consistently good birdwatching.

> **HUNTING AND FISHING** You may fish in Rice River and Mandy Lake. Boats are permitted with electric motors only. Anglers most often find **northern pike**, along with the occasional **walleye**, **large-mouth bass**, and **yellow perch**. There is hunting allowed on certain areas of the refuge for **grouse**, **rabbits**, **squirrel**, and **deer** (archery only), but there is no waterfowl hunting. Contact the refuge for details on seasons and regulations.

Mammals include mice, voles, and shrews, which tunnel through the refuge's grass and leaf litter. Beaver, porcupine, woodchuck, and badger are also present. This is black bear country, and they are sometimes encountered on the refuge trails. Thankfully, this most timid member of the bear family usually flees when meeting up with a human.

Painted and snapping turtles, several frog species, garter and green snakes can be found on the refuge. And unless you take precautions, ticks, mosquitoes, and blackflies will plague you, particularly in the warm months.

ACTIVITIES

The auto-tour and hiking trails offer good opportunities for wildlife observation, and the observation tower on the north shore of Rice Lake presents a magnificent panoramic view of the refuge. The hiking trails are level to gently sloped and can be wet and muddy. The refuge sports 3.75 miles of groomed cross-country ski trails when the snow flies, and it also welcomes snowshoeing. A small picnic area lies on the north side of Twin Lakes. Neither camping nor swimming is allowed.

NEARBY REFUGES

■ **Sandstone Division** The refuge's Sandstone Division lies 40 miles to the southeast and features forested uplands pierced by logging roads that serve as hiking trails. The Kettle River cuts across the west side of the unit, and its topography is generally flat to rolling except where the river has cut 100-foot-deep canyons in the underlying bedrock. The refuge lies approximately 2 miles southeast of Sandstone on Highway 20.

■ **Mille Lacs NWR** Of special note is the Mille Lacs NWR, 15 miles southwest of Rice Lake, which is administered by Rice Lake NWR. The refuge consists of two islands in Mille Lacs Lake on which common terns nest. Totaling less than an acre of dry ground, it is the country's smallest NWR.

Prairie smoke

A river valley is a potent, life-sustaining force anywhere on earth. A river valley situated in a meetingplace of two vast and distinct natural worlds is doubly dynamic. Here, just an hour north of the habitat of 4 million people, at 30,000-acre Sherburne NWR, prairie-oak savannah, deciduous woodlands, and rivers and marshes appear in near-limitless combinations, each shading into the next, in a region where forest and prairie overlap. As a result of ongoing restoration efforts, a sense of wildness is returning to this expansive refuge.

HISTORY

A great deal has come and gone on this land. Native American village sites discovered on the refuge date back to A.D. 1300; people have lived in this area for some 10,000 years, Beginning in the 1870s, European settlers harnessed the region, converting oak savanna, and in the 1920s building a series of ditches to drain wetlands. Interest in the possibility of establishing a refuge began in the early 1940s; Sherburne was established in 1965, and 10 years later land acquisition was nearly complete. What followed was an ambitious process of turning back time—removing barns and other buildings, burying foundations, and reseeding croplands to native prairie grasses.

Sherburne's long-term goal—restoring wetlands, prairie, and oak savanna to presettlement conditions—continues today. Thousands of acres are burned each year when conditions allow, opening up brush-choked areas and reinvigorating the fire-tolerant oak savannah.

GETTING THERE

From the town of Zimmerman, MN, on US 169 (about 50 mi. north Minneapolis–St. Paul), travel 4 mi. south to Sherburne County Road 9, turr west; continue 4 mi. to refuge entrance, where a kiosk contains information and leaflets; refuge headquarters is 1.5 mi. ahead.

■ **SEASON:** Refuge open year-round; designated wildlife sanctuary areas closed to public entry March through Aug.

■ **HOURS:** Daylight hours; refuge headquarters open weekdays 8 a.m.–4 p.m.

■ **FEES:** Free access.

■ **ADDRESS:** 17076 293rd Ave., Zimmerman, MN 55398

■ **TELEPHONE:** 612/389-3323

TOURING SHERBURNE

■ **BY AUTOMOBILE:** The 7.3-mile Prairie's Edge Wildlife Drive traverses all major habitats and is open during daylight hours from late April through October.

■ **BY FOOT:** Excellent opportunities for hiking abound. The Blue Hill trail network is a gem, with opportunities to walk amidst tallgrass prairie and a few wetland sites and through Sherburne's lovely woodlands. In addition, all refuge service roads are open to foot travel between September and February, and open hiking anywhere on refuge lands is permitted during this same period. In winter, hiking trails and many other areas provide outstanding cross-country skiing and snowshoeing, permitted from September through February.

■ **BY BICYCLE:** Bicycles are permitted on the Prairie's Edge Wildlife Drive, on public roads crossing the refuge, and refuge service roads between September and February. No off-road or off-trail riding permitted; hiking trails are closed to bicycles.

■ **BY CANOE, KAYAK, OR BOAT:** Some hunters use nonmotorized rowboats during migratory bird season, though access is difficult. Canoeing is the way to go here. Canoes are permitted on Battle Brook south of Little Elk Lake and on the St. Francis River south of Battle Brook. With its picturesque meanders, a float down the St. Francis can be a long, languid expedition; with the exception of spring, the river is well suited to all skill levels and rewards with great wildlife viewing.

WHAT TO SEE

■ **LANDSCAPE AND CLIMATE** A great mound cloaked in woodlands and oak savanna, Blue Hill is the highest point on this otherwise level refuge. Composed of sand and gravel "outwash" deposited 12,000 years ago, the hill is a glacial remnant. Other reminders of that era live on in the form of wetlands, where depressions were left by slabs of ice stranded as glaciers receded. Soils across much of Sherburne are coarse and extremely porous—vegetation grows like mad with reliable rainfall, but withers away just as rapidly if precipitation fails. Prairie-oak savanna evolved in accord with this dynamic climate between true prairie and deciduous forest, which included wildfires when the area dried out. Fire suppression since settlement allowed woodlands to encroach further upon oak savanna areas, which, coupled with clearing for settlement, virtually eliminated them in less than 100 years. Oak savanna restoration is a primary goal of the refuge today.

Annual precipitation here may reach 29 inches or more, with much of it occurring between June and August; the months of winter bring 30 or more inches of snow. The St. Francis River is subject to cyclical spring flooding. Summers are generally mild, whereas late fall and winter can be frigid, with stretches when temperatures are below zero—sometimes *well* below zero.

■ **PLANT LIFE** The sheer diversity of Sherburne's native plant life is stunning; space permits only the sketchiest of sketches. Visitors with enthusiasm for trees,

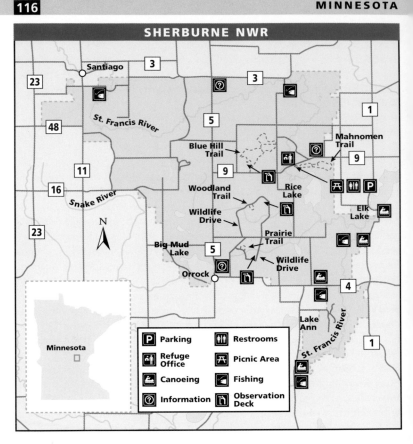

SHERBURNE NWR

shrubs, ferns, vines, wildflowers, and grasses will be overwhelmed here. The refuge is still very much a work-in-progress, as habitat restoration continues.

Woodlands Sherburne's historic oak savanna, with pin oak and fire-tolerant bur oak the dominant species, survives in remnants scattered across the refuge. This extremely rare community features oaks either widely scattered or in small stands, with tallgrass prairie beneath. Savanna restoration involves eliminating a wide array of encroaching or nonnative trees. Through prescribed burning and limited timber cutting, these tracts grow smaller each year. Seedling bur oaks are planted where native prairie has been reestablished.

Also present to a lesser degree are deciduous woodlands with a stunning diversity of trees, shrubs, and wildflowers. There are four species each of maple, birch, and oak; two species each of aspen and cedar; shrubs such as hazelnut, gooseberry, and four varieties of dogwood; and a wondrous assortment of woodland wildflowers—Solomon's seal, Turk's-cap lily, and jack-in-the-pulpit.

Adjacent to wetlands and other low-lying sites are a light scattering of tamarack, black spruce, and their bog associates—leatherleaf, cinnamon fern, spaghnum moss, cinquefoil, and Labrador tea. Along the St. Francis River and other wet sites are no fewer than eight species of willow.

Grasslands Sherburne's native and restored tallgrass prairie is as rich as they come. Big bluestem, switchgrass, Indian grass, and little bluestem are dominant grasses, though there are many others. Wildflowers bloom from early spring through August: prairie smoke, leadplant, the vivid orange of butterfly weed, the shrubs, ferns, vines, wildflowers, and grasses will be overwhelmed here. The refuge is still very much a work-in-progress, as habitat restoration continues.

Woodlands Sherburne's historic oak savanna, with pi oak and fire-tolerant bur oak the dominant species, survives in remnants scattered across the refuge. This extremely rare community features oaks either widely scattered or in small stands, with tallgrass prairie beneath. Savanna restoration involves eliminating a wide array of encroaching or nonnative trees. Through prescribed burning and limited timber cutting, these tracts grow smaller each year. Seedling bur oaks are planted where native prairie has been reestablished.

Also present to a lesser degree are deciduous woodlands with a stunning diversity of trees, shrubs, and wildflowers. There are four species each of maple, birch, and oak; two species each of aspen and cedar; shrubs such as hazelnut, gooseberry, and four varieties of dogwood; and a wondrous assortment of woodland wildflowers—Solomon's seal, Turk's-cap lily, and jack-in-the-pulpit.

Adjacent to wetlands and other low-lying sites are a light scattering of tamarack, black spruce, and their bog associates—leatherleaf, cinnamon fern, spaghnum moss, cinquefoil, and Labrador tea. Along the St. Francis River and other wet sites are no fewer than eight species of willow.

Grasslands Sherburne's native and restored tallgrass prairie is as rich as they come. Big bluestem, switchgrass, Indian grass, and little bluestem are dominant grasses, though there are many others. Wildflowers bloom from early spring through August: prairie smoke, leadplant, the vivid orange of butterfly weed, the electric blue of wild lupine, hoary pucoon, blazing star, bergamot, and many varieties of aster. It goes on like this—five species of milkweed, nine species of native sunflower, at least ten native species of goldenrod.

Wetlands Along the St. Francis River and in other areas are 24 wetland impoundments created by dikes and water-control structures, which have restored water once drained from these low-lying areas. Throughout the year, each pool is raised or lowered to mimic natural cycles, stimulating growth of such emergent plants as cattail, hardstem bulrush, and smartweed. Wild rice is present in several areas. A great variety of sedges are found here—some 25 species are recorded—

Badger

chipmunk, and white-tailed deer. Many other mammals are present but elusive—gray fox, mink, bobcat, and their preferred prey: meadow and prairie voles, masked shrew, ground squirrels, and moles.

Reptiles and amphibians A great diversity of frogs are here, including the green, northern leopard, wood, two species of tree frog, along with the western chorus frog. Snakes are equally diverse—the smooth green, redbelly, hognosed, and bullsnake. The northern prairie skink is present, as are two salamander species, the tiger and blue-spotted. Painted and snapping turtles are seen frequently, and careful observers may also see the lovely Blanding's turtle.

ACTIVITIES

■ **CAMPING:** Camping is not permitted on the refuge. Primitive and drive-in camping are available at Sand Dunes State Forest, which adjoins the refuge to the south.

■ **SWIMMING:** There is no swimming allowed inthe refuge waters.

■ **WILDLIFE OBSERVATION:** Sherburne's active volunteer program yields benefits for wildlife enthusiasts. On evenings and weekends, "roving interpreters" staff Wildlife Drive, with binoculars and spotting scopes at the ready. These folks are savvy in everything from bird species to wildflower identification. May 10–20 is typically the peak period for the spring migration of warblers through the area; the blue-winged and golden-winged warblers are two notable species that may be seen here.

HUNTING AND FISHING Fishing is permitted in the St. Francis River only—river access is located where county roads cross the river. **Northern pike**, **bullhead**, and **bluegill** are common catches. State regulations apply; contact the refuge for details.

Small game, **waterfowl**, and **white-tailed deer** are hunted on the refuge, in designated areas only. Contact the refuge for details, brochures, and maps.

■ **PHOTOGRAPHY:** Bald eagles in the past have nested near Wildlife Drive, and photographers with long lenses have obtained good shots of parents, nest, and young. Observation decks along Wildlife Drive are great for setting up tripods. Many species may be encountered along the drive; wildlife here is skittish, and vehicles make the best photo blinds.

■ **HIKES AND WALKS:** The Blue Hill Trail system features a series of loops, the largest traversing about 4.5 miles, with smaller combinations possible, including a one-way hike of about 1 mile from the parking area to an observation deck. The Mahnoman Trail system, too, offers several loops, the shortest just over 1 mile, the longest about 2.6 miles. Two half-mile-long footpaths—Prairie Trail and Woodland Trail—are along the auto-tour route.

■ **SEASONAL EVENTS:** Lots of fun things happen here: the Wildlife Festival and Open House in October; guided birding tours for beginners, families, and advanced birders during International Migratory Bird Day in May; and Winter Fun Day in February, including a demonstration dogsled team, and use of cross-country ski equipment and snowshoes.

■ **PUBLICATIONS:** Bird checklist; brochures on prescribed burning, volunteer opportunities, hunting guidelines, general visitor information. Plant and animal lists are forthcoming. *The Prairie's Edge* is a quarterly publication of the Friends of Sherburne NWR, with calendar of events and natural history information.

Tamarac NWR
Rochert, Minnesota

Bald eagle

More than half of this 42,724-acre refuge is forested, a tapestry of conifers and deciduous species unlike any other in the country. The namesake species of this exceptional refuge is tamarack, a deciduous conifer that emerges from winter's doldrums in the loveliest shade of pale green and in autumn turns a blazing gold.

It seems as though the remaining half of Tamarac NWR is water. Cold, clear, and gravel-bottomed, lakes of all size and shape are tucked amid the woodlands, and three rivers meander through hills and plains, fueling the abundant marshes and oxbow sloughs. Wild and diverse, home to timber wolves, loons, and one of the country's largest nesting populations of bald eagles, Tamarac is a feast for naturalists.

HISTORY

The myriad lakes, rivers, and lush forests of Tamarac were central to the lives of two major Indian tribes, the Dakota (Sioux) and Chippewa, who hunted deer and waterfowl and fished the local waters. Each fall the tribes filled their canoes with wild rice and set up camps to harvest maple sugar in spring. Disputes and battles over the area were common until the 1700s, when the Chippewa managed to push the Dakota deeper into their western territory once and for all.

Today the northern half of the refuge lies within the White Earth Indian Reservation, Chippewa lands set aside in 1867. A number of historic markers at Tamarac interpret Native American culture and history. Burial sites, rice-harvesting campsites, and ancient travel routes are all part of the landscape.

Spinning tall tales of Paul Bunyan and his blue ox, Babe, a generation of lumberjacks felled the region's original stands of white and red pine between 1890 and 1930. Homesteaders followed, but the land was poorly suited to farming. The refuge was established in 1938 and further enhanced during the 1960s by the establishment of a Job Corps Conservation Center. Because of resistance by sev-

TAMARAC NWR

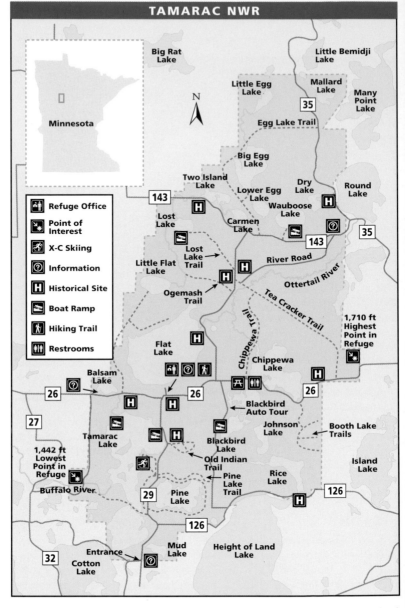

eral area gun clubs with influential members, Tamarac did not acquire its final third of acreage until the 1960s.

Tamarac is adjacent to the Detroit Lakes area, the limitless waters of which attract outdoor recreationists of all stripes from throughout the Midwest, year-round. Lakeside cabins and resorts dot the region.

GETTING THERE

From Detroit Lakes on US 10: Follow MN 34 east to County Rd 29, turning north (left); continue 8 mi. to refuge headquarters and Visitor Center.

■ **SEASON:** Refuge open year-round.

■ **HOURS:** Public use hours: 5 a.m.–10p.m. The Visitor Center—with exhibits, bookstore, observation deck, auditorium—is open weekdays year-round, 7:30 a.m.–4 p.m. The Visitor Center is open on weekends from Memorial Day through mid-Oct.

■ **FEES:** None.

■ **ADDRESS:** 35704 County Highway 26, Rochert, MN 56578

■ **TELEPHONE:** 218/847-2641

TOURING TAMARAC

■ **BY AUTOMOBILE:** County roads allow quick access to trailheads and nat-ural areas but provide only a limited sense of the refuge; the 10-mile Blackbird Auto Tour traverses forests, wetlands, and lakes, with many opportunities for wildlife viewing, photography, and the like.

■ **BY FOOT:** Old Indian Historic Trail and Visitor Center Nature Trail are desig-nated hiking trails; Pine Lake Trail follows the refuge auto tour, though traffic is nonexistent. All refuge grounds south of County Road 26 are open to public use year-round, including hiking, snowshoeing, skiing, hunting, and fishing. Several unimproved refuge roads within this area, closed seasonally to vehicles, are open to foot travel. The 2,000-acre Tamarac Wilderness Area (roadless and without des-ignated trails) is open to foot travel during fall hunting season.

■ **BY BICYCLE:** Not the best means of seeing this refuge, bikes are best suited to get from one area to another for exploration on foot. Bikes are permitted on roads open to vehicular traffic, including County Roads 29, 26, and 143, as well as the refuge service road and along the Blackbird Auto Tour.

■ **BY CANOE, KAYAK, OR BOAT:** Boating, including the use of motorized boats, is permitted on several refuge lakes, including Tamarac, Wauboose, Lost, Blackbird, and Cotton. All feature boat ramps and are popular with anglers.

WHAT TO SEE

■ **LANDSCAPE AND CLIMATE** This is the heart of Minnesota's glacial lake region, the benchmark for the state's license plate moniker, "Land of 10,000 Lakes." In all likelihood there are more. The refuge occupies a biological crossroads, with three major plant and animal communities represented: prairie species of the Great Plains, the "north woods" or boreal forest of the northern United States and Canada, and the deciduous hardwood forests that reach to New England. Prior to settlement, wildfires regenerated the area's tallgrass prairie and its forests, by thin-ning out dense stands of undergrowth and allowing some species, such as the jack pine, to disperse seeds.

The watershed tips northward; the Egg, Ottertail, and Buffalo rivers flow through Tamarac en route to the Red River Valley in North Dakota, and on to Hudson Bay. Situated atop this drainage, refuge waters receive no runoff from other areas; the result is water of very high quality. Elevations vary from 1,442 to 1,710 feet in a series of low, dipping hills and ridges.

The refuge climate is heavily influenced by arctic and Canadian air flows. Cool summers and cold, lengthy winters are the norm. Yearly precipitation averages 24 inches; about 46 inches of snow accumulate here each winter.

■ **PLANT LIFE**

Open water At the top of the Red River watershed, Tamarac is blessed with great amounts of freshwater in many forms, and water of exceptional purity. Its 21 natural lakes support a thriving native fishery of walleye, northern pike, and black crappie. Many lakes yield prolific harvests of wild rice. Shorelines feature some amount of cattail and bulrush, though in many areas the forest reaches to the water's edge.

The Egg and Buffalo rivers originate here. Narrow and slow moving, the Egg serves as a natural inlet and outlet for several lakes. A third river, the broad Otter Tail, meanders across level portions of the refuge, with a variety of oxbow lakes and cattail-bulrush flats to its credit; in areas with some relief, its flow approaches whitewater.

Spruce-tamarack bog Some 1,185 acres feature this lovely stuff, with tamarack and a few black spruce anchoring a deep, spongy mat of peat. Sphagnum moss, leatherleaf, bog rosemary, pitcher plant, sundew, and Minnesota's state flower, the showy lady's slipper, a white-to-pink orchid, are a few understory species.

Forest ponds The refuge plans to inventory and study these often-overlooked wetlands, of which there may be thousands in the refuge. Very small ephemeral pools, tucked away in hardwood and coniferous forests, serve a wide variety of creatures—from salamanders to beetles—during one or more critical stages of their life cycles. The role of these wetlands in the greater scheme is not well understood.

Marsh The classic marsh is found throughout Tamarac. A near 50-50 mix of open water and emergent thickets of cattail and bulrush; fingernail clams, fairy shrimp, and aquatic plants such as milfoil provide a bounty for waterfowl. Where possible, water levels are adjusted for maximum growth of wild rice.

Prairie potholes Tamarac represents the easternmost limits of this

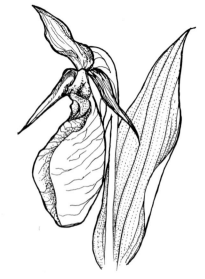

Lady's slipper

seasonal grassland wetland. These are dimples and depressions in the landscape that recharge with rain and snowmelt each spring. By the time migratory waterfowl return for breeding, a soup of insect larvae and fairy shrimp is ready to be consumed. By midsummer most potholes here are dry.

Shrub swamp This swamp encompasses 10 percent of the refuge (4,172 acres), forming a transition between marshes and upland areas, such as forests, and encircling the shallow edges and inlets of lakes. Alder, willow, and bog birch are dominant species. A fine sample can be seen from the auto tour along Blackbird Lake.

Forests The deep woods of Tamarac are a rich collage of trunks, needles, and greenery. Stock-straight sugar maple and basswood, gnarled moss-dappled trunks of black spruce, the frondlike limbs of balsam fir with pale green tips of new growth. The smooth, vivid white of paper birch alongside the armored black trunk of a white pine soaring clear of the rest.

Tamarac's forests are unique in their diversity. Both northern hardwood species, which are dominant to the south and east, and boreal forest, which becomes dominant to the north, coexist in a rich mosaic of species. Sugar maple and basswood, paper birch, aspen, and bur and pin oak are joined by white and red pine, balsam fir, tamarack, and black spruce. Aspen parks are managed aggressively through seasonal harvesting to maintain a diversity of age groups. The dense understory includes red osier dogwood, juneberry, and chokecherry; bloodroot, trillium, and giant hyssop are a few of the many forest wildflowers. Shafts of sunlight reach through to bright patches of jack-in-the-pulpit.

A few titanic white and red pines are scattered through the refuge. Young trees at the time of timber harvesting, these old-growth remnants offer a glimpse of the presettlement forest.

Grasslands Altered by early homesteaders and agriculture, the 1,500 acres of grasslands retain pockets of native big bluestem, indicating that the area supported a more extensive tallgrass prairie prior to settlement. Most of this land today is seeded to native grasses, dense nesting cover for waterfowl, or croplands for wildlife.

■ **ANIMAL LIFE** Only in a place this diverse is it possible for the badger, that low-slung rendering machine of open prairie, to live in close proximity to its cousin the fisher, a sleek, luxuriantly furred carnivore of the coniferous forest. The black tern, by and large a prairie species, nests here; so too does that emblem of wild northwoods lakes, the common loon. Both are readily encountered. The brown thrasher and bobolink nest on site, as do the rose-breasted grosbeak and golden-winged warbler. Nothing is too improbable here.

Birds Extirpated around the turn of the century, trumpeter swans were reintroduced in 1987. Their eight established nesting territories produced 19 cygnets in 1998; cygnets are now returning with their parents in spring, and the birds at this time are flourishing. Some 30 bald eagles were fledged here in 1997; several immense nests are clearly visible in the tops of ancient pines, one of them along the auto-tour route.

The combination of forest and marsh makes ideal habitat for the wood duck; Tamarac features a very large nesting population of these striking birds. The ring-necked duck and blue-winged teal are the other prominent nesting duck species,

Fisher

Common goldeneye

though canvasback, lesser scaup, bufflehead and common goldeneye may also be seen. The pied-billed and red-necked grebes are commonly seen in summer with their young. During spring and fall migration, 30,000 or more ring-necked ducks pass through, the birds in fall gathering to feast on wild rice.

Tamarac's diverse community of woodland songbirds makes it a favorite destination for birders. Uncommon nesting species include the winter wren, hermit thrush, warbling and yellow-throated vireos, eastern towhee, pine sisken, and scarlet tanager. Warblers are greatly varied—the northern parula, mourning, black-throated green, pine, and black-and-white are uncommon nesting species; the ovenbird, American redstart, and chestnut-sided warbler are common nesters. As many as 14 other warbler species pass through during spring and fall migration.

Mammals A single pack of 8 to 12 timber wolves drifts through the forests, rarely seen, though the sight of a paw print in soft ground—which may be discovered with some effort—is fairly thrilling in its own right. Tamarac's white-tailed deer population averages 22 animals per square mile, and the wolves are very pleased with this arrangement. Other notable forest mammals include the black bear, bobcat, northern flying squirrel, and seven species of bats, along with porcupine, raccoon, gray fox, and ermine. Moose inhabit the refuge but are not often seen.

Amphibians In marshes, bogs, and forest ponds are many frogs—striped chorus frog, wood frog, spring peeper, gray tree frog, and mink frog, as well as the northern leopard and green frogs. Snapping and painted turtles ply the marshes, rivers, and lakes.

ACTIVITIES

■ **CAMPING:** Not permitted. Near-limitless opportunities exist in close proximity to the refuge on state lands, county properties, and private campgrounds.
■ **SWIMMING:** Swimming is not permitted in refuge waters.
■ **WILDLIFE OBSERVATION:** Spring is slow to come to Tamarac, but the wait is well worth it. In late April and early May, male ruffed grouse station themselves

atop fallen logs and "drum" for mates—a soft, percussive thrumming of wingbeats that wafts through the forest. At the same time, trumpeter swans and bald eagles begin to nest. Between late May and early June, songbirds pass through, and white-tailed does with dappled fawns graze in meadows. It may be possible to hear wolves and pups of the year howling at this time.

■ **PHOTOGRAPHY:** Those who appreciate autumn colors will find Tamarac's fall display as varied in hues and species as any in the Midwest. Northwoods images abound here in all seasons: misty, glass-flat lakes, old-growth stands of white and red pine, wolf tracks in the snow, skeins of geese and ducks, and a fine display of woodland wildflowers between May and July.

■ **HIKES AND WALKS:** Old Indian Historic Trail is an interesting piece of the region's Native American history. It winds through a cathedral-like forest of mature sugar maples and basswood and traverses several wetland areas. Birding is productive for songbirds and wetland species. A very short walk with high scenic values is the Sugarbush Boat Access; the forest canopy high above all but erases the sky, and the fall colors are nothing short of spectacular.

■ **SEASONAL EVENTS:** The annual Detroit Lakes Festival of Birds, in May, features trips to Tamarac and other area refuges, along with workshops, speakers, trade shows, and arts and crafts; contact the Detroit Lakes Regional Chamber of Commerce (800/542-3992) for information. The annual Fall Open House at Tamarac includes arts and crafts booths and speakers; contact refuge headquarters for details. Other annual events include National Wildlife Refuge Week in October; bird surveys in spring, summer, and fall; and summer programs. Contact the refuge or the Tamarac Interpretive Association.

■ **PUBLICATIONS:** *Tamarac Highlights*, published twice yearly by the Tamarac Interpretive Association and Tamarac NWR. Also checklists of birds and mammals, auto-tour guide, general brochure, and informational materials on wild rice. The Detroit Lakes Chamber of Commerce publishes an excellent visitors' guide with information on lodging, birding, and other outdoor activities in the region.

HUNTING AND FISHING
Tamarac, Black Bird, Lost, Pine, and Waboose lakes are open to **fishing** at various times of the year; contact refuge for details.

You may hunt **waterfowl**, **white-tailed deer**, **upland birds**, and **small game** in accordance with state regulations and seasons; contact the refuge for more detail.

Upper Mississippi NW & FR

Winona District, Winona, Minnesota; La Crosse District, La Crosse, Wisconsin; McGregor District, McGregor, Iowa; Savanna District, Savanna, Illinois

Observation platform, Upper Mississippi NW & FR

A vast and varied labyrinth of forests, islands, secluded side channels, and deep waters, the Upper Mississippi River National Wildlife and Fish Refuge is a 261-mile-long riverine corridor. Encompassing some 194,000 acres along the Mississippi River in the states of Minnesota, Wisconsin, Iowa, and Illinois, the refuge—divided into four management districts—maintains some of the more intact natural communities left in a region greatly altered by civilization. It is a vital migratory route for immense numbers of bird species, from warblers to swans and eagles; its woodlands, sandbars, sheltered coves offer secure nesting sites for hundreds of other bird species; and its waters, though degraded in most every conceivable manner, are a stronghold for 45 species of reptiles and amphibians, 118 species of fish, including several endangered varieties, and more than 40 species of freshwater mussels.

Each state's management district offers access for exploration by various means, from canoes and small motorized craft to hiking trails and a few unimproved roads. Each district, too, features a Visitor Center, most with interpretive exhibits and more detailed information about plants, animals, and conservation issues and strategies. Observation areas, developed for seasonal spectacles such as waterfowl and bald eagle migration, are found on or adjacent to each district.

HISTORY

The Upper Mississippi Valley gave rise to a highly sophisticated agrarian culture some 2,000 years ago, with riverside villages, extensive trade networks, and elaborate religious proceedings. Burial mounds of these early people may still be seen across the region. The first Europeans to see the river were Hernando DeSoto and later the French explorers Jacques Marquette and Louis Jolliet. The Indian tribes they encountered, such as the Fox, Winnebago, and Ojibwa, maintained cultures of agriculture and village life, augmented with fishing and hunting. "Mississippi" was an Algonquian word, meaning "father of waters." France sold the western portion of the river basin to the United States as part of the 1803 Louisiana Purchase.

Long an important travel corridor, river transportation on the Mississippi grew enormously after the 1812 invention of the steamboat. As agriculture flourished on adjacent fertile plains, commercial river traffic increased significantly. By the early 1900s, unregulated market hunting and fishing had pushed waterfowl and other species to their limits. Will Dilg, founder of the Izaak Walton League, led the effort to secure permanent protection for Mississippi River migratory birds and sport fish such as the black bass. The refuge, formally established in 1924, was the first to include fisheries in its conservation efforts.

Beginning in the 1930s, the river's character and ecology would be substantially altered by a series of locks and dams developed by the Army Corps of Engineers.

GETTING THERE

Refuge headquarters is located in the city of Winona, MN, about 150 mi. southeast of Minneapolis–St. Paul. There are four district management offices with maps, Visitor Centers, wildlife checklists, and other information, Their addresses are: Winona District: Located in the city of Winona, MN, about 100 mi. southeast of Minneapolis–St. Paul on US 61; La Crosse District: Located in the town of Onalaska, WI, 3 mi. north of the city of La Crosse, WI; just south of I-90; McGregor District: Located in the town of McGregor, IA, about 72 mi. north of the city of Dubuque, IA, on US 18; Savanna District: Located in the town of Savanna, IL, about 77 mi. southwest of the city of Rockford, IL, on US 52.

■ **SEASON:** Open year-round.

■ **HOURS:** All hours.

■ **FEES:** None.

■ **ADDRESS:** Refuge headquarters: 51 E. 4th St., Room 263, Winona, MN 55987; Winona District: 51 E. 4th St., Winona, MN 55987; La Crosse District: 555 Lester Ave., Onalaska, WI 54650; McGregor District: P.O. Box 460, McGregor, IA 52157; Savanna District: P.O. Box 336, Savanna, IL 61074

■ **TELEPHONE:** Refuge headquarters: 507/452-4232; Winona District: 507/454-7351; La Crosse District: 608/783-8405; McGregor District: 319/873-3423; Savanna District: 815/273-2732

TOURING UPPER MISSISSIPPI

■ **BY AUTOMOBILE:** The refuge offers limited opportunities for wildlife viewing along riverside roads, boat launches, and at parking areas for dams, dikes, and some scenic overlooks.

■ **BY FOOT:** Hiking is permitted year-round in all open public-use areas. Developed trails are hard to come by. Unimproved footpaths and boat access roads are abundant and provide for exploration of backwaters and bottomland forests. Several dams and dikes along the refuge offer safe and improved foot access for wildlife viewing. Check with staff at the district office for the best options.

■ **BY BICYCLE:** Bicycling is permitted year-round on gravel boat access roads, improved county roads, and other "river roads" adjoining each district. Bicycles are not the best means of exploring here.

■ **BY CANOE, KAYAK, OR BOAT:** Taking to the refuge waters is by far the most popular and productive means of seeing the river and associated wild lands. Power boats and houseboats have their places, allowing visitors to cover large swaths of the river and to navigate deeper, open waters. But canoes, kayaks, and other small craft are ideal for exploring literally hundreds of miles of marshlands, hidden backwater channels, lakes, and islands. Overnight primitive camping is permitted on refuge islands—canoeing a stretch of river over several days, camping each night, is a very attractive combination. Be aware of large pleasure boats or barges; small boats and canoes can easily be capsized by heavy wakes.

WHAT TO SEE

■ **LANDSCAPE AND CLIMATE** The nation's second-longest river at 2,348 miles, the Mississippi and its watershed includes all or part of 31 states, or about 40 percent of the nation; its total drainage area of 1,250,000 square miles is third-largest on earth.

Originating in Lake Itasca, MN, at an elevation of 1,463 feet, the river flows rather unassumingly through a series of glacial lakes. Below Minneapolis–St. Paul, its floodplain is bounded by a series of bluffs, which range from 200 to 300 feet in height and constitute a defining feature of the river throughout the refuge. Between the Twin Cities and Saint Louis, MO, are many sizable tributaries, including the Illinois, Black, Wisconsin, Chippewa, Des Moines, and Iowa rivers. At Saint Louis, the Mississippi is joined by the Missouri River, which by itself accounts for 40 percent of the entire drainage area. At Cairo, IL, the formidable Ohio River enters from the east.

The dams, dikes, and levees along the Mississippi and its major tributaries have mitigated flooding and allowed agriculture and urban areas to encroach further upon floodplains. Flooding, however, will always remain a part of the watershed. The most recent and substantial occurred in 1993, when the Mississippi and Missouri rivers inundated some 16 million acres in Iowa, Illinois, Wisconsin, Minnesota, Missouri, Nebraska, South Dakota, and Kansas.

The Mississippi in general forms a north-south boundary between the lush deciduous forests of the East and the open plains and grasslands of the West. Warm, humid air from the Gulf of Mexico enters the upper portions of the valley, mixing with cooler, drier air from the west and north. Precipitation in this upper region ranges from 20 to 40 inches annually. Mean annual temperatures are 40 to 50 degrees.

■ **PLANT LIFE**
Open water and wetlands Along these 261 miles, the Mississippi River ranges from 1.5 to more than 2.5 miles in width. Throughout the refuge, as along most of its length, the river is harnessed by a sequence of locks and dams. Within each region between impoundments, three general zones occur. The first several miles of water below a dam most closely approximate the Mississippi's natural free-flowing state: Most of the dense, mature forests are here, along with islands, many braided channels, and deep sloughs; the natural tendency of the current to dismantle and rearrange the riverbed is greatest in this reach, creating holes and irregularities that benefit fish and other aquatic life. Below this region, the river's backwaters spread out over a ghost landscape of submerged woodlands and farm fields. Water depths range from a few inches to 3 or 4 feet. In the shallower areas are extensive marshes; arrowroots, lotus, water lily, cattail, and bulrush form dense thickets, creating food, nesting cover, and nursery sites for hatchling fish. Rich and productive over many years, the inevitable buildup of sediments within

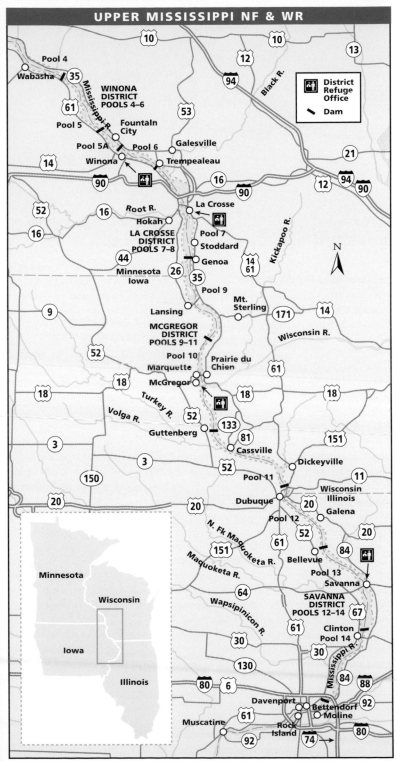

Canvasback duck

impounded navigation pools is now degrading these aquatic habitats at a rapid rate. A significant loss of wetland habitat is expected within 50 years.

In the main channels of this middle zone, current velocity diminishes as it nears the massive "hydraulic cushion" of impounded water below. Siltation occurs here as well. It's only fitting that in this utterly unnatural scheme, yet another bit of human meddling—the submerged wing dam—actually offers some benefits. These structures force the current toward the center of the channel, boosting its speed, which causes sediment deposition along the shore and scouring in the main channel. The wing dams—along with a continuous program of dredging problem stretches and piling sediment at disposal sites—help the Army Corps of Engineers maintain a 9-foot-deep channel for commercial barge traffic. Wing dams do create depth variation: water levels may be 7 feet in front of a structure, and 18 feet behind it; temperature and oxygen levels vary accordingly, which is a good thing for fish, including the endangered pallid sturgeon. Researchers monitoring radio-implanted sturgeon have found they spend a good deal of time around wing dams. The concrete rubble of a dam is another serviceable, if alien, habitat, housing great densities of invertebrates, such as caddis flies, a staple in the diet of fish, amphibians, and insect-eating birds.

Below this middle zone is the immense pool of motionless water behind the dam. Siltation, the Mississippi River's number-one enemy, is prolific here, converting large portions of what were once gravel-bottomed channels into relatively stagnant, featureless expanses of sand and muck. Aquatic plant diversity is poor in these reaches, where the activities of carp and powerboaters stir the water, increasing turbidity and lowering light penetration.

Two more important features of the river are its riverine lakes and river deltas. On many islands throughout the refuge are large and small lakes. Shallow, often gin-clear, riverine lakes were inundated each year by spring flooding before dam installation. It's down to once every three or so years now, and sedimentation has increased. Wild celery, an excellent food source for wildlife, occurs here with sago pondweed and millfoils. River deltas form where tributaries deposit loads of sediment. Emergent plants and, later, shrub and forest communities develop on these fertile landforms, some of which are enormous. Tributary waters are often cooler than those of the Mississippi and add a fresh dose of oxygen.

Forests A bottomland deciduous forest cloaks thousands of acres: islands, adjacent bluffs, and much of the floodplain. This is a densely canopied forest of silver maple, green ash, cottonwood, American elm, black willow, swamp white oak, and box elder. Nelson-Trevino Bottoms, on the Winona District, is only one of many examples. The often dense understory features poison ivy, stinging nettle, and reed canary grass. Cardinal flowers and wild iris bloom along the banks.

■ **ANIMAL LIFE** The ecosystem of the Mississippi River, imperiled though it is, remains a place of beauty and diversity, with hints of its once extensive wilderness.

Birds As both a migratory corridor and nesting ground for birds, the refuge has been recognized by the American Bird Conservancy and Birds International as one of the "globally important bird areas" of the United States. Mature cottonwoods serve as rookeries for large numbers of great blue herons, great egrets, along with yellow-crowned and black-crowned night-herons. In 1998, the refuge hosted 85 bald eagle nests, which fledged 128 young, the highest total yet. Trumpeter swans, extirpated from the watershed decades ago, are seen today; biologists are hopeful a pair may nest in the future. A newcomer is the American white pelican. These enormous birds have moved into the region in growing numbers; no nests have been recorded yet, though flocks of more than 100 birds are occasionally seen in summer, and refuge biologists are tagging pelicans to study their movements. Canvasback ducks nest on the river in sizable numbers; during migration they follow a route from Chesapeake Bay to the Canadian provinces, and stop at the refuge—some 300,000 canvasbacks were here in 1998. Black terns nest on floating pads of decayed vegetation amidst lily pads, bulrushes, and cattail thickets.

Songbird diversity is rich. A few of many notable species include the American redstart, prothonotary warbler, yellow-billed cuckoo, scarlet tanager, swamp sparrow, yellow-throated vireo, and blue-gray gnatcatcher. Woodpeckers—red-headed, pileated, red-bellied—are abundant. The ruby-throated hummingbird is common in summer, visiting thickets of wildflowers. The barred owl and red-shouldered hawk are also present

Mammals Another cause for optimism is the growing number of river otters, an "indicator" species for overall river health. Mink, muskrat, beaver, raccoon, Virginia opossum, the occasional black bear, and white-tailed deer inhabit the floodplain. Present but elusive are red and gray fox, and coyote. Fox squirrels and eastern chipmunks are abundant.

Reptiles and amphibians In the marshes, forests, and other areas are many reptiles. Snakes include the northern water snake, hog-nosed snake, black snake, and some massasauga rattlesnakes. On the northern end of the refuge, the lovely Blanding's turtle survives; wood, softshell, snapping, and map turtles are present as well.

Beginning in mid-May and continuing through July, the frogs make noise: lots of frogs, lots of noise.

Snapping turtle

Chorus frogs, wood frogs, green frogs, spring peepers, and two varieties of tree frog, along with leopard and some bullfrogs, chirp and croak the nights away. Salamanders, such as the mudpuppy and eastern tiger, are widespread.

Fish and invertebrates Fish and freshwater mussels are included in the conservation efforts of the refuge. Two prehistoric species, the paddlefish and endangered pallid sturgeon, survive here; little is known about the sturgeon other than the fact it has been adversely affected by dams. Mussels, too, are under threat; the Higgins' pearly eye, native only to the Mississippi and a few tributaries, is also endangered. Many others—the washboard, three ridge, pigtoe—are widespread, though they now compete with the zebra mussel, a European exotic that is difficult to control. Other fish here include walleye, northern pike, largemouth and smallmouth bass, sunfish, and crappie.

ACTIVITIES

■ **CAMPING:** Camping is permitted on refuge islands year-round; dead wood on the ground may be used for campfires. Contact a district office for more information.

■ **SWIMMING:** Swimming is permitted in many public-use areas, such as boat landings.

■ **WILDLIFE OBSERVATION:** Large numbers of tundra swans move through the refuge during spring and fall migration, along with a splendid array of shorebirds, warblers, raptors, and waterfowl. Bald eagles winter on the refuge in sizable numbers; several districts maintain staffed viewing areas where visitors can watch these great birds fishing, hunting, and soaring.

■ **PHOTOGRAPHY:** Wildlife and floodplain scenery are best photographed from the river. Autumn colors in the forest are magnificent. Wild turkey are common, so try to catch males perform their stately courtship displays in the forests in spring.

■ **HIKES AND WALKS:** Many public lands adjoin the refuge along its 261 miles: city, county, and state parks and federal lands. These areas offer the most accessible walking for visitors seeking improved trails.

> **HUNTING AND FISHING**
> Fishing is permitted in accordance with the regulations of each state. Species and seasons vary by state, as do other regulations. Contact the refuge for details.

■ **SEASONAL EVENTS:** Each district maintains a calendar of events. The refuge celebrates National Wildlife Refuge Week in October with special events.

Crescent Lake NWR
Ellsworth, Nebraska

Barn owl

Craving solitude? Look no further than the Nebraska Sandhills. The state begins in the realm of midwestern humidity and cornfields and ends in semiarid plains rolling toward snow-capped peaks. Right smack in the middle are the scalloped hills and expansive, sky-blue lakes of the Nebraska Sandhills. Big cities are far, far away—even Omaha is at the other end of the state. And square in the heart of the Sandhills lies Crescent Lake NWR.

These 70 square miles of refuge offer the adventuresome visitor a level of solitude even the Rocky Mountains would be hard-pressed to match. Crescent Lake is a place to wander, a place to visit when there are no concerns for schedules or obligations. It is too big to hurry through, and quite frankly, the roads won't allow it. Pack a breakfast, lunch, and dinner; fill the gas tank, and check the spare tire. The town of Alliance is an hour to the northwest; due south 40 minutes is Oshkosh. After a long day in the embrace of the Sandhills, a cozy room for the night can be had at either place.

HISTORY

Near the Nebraska-Wyoming border about 100 miles west of Crescent Lake, the 1851 Horse Creek Council was a gathering of Plains Indian tribes—Assinoboins, Arikaras, Sioux, Cheyenne, Arapahos, Shoshones, among several others—the likes of which had never occurred before, or since. Convened by Tom Fitzpatrick, legendary mountain man turned U.S. Indian Agent, all members present agreed to a general regional peace and to cease harassment of wagon trains ferrying settlers west. Three years later, the historic agreement would unravel when a minor dispute over a sickly cow triggered a bloodbath between the U.S. Cavalry and a Sioux camp. Out of this disagreement the war between the United States and the Plains Indians would begin.

Between the 1870s and 1880s, Plains Indian culture and the vast bison herds

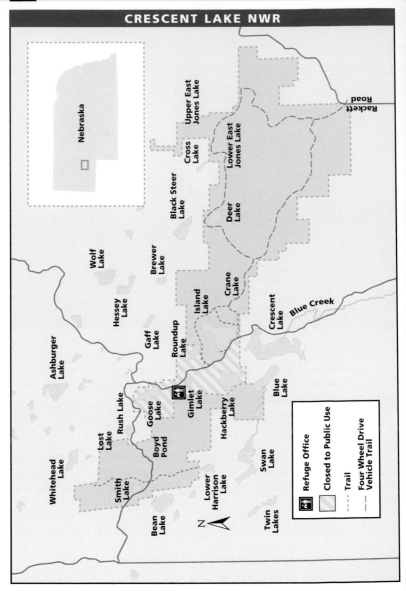

CRESCENT LAKE NWR

Nebraska

Rackett Road

Upper East Jones Lake

Lower East Jones Lake

Cross Lake

Black Steer Lake

Deer Lake

Wolf Lake

Brewer Lake

Hessey Lake

Crane Lake

Island Lake

Crescent Lake

Blue Creek

Ashburger Lake

Gaff Lake

Roundup Lake

Rush Lake

Goose Lake

Gimlet Lake

Hackberry Lake

Blue Lake

Lost Lake

Boyd Pond

Whitehead Lake

Smith Lake

Lower Harrison Lake

Swan Lake

Bean Lake

Twin Lakes

N

Refuge Office

Closed to Public Use

Trail

Four Wheel Drive Vehicle Trail

were decimated, and the Sandhills became cattle country, open range for immense herds of Texas longhorns. Homesteaders followed through the turn of the century, but the porous ground here—almost pure sand—was ill-suited to crops. By the 1920s, growing national concern over declining waterfowl populations led to consideration of the Sandhills, with its mosaic of natural wetlands and lakes, as a wildlife refuge. The initial land purchase for Crescent Lake NWR was completed in 1931.

A 25,000-acre area of Crescent Lake received nomination for wilderness status in 1972, though no final decision has ever been made. A portion of these lands has been named the Prairie Primitive Area, to emphasize the fact that special management considerations are in effect—a general policy of minimal disturbance by vehicles—but that the area, at this time, is not quite an official wilderness. Reintroduction of bison is currently being considered.

GETTING THERE

From Alliance, NE, travel 24 mi. east on NE 2, to the town of Lakeside, turning right (south) onto unimproved Country Road 181; continue 28 mi. to refuge boundary.

- ■ **SEASON:** Refuge open year-round.
- ■ **HOURS:** Open daylight hours.
- ■ **FEES:** Free access.
- ■ **ADDRESS:** Refuge office: 10630 Road 181, Ellsworth NE 69340; Crescent Lake Complex Headquarters: 115 Railway St., Ste. C109, Scottsbluff NE 69363
- ■ **TELEPHONE:** Refuge office: 308/762-4893; complex headquarters: 308/635-7851

TOURING CRESCENT LAKE

■ **BY AUTOMOBILE:** The self-guided auto tour, with 19 interpreted stops, traverses the very best of the refuge. As currently designed, however, visitors arriving from the north or west must travel backward along the route to reach its beginning near Crescent Lake. The entrance road from the south, out of the town of Oshkosh, allows a visitor to reach stop one on the tour without backtracking. Some refuge roads are passable only by 4-wheel-drive or high-clearance vehicles. Most of these are marked with signs.

■ **BY FOOT:** The refuge has no designated or improved trails; foot travel is permitted on a vast network of unimproved trails, refuge roads, and primitive 4-wheel-drive jeep trails.

■ **BY BICYCLE:** Energy, skill, and resolve are necessary for cyclists here; the terrain is greatly varied, and most all roads are composed of loose, often deep sand. It's tough going. All refuge roads and jeep trails are open to those who wish to try.

■ **BY CANOE, KAYAK, OR BOAT:** Nonmotorized watercraft (electric motors OK) are permitted on Island Lake only.

Evening primrose

WHAT TO SEE

■ **LANDSCAPE AND CLIMATE** The Great Plains and Nebraska Sandhills owe their existence to the Rocky Mountains; through eons of uplifting and erosion, alluvial deposits—including volcanic ash and sand—have made their way eastward, transported by wind and water. Geologically young, the 19,000-square-mile Sandhills region has been stabilized by plant communities. "Blowouts," in which the upper portion of a dune is sheared off by wind, are less common today, though they remain a feature of the refuge.

Beneath this restless landscape lies the Ogallala Aquifer, a great subterranean

Mule deer buck

lake. The natural lakes and wetlands at Crescent Lake are low spots where groundwater from the aquifer emerges from the porous soil. Given the greatly variable climate—including precipitation, which replenishes the aquifer—the waterscape is equally dynamic, with lakes and wetlands bankfull some years, and very low in others.

The 100th meridian—that all-important dividing line between the humid air masses of the East and drier, western air—passes through the heart of this region, one factor in the roller coaster of a climate. January 1997, for example, featured a high of 65 degrees, and a low of -20 degrees; in March, the high reached 81 degrees, with a low of 3 above. Annual precipitation averages some 17.5 inches. Elevations here average 3,800 feet.

■ PLANT LIFE
Open water Many shallow freshwater lakes—including Island, Smith, Martin, Crane, Goose, Blue, and several others—encompass more than 2,000 acres. In a wet year these waters are 6 to 8 feet deep, just enough to support a stocked fishery of bluegills, yellow perch, largemouth bass, walleye, and crappie. All are natural lakes; several are diked, enabling refuge staff to manage water levels for control of cattail and hardstem bulrush, which can overtake shallows and reduce habitat for waterfowl. On the largest lakes, emergent vegetation is minimal and prairie grasses roll down nearly to the water's edge.

Wetlands Crescent Lake's 8,251 acres of wetlands are low, sandy basins where the water table reaches the surface. Most were formed during periods of extreme drought, when the scouring action of winds pushed sand from low-lying areas onto dunes. Through the natural cycle of the seasons, wetlands are full in spring and diminish through summer and fall, recharging again over the winter.

Temporary wetlands on site capture spring rains and snow and last only a few weeks, though they provide critical habitat for migrating waterfowl and shorebirds. Marshes maintain some amount of water throughout the year and often include emergent vegetation, such as cattail and hardstem bulrush. About 4,755 acres of wet meadows occur in many of the long, narrow valleys between hill and

DIFFERENTIATING DEER Both white-tailed and mule deer are common at Crescent Lake—how to tell one from the other? Tails and ears are a starting point. True to its name, the underside of the tail of a white-tailed deer is pure white; when alarmed it bounds off with tail held high. The mule deer's tail is smaller, with a black tip, and its name is no accident—the ears of a mule deer are significantly larger, like those of a mule.

Watch the deer as they run. White-tails bound in high, graceful arcs or just flat-out gallop. Mule deer perform a wonderful routine known as "stotting," bouncing along as though powered by pogo sticks. The appearance of antlers on bucks in fall offers another means of identification. Each antler of a white-tailed buck features one prominent beam, more or less horizontal, with secondary tines protruding upward from it. The "mulie" buck, by contrast, has two major, Y-shaped beams on each antler, which continue to fork near the tops.

dunes; these too are an expression of groundwater close to the surface. Switchgrass and Indian grass dominate, growing in dense stands 3-4 feet high and offering ideal nesting cover for waterfowl and bedding areas for deer.

Grasslands More than 37,000 acres of mixed-grass prairie carpet the swales, flats, "choppies," dunes, and ridges of Crescent Lake. Eastern tallgrasses, midgrasses, and western shortgrass varieties are all found here: Prairie sand reed, sandhills muhly, big and little bluestem, needle and thread, and blue grama are typical grass species. Chokecherry, yucca, sand cherry, prairie rose, and a splendid assortment of wildflowers—milkweed, prickly poppy, bush morning glory, spiderwort, evening primrose, and prairie coneflower, among others—are also present.

Crescent Lake is a stronghold for blowout penstemon, an endangered wildflower found in only five counties of Nebraska. Its large, showy blossoms of blueish purple appear in clusters on stalks 18 inches high. In addition to its beauty, this plant is perfectly adapted to life in the dynamic Sandhills. Its seeds may lie dormant below ground for years, awaiting a "blowout," when winds obliterate the crown of a dune; as soon as there is an opening of bare sand, the penstemon moves in. Its function is to stabilize the dune, enabling grasses to move in. Once this happens, the penstemon, which does not compete well, is crowded out. As private landowners have succeeded in stabilizing sandhills, the penstemon has found fewer opportunities to reproduce. Perhaps 550 or so plants survive on the refuge; staff and volunteers dedicate a good deal of time each year to maintaining blowouts; in 1997 some 2,000 seedlings were planted.

■ ANIMAL LIFE

Birds Crescent Lake's birdlife is dazzling. A pair of bald eagles has begun nesting near Hackberry Lake, and a pair of trumpeter swans at this time have serious ideas of following suit. During spring and summer, a rich variety of marsh-associated birds are seen—American white pelican, western and eared grebes, white-faced ibis, black tern, Forster's tern, black-crowned night-heron, and American bittern. Nesting shorebirds include the American avocet, black-necked stilt, willet, and upland sandpiper; nesting waterfowl include the blue-winged teal, canvasback, ruddy duck, and mallard. Numbers and diversity of shorebirds and waterfowl climb substantially during spring and fall migration.

The array of grassland species is equally rich. The long-billed curlew is a favorite of visitors and readily seen. Songbirds include the dickcissel, lark sparrow, grasshopper sparrow, lark bunting, eastern and western kingbird, and blue grosbeak. Rarities include Bell's vireo and MacGillivray's warbler. Burrowing owls are present in summer, along with short-eared owls; the barn owl, a species of special concern here, occupies man-made nest boxes placed on windmills and fire towers. The eastern screech owl may also be seen or more likely heard.

During the course of the year, especially spring and fall migration, a tremendous array of raptors may be seen: the peregrine and prairie falcon, golden eagle, broad-winged hawk, sharp-shinned hawk, osprey, and in the winter, rough-legged hawk. The red-tailed and Swainson's hawk, along with the American kestrel and northern harrier, nest on the refuge.

Mammals Suffice it to say that burrowing animals and sand do not go together. Loose and drifty, the sandhills are a sort of purgatory for prairie dogs, badgers, burrowing owls, and other grassland subterraneans. Badgers and burrowing owls are present, but in very small numbers. The prairie dogs don't bother.

These remote expanses probably do harbor one of the country's rarest and most elusive mammals, the swift fox. Solitary, mostly nocturnal, it is a smallish fox, yellow to buff colored on top, whitish below, with a black-tipped tail. Over

Black-tailed prairie dog on its haunches

short distances it can reach speeds of 25 miles per hour—a swift fox indeed. A candidate for endangered-species listing, the animal is almost never encountered—a year may pass without a sighting by refuge staff— though it has been glimpsed now and again.

As a midcontinent crossroads, Crescent Lake is home to several mammals normally seen great distances from here. Both white-tailed deer and mule deer thrive in the Sandhills, and visitors can sharpen their identification skills for picking out each species(see sidebar, p. 137). Both the desert and eastern cottontail rabbits are present. The Ord's kangaroo rat, a spring-loaded creature found as far west as Nevada, is abundant; the silky pocket mouse, with a range extending south into Mexico, is also abundant—look for its tiny burrows, about the width of a finger, at the base of plants and on the steeper sides of hills. Other common mammals include the muskrat, coyote, long-tailed weasel, plains pocket gopher, and both white-tailed and black-tailed jackrabbit.

Reptiles and amphibians One of the rare creatures here is the yellow mud turtle, another candidate for listing. A stop along the auto tour interprets this reptile's life cycle. The ornate box turtle, a colorful, high-backed grassland species, is fairly common. Bull snakes inhabit the grasslands and road edges; when alarmed, these large snakes rise up to mimic a rattlesnake, which they resemble in color and markings though they have no venemous bite. Chorus frogs sing in the marshes and wet meadows in spring.

ACTIVITIES

■ **CAMPING:** Camping is not permitted on the refuge. Camping opportunities are found south of the refuge on the shores of Lake C. W. McConaughy, an impoundment on the North Platte River.

■ **WILDLIFE OBSERVATION:** No fewer than 45 sharp-tailed grouse leks (dancing grounds) are here; the mid-April courtship period is busy and an observation blind is available for watching the action. Border Lake is a good bet for shorebird species. Smith Lake is home to the refuge's black-crowned night-heron colony. A nesting community of great blue herons and double crested cormorants is found at Crane Lake. Spiderwort, yucca, prickly pear cactus, and the endangered blowout penstemon bloom in June, though August is by far the best month to see wildflowers across the refuge; the display can be sensational.

■ **PHOTOGRAPHY:** Given the relative uniformity of the landscape, sweeping panoramas of the Sandhills may result in uninteresting photographs; for best results, position something—a shrub, ridgeline, lake, a person—in the foreground, or opt for close-ups instead. Experienced wildlife photographers will find prime opportunities for shorebirds and prairie songbirds. Wildflowers are best photographed very early or very late in the day, when color values are highest.

> **HUNTING AND FISHING**
> **Deer, grouse,** and **pheasant** hunting are allowed on the refuge, in accordance with state seasons and regulations. Steel shot is required for bird hunting. Contact the refuge for further details.
>
> **Fishing** is permitted year-round on Island Lake. Smith Lake is open to ice fishing Nov. 1–Feb. 15; contact refuge for details.

■ **HIKES AND WALKS:** Jeep trails crisscross the refuge, following the shorelines of lakes and marshes, and traversing the prairie hills. Many of the more commonly traveled routes open to vehicles are marked on the refuge brochure's map. Those seeking more specific route information should contact the refuge.

■ **SEASONAL EVENTS:** Group tours are available on request; contact the Complex Headquarters in advance of visiting. A 1997 project to improve habitat for blowout penstemon, involving volunteers from The Nature Conservancy and the University of Nebraska, may well become an annual April event. The refuge celebrates National Wildlife Week in October with special events.

■ **PUBLICATIONS:** Bird checklist, auto-tour guide, general visitor brochure with map, public-use regulations.

Fort Niobrara NWR
Valentine, Nebraska

Bison herd, Fort Niobrara NWR

The wind arrives from many directions and in many seasons, pulsing over the sandhill ridges and dunes it has shaped and reshaped for eons. In summer, when the hills are deep in swaying stems of grass, the wind blows from the south, southwest, or due west, wrung of moisture by the Rocky Mountains. Through the winter it drives in from the northwest, west, and north, pushing squalls and Arctic fronts over the landscape.

The wind is a constant in Nebraska's Sandhills region, where the landscape hints at the tangled pine forests and aspen parks of the far-off north woods. Indeed, this is a terrain that offers traces of many distant worlds. At 19,131-acre Fort Niobrara NWR, the more intangible aspects of these distant worlds are made real in the form of a variety of wildlife and forests and the glorious Niobrara River, a spring-fed ribbon of life that has carved out one of the most quietly spectacular canyons to be found anywhere. Here, and at nearby Valentine NWR, part of the Niobrara-Valentine Refuge Complex, is a powerful reminder that no part of the natural world exists in isolation from another.

HISTORY

All manner of ghosts, human and otherwise, inhabit the quiet expanses here. For millions of years, more than 20 prehistoric mammal species roamed today's Sandhills, disappearing with the Ice Age. Bones of long-jawed mastodons, three-toed horses, and the giant bison have all been excavated on the refuge. Their successors—plains bison, elk, grizzly bear, pronghorn—appeared in equally large numbers, sustaining a thriving Sioux culture. As the frontier pushed westward, the bison vanished, and the Sioux were confined to the Rosebud Reservation. Fort Niobrara was erected in 1879 to protect settlers and homesteaders. No battles were fought, and the fort was abandoned in 1906; a few foundations, one building, and earthworks may still be seen today. In 1912, J. W. Gilbert of Friend,

Nebraska, offered 6 bison and 17 elk to the federal government if land could be found for them. The old fort and adjacent lands became the nucleus of today's refuge that same year. In 1936 a herd of Texas longhorn cattle arrived; descendants of the Open Range era, they graze the prairie today. Recognition of the area's rich biological diversity led to creation in 1960 of the 200-acre Ponderosa Pines Natural Area; in 1976, the 4,635-acre Fort Niobrara Wilderness was established. Despite a good deal of local opposition, a 70-mile portion of the Niobrara River Canyon received federal Wild and Scenic status in 1991.

GETTING THERE

From Valentine, travel east on Hwy 12 for 4 mi., turning right onto refuge entrance road and Visitor Center.

■ **SEASON:** Refuge open year-round.

■ **HOURS:** Open daylight hours. Visitor Center—with exhibits on wildlife, regional history, prehistoric life—is open Mon.–Fri. year-round, 8 a.m.–4:30 p.m., closed federal holidays.

■ **FEES:** Free access.

■ **ADDRESS:** Hidden Timber Route, HC 14, Box 67, Valentine, NE 69201

■ **TELEPHONE:** 402/376-3789

TOURING FORT NIOBRARA

■ **BY AUTOMOBILE:** The refuge has a very good 3.5-mile auto tour with an excellent self-guided brochure and numbered stops; the Niobrara prairie dog town, along with exhibition pastures of bison, elk, and longhorn cattle, is included in the tour; also some historic sites and a scenic overlook of the Niobrara River.

■ **BY FOOT:** There are outstanding hiking possibilities for all energy levels. Fort Falls Nature Trail leads in just 150 yards to a scenic waterfall and continues for nearly a mile to the Niobrara River Canyon; a short trail leads from the exhibition pasture to a prairie dog colony; unimproved trails parallel the Niobrara River from the Cornell Canoe Launch; the adventurous will want to explore the wilderness.

■ **BY BICYCLE:** Bicycling is permitted only on refuge roads and the hidden timber county road; still, it's a good way to get the big picture of this far-flung prairie world, as well as herds of bison, elk, and longhorn cattle—use caution around these dangerous animals.

■ **BY CANOE, KAYAK, OR BOAT:** Canoeing the 70-mile Wild and Scenic corridor of the Niobrara River, 25 miles of which flows through the refuge, is an exceptional experience; the gentle river twists through a splendid canyon rising 100 to 200 feet overhead, with steep side drainages cloaked in forests. The Fort Niobrara Canoe Launch is the put-in; private and public landings, and many riverside campgrounds, are scattered downriver; contact the refuge for a map; for canoe rentals, call the Valentine Chamber of Commerce at 800/658-4024.

WHAT TO SEE

■ **LANDSCAPE AND CLIMATE** The Great Plains and Nebraska Sandhills owe their existence to the Rocky Mountains; through eons of uplifting and erosion, alluvial deposits—including volcanic ash and sand—have made their way eastward, transported by wind and water. Geologically young, the 19,000-square-mile Sandhills region remains dynamic; stabilized by plant communities and the efforts of people, these dunes continue to redistribute themselves and, in some areas, to claim new territory. Beneath this restless land lies the Ogallala Aquifer, a great subterranean lake. It saturates the porous sand and rock layers, creating lakes, wetlands, and wet meadows; in the canyon of the Niobrara River, cut 300 feet into the Plains, water from the aquifer seeps out of cliff walls and feeds tributary streams, replenishing the river.

The 100th meridian, the dividing line between the humid air masses of the East and drier, western air, cuts through the middle of this region. The result is a landscape of stunning biological diversity. This is the only area in the United States where plants and animals from the Rocky Mountain coniferous forests, eastern deciduous forests, northern boreal forest, mixed-grass prairie, and sandhills prairie intermingle. The refuge plays a vital and successful role in maintaining this richness—most every feature of the presettlement natural community is alive and well here today.

True to its location, the climate is highly variable. Annual precipitation averages 18 inches, including 37 inches of snow on average; most precipitation, however, occurs between May and September. July and August, the warmest months, feature an average high temperature of 85 to 87 degrees Fahrenheit, though extremes above one hundred degrees are not uncommon. Elevations here range from 2,000 to about 2,800 feet.

■ PLANT LIFE

Open water Originating on the plains of Wyoming, the Niobrara River flows 300 miles to its confluence with the Missouri in northeastern Nebraska. Along its 9 miles through the refuge it is braided and shallow on the western end, deeper and narrower to the east. The region's geology, coupled with the pulse of the Ogallala Aquifer, result in a series of waterfalls along its course; one of the most dramatic is just east of the refuge at Smith Falls State Park, though several lovely examples are on the refuge as well. A series of man-made impoundments on the refuge are found at the headwaters of several tributaries of the river. Capturing spring water, rimmed with cattails and bulrush, they provide a critical water supply for bison, elk, and other refuge wildlife.

Grasslands Sandhills prairie dominates south and west of the river corridor,

Sandhill prairie and wetland

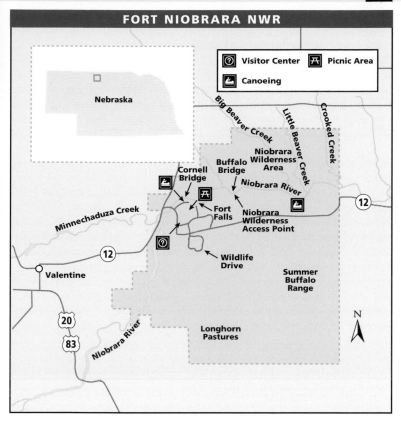

unrolled over an undulating terrain of 10- to 100-foot-high dunes, sculptured by wind into a series of paralleling ridges and narrow valleys. Eastern tallgrasses, midgrasses, and the western shortgrass varieties are found here—sand bluestem, little bluestem, prairie sandreed, and switchgrass. Common shrubs include prairie rose, sand cherry, yucca, and leadplant. Wildflowers are profuse: milkweed, spectacular sunflower displays, spiderwort, several penstemon species—including blowout penstemon, an endangered plant—are just a few.

Mixed-grass prairie occupies tablelands north of the Niobrara River. Blue grama, sideoats grama, needle-and-thread, and threadleaf sedge are dominant grasses. Other plants include prickly pear cactus, yucca, silver-leaf scurf pea, and a host of wildflowers—including prairie coneflower, gayfeather, and evening primrose, among others.

Forests The varied topography of the Niobrara River canyon, with its many benches, steep side canyons, and waterfalls, supports a forest like no other in the country. Courtesy of the Rocky Mountains is a ponderosa pine savanna and forest, occupying steep cliffs and upper slopes of the canyon; serviceberry, juniper, and chokecherry are dominant in unbroken forest. In the coolest reaches—around springs, on north-facing slopes, and other sheltered sites—is a northern boreal forest community of quaking aspen, paper birch, and bigtooth aspen, with an understory of ferns, club mosses, and sedges typical of northern bog communities. Eastern red cedar has invaded some of these sites and is now dominant in a few areas. Down on the floodplain and in side canyons is a blend of eastern deciduous forest species, including basswood, American elm, green ash, and bur oak.

Also present on some upland sites are planted shelterbelts of nonnative honey locust and eastern red cedar, along with native elm, ash, and ponderosa pine. Each major forest type is at the extreme limits of its range.

Wetlands Small pockets of riverine wetlands occupy the floodplain of the Niobrara River. Some consist of flooded woodlands, with cottonwood and peachleaf willow and western snowberry; others feature emergent vegetation such as cattails, bulrush, and phragmites, with prairie cordgrass and sedges. Beavers have impounded a few streams in the wilderness area, creating ponds and wet areas as well.

■ **ANIMAL LIFE** The beauty and unique diversity of Fort Niobrara's plant communities are matched by its animal inhabitants. Species native to the Rocky Mountains, eastern hardwood forests, northern boreal forest as well as the Great Plains may all be encountered here.

Birds Fort Niobrara is one of the few remaining strongholds for the greater prairie chicken, a once abundant species diminished by the conversion of grasslands to agriculture. During April and early May, male prairie chickens gather on booming grounds for their annual spring courtship rituals, facing off with one another in a sometimes frenzied display of spinning, noise-making, and display of their hornlike head feathers. Sharp-tailed grouse engage in their own dancing activities through the same period. Yet another showy bird, the Merriam's turkey, emerges from brushy thickets and forest edges for spring mating activities during this period, the large, colorful males, or toms, strutting and gobbling before hens. An observation blind is usually set up on site for visitors to see the action.

The river corridor, with its cliffs, pine forests, and floodplain thickets of willows and hardwoods, is a songbird haven. Bur Oak Picnic Area and Fort Niobrara Canoe Launch are hot spots; watch for warblers— common yellow-throat, yellow-breasted chat, prothonotary and golden-winged—and other species: Townsend's solitaire, lazuli bunting, brown thrasher, eastern and western kingbirds, great crested flycatcher, black-headed grosbeak, eastern bluebird, rufous-sided towhee, loggerhead shrike, and olive-sided and alder flycatchers. The western wood pewee,

Common yellow-throated warbler

ovenbird, rock wren, and northern oriole all nest on site but are seen less frequently.

Mammals The notable megafauna—bison, elk, and a herd of longhorn cattle, descendants of the herds trailed up here from Texas to supply the reservation and Fort Niobrara with beef—are seen along the auto tour, grazing in display pastures. They occupy more remote areas of the refuge in a free-roaming state, including the wilderness area.

Texas longhorn and calf

The refuge hosts a thriving black-tailed prairie dog town; it is great fun to watch these sociable little grazers, whose burrowing activities and endless clipping of grasses create niches for many other prairie creatures. Five pairs of burrowing owls reside amidst the "dogs," and may be seen by patient observers; a host of prairie songbirds—upland sandpiper, grasshopper sparrow, field sparrow, and lark sparrow, along with raptors such as the northern harrier and Swainson's hawk—hunt here through the summer.

Both mule deer and white-tailed deer inhabit the forested breaks and adjacent prairie lands, with a small number of pronghorn present as well. Elusive mammals—the bobcat, coyote, long-tailed weasel, Ord's kangaroo rat, white-tailed and black-tailed jackrabbits, beaver, and gray fox—inhabit the woodlands, river corridor, and prairie lands. Seven bat species are common here, including the keen myotis, silver-haired bat, and red bat.

ACTIVITIES

■ **CAMPING:** Camping is not permitted on the refuge, but many private and public campgrounds are close by.

■ **WILDLIFE OBSERVATION:** Although Fort Niobrara is not known for great abundance or diversity of waterfowl, spring and fall migrations are the most productive times for watching. Shorebird diversity is relatively high during migrations, and a number of raptors pass through. The golden eagle, rough-legged hawk, prairie falcon, merlin, osprey, and bald eagle are sighted in spring and fall. Bald eagles are seen reliably in winter along the Niobrara River. Every few years in spring or fall a few whooping cranes appear.

■ **PHOTOGRAPHY:** Inquire about observation blinds for photographing prairie chickens, wild turkeys, and sharp-tailed grouse during spring courtship. Elk, bison, and longhorn cattle are easily photographed along the auto tour. Wildflowers bloom in great diversity from spring through fall.

■ **HIKES AND WALKS:** Buffalo Bridge is the best point of access for the Fort Niobrara Wilderness Area. Paddlers can beach their canoes here and walk in; foot travelers merely cross the bridge heading north. Plan on four hours of cross-country hiking to reach some of the more remote areas.

SEASONAL EVENTS: Niobrara's Junior Ranger Program is popular for youth in the region. The fall round-ups and auctions of bison and longhorn cattle are very popular; contact the refuge for best dates to visit. Birding hikes and walks are offered seasonally, including the spring celebration of International Migratory Bird Day. Kids Fishing Day is held each September.

Rolling prairie hills, Valentine NWR

SATELLITE REFUGE

■ **Valentine NWR** Valentine NWR encompasses vastness (71,516 acres) and includes the largest sand dune in the Western Hemisphere; like Niobrara, wildlife diversity is largely unchanged since presettlement times. The mosaic of sandhills, wetlands, and wet meadows here—more extensive than at Niobrara—is a haven for wading birds and shorebirds; trumpeter swans nest on site. The rare prairie fringed orchid survives here. A wild and marvelous place; visitor amenities are very limited.

■ **ADDRESS:** HC 14 Box 67, Valentine NE 69201
■ **TELEPHONE:** 402/376-3789

Arrowwood NWR
Pingree, North Dakota

Refuge wetlands, Arrowwood NWR

It's a crisp April morning on the prairie at Arrowwood NWR. At first light the dancers appear. They are sharp-tailed grouse, males, ready for courtship. As female grouse arrive, one dancer begins. Its wings are held outstretched, tips brushing the grass, head lowered in a deferential bow. The bird patters and spins on quick feet, whirling in place; its vivid magenta throat pouch opening and closing with a rapid *pop-pop* sound. Another male joins in, then another. For several minutes it is all motion and whirring and sound. The spectators, a bevy of female grouse, appear unimpressed, and finally wander off; the males follow.

HISTORY

Arrowwood was established in 1935 by President Franklin D. Roosevelt; the 15,934-acre refuge maintains waterfowl breeding grounds and native prairie.

GETTING THERE

From Jamestown, travel northwest on ND 281 for 40 mi. to the town of Edmunds. Turn right just past Edmunds Kensal Road and continue 5 mi. to refuge headquarters.
- **SEASON:** Open year-round.
- **HOURS:** Daylight hours; refuge headquarters: 7:30 a.m.–4 p.m. weekdays.
- **FEES:** None.
- **ADDRESS:** 7745 11th St. SE, Pingree, ND 58476
- **TELEPHONE:** 701/285-3341

TOURING ARROWWOOD

- **BY AUTOMOBILE:** A 5.5-mile self-guided tour route explores prairie and marshlands. Lucky visitors at certain times of year may pass through the prairielands and see a herd of grazing bison.

■ **BY FOOT:** There are ample opportunities for hiking and cross-country skiing on the refuge. A short interpretive trail begins at the picnic area; most all prairielands and lakeshores are open to exploration along undeveloped trails.

■ **BY BICYCLE:** Bicycling is another great option. The auto-tour route is considered a fine ride, and several trails are also open seasonally. Contact the refuge office before biking for guidelines and recommended routes.

■ **BY CANOE, KAYAK, OR BOAT:** Taking to the refuge waters is highly recommended for both scenic values and wildlife viewing. All three of Arrowwood's lazy riverine lakes are open to canoes; it is possible to see the refuge from end to end by water.

WHAT TO SEE

■ **LANDSCAPE AND CLIMATE** Arrowwood is included in North Dakota's Drift Prairie region, a large band of glaciated hills and ridges; receding glaciers left behind masses of "drift," soil and rock deposits that insulated melting ice to create the myriad "pothole" wetlands of the region. Shallow and slow-moving, the James River forms the core of the refuge; its four "lakes" are naturally formed basins, one-eighth to one-quarter of a mile wide. From the river bottom, the land rises quickly into hills cloaked in prairie and scattered woodlands, at an elevation of 1,540 feet.

On average, this area of east-central North Dakota receives 18.36 inches of precipitation annually, roughly 2 inches more than falls in the westernmost reaches of the Drift Prairie. Winter (or at least winterlike temperatures) can last five months. Summers are a bit milder and wetter than exist farther west. In the recent past, the area has been a place of extremes—drought years persisted from 1987 to 1992, followed by five consecutive flood years.

■ **PLANT LIFE**
Open water The distinction between river and lake is somewhat blurry at Arrowwood, where the James River has formed a series of shallow basins—in effect, lakes—linked by narrow natural channels. Today each basin—Arrowwood,

Marbled godwits

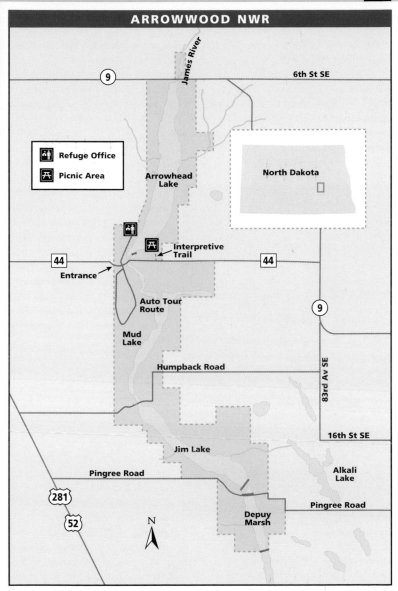

ARROWWOOD NWR

Refuge Office

Picnic Area

James River

9

6th St SE

North Dakota

Arrowhead Lake

Interpretive Trail

44   44

Entrance

Auto Tour Route

9

Mud Lake

Humpback Road

83rd Av SE

16th St SE

Jim Lake

Pingree Road

Alkali Lake

281

Pingree Road

52

N

Depuy Marsh

Mud, and Jim lakes, and Depuy Marsh—has an artificial dike at its outlet end. Under normal conditions, these basins are 3 to 6 feet deep and great producers of sago pondweed, a waterfowl delicacy. Between 1992 and 1997, however, the water cycle was anything but normal. Five consecutive years of spring floods raised water levels to as high as 20 feet, obliterating nesting and feeding habitats and preventing the refuge from manipulating water levels to the maximum benefit of shorebirds, ducks, geese, and swans.

The flooding exacerbated an ongoing water problem involving flow rates on the James from an downstream impoundment. With a gradient of just 12 inches per mile below the refuge, water takes its time flowing through. The timing and amount of water released downstream continue to offset refuge efforts to create mudflats, nesting habitat, and pondweed growth at different times of the year. Refuge management began working with the U.S. Bureau of Reclamatioon to come up with a solution. In the late 1990s, some of the waterfowl and shorebirds that would otherwise stop or nest at Arrowwood were passing it by.

In addition to the four basins, the refuge features a number of prairie pothole wetlands, ranging from the temporary variety, which fill and dry over a matter of weeks in early spring, to seasonal and semipermanent potholes, which feature some emergent vegetation, including sedges and reed canary grass, and remain wet through most or all of the nesting season.

Grasslands Arrowwood features some 11,000 acres of grasslands, more than 8,000 of which is native mixed-grass prairie. This includes grasses found in the

Purple prairie clover

tallgrass biome farther east and in the shortgrass prairie to the west. Big bluestem, one of the showiest tallgrass constituents, is abundant here, along with sideoats grama, needle and thread, and wheatgrasses. Wildflowers abound—pasqueflower, blanketflower, oxeye daisy, false dandelion, wild rose, purple prairie clover, fireweed, and blue phlox, among others.

For years the refuge has used prescribed burning and some livestock grazing to keep its native prairie vigorous—fire and grazing mitigate encroachment by shrubs such as buckbrush and snowberry, and such nonnative grasses as Kentucky bluegrass and smooth brome. Today, visitors are in for a real treat—the natives are back. Two area landowners who raise bison have worked out a grazing plan with Arrowwood; the herds are here in summer,

devouring the brome and bluegrass and gracing the prairie with their inimitable presence. Refuge management is thrilled and eagerly monitoring effects on native grasses and wildflowers.

Forests About 118 acres of Arrowwood consist of bottomland forest, a mix of native and introduced trees, such as green ash, cottonwood, and oak, with thickets of buckbrush, buffaloberry, and snowberry. These woodlands cover some of the slopes adjacent to the James River, as well as several coulees on site.

Human-made About 780 acres are croplands, along with planted nesting cover for waterfowl. Another 3,000 acres of grasslands are seeded and yield hay for winter wildlife.

■ **ANIMAL LIFE** In a normal year, the blue-winged teal and redhead, canvasback, and wood ducks are commonly seen nesting here, with at least 10 more duck species and Canada geese. Muskrat and mink inhabit the lakes, as do beaver.

Shorebirds nesting in grasslands or near water include the willet, marbled godwit, American avocet, and spotted sandpiper. During spring and fall migration, white-fronted geese, tundra swans, great egrets, and a far higher diversity of shorebirds are seen; bald eagles are also sighted regularly.

For 36 years Arrowwood maintained a small but stable black-tailed prairie dog town. A suspected outbreak of sylvatic plague wiped out the colony in 1995. New residents were introduced the following year, with only a handful surviving. The refuge continues to bring in fresh recruits in the future and is determined to keep at it until the town is bustling again.

The woodlands host white-tailed deer, short-eared owls, an occasional cow moose with calf, and a fair number of songbirds, including the orchard and northern oriole. Songbird diversity is highest on the prairie, where the great crested flycatcher, dickcissel, bobolink, and black-billed cuckoo reside in the summers. Badgers, red fox, and sharp-tailed grouse are seen here as well. An effort to reintroduce the native lesser prairie chicken in 1993 was unsuccessful; only a handful of the birds remain in the region. Arrowwood appears to have suitable habitat for the Dakota skipper, a butterfly proposed for threatened species listing in 1996; the refuge staff began a survey of all butterfly species on the refuge.

ACTIVITIES

■ **CAMPING:** No camping is allowed on the refuge. Primitive and developed camping is available at the Jamestown Reservoir, about 25 miles south of Arrowwood

■ **SWIMMING:** There is no swimming permitted in the refuge waters.

■ **WILDLIFE OBSERVATION:** The spring courtship displays of sharp-tailed grouse are extremely popular at Arrowwood; a viewing blind, available on a reservation basis, is often booked throughout the 8-week period of activity. The auto-tour route is another good spot for viewing grouse. Chase Lake NWR, 30 miles away, hosts the largest American white pelican colony in North America; some

Dickcissel

20,000 pelicans nest here. Binoculars or spotting scopes are necessary for prime viewing; contact the refuge at 701/285-3341 for details.

■ **PHOTOGRAPHY:** A snapshot of dancing grouse is likely to disappoint without the use of a 200-400 mm telephoto lens and a fast-speed film (rated ASA 250 or higher). A lens hood is helpful. On an unusually overcast dawn, consider using a tripod and cable shutter release. Inquire with refuge headquarters about reserving the viewing blind well in advance; portable blinds may be permitted.

■ **HIKES AND WALKS:** Park along Humpback Road (do not block traffic), and walk north or south to explore either Mud or Jim lake. It is possible to wander the shorelines. For a good view, walk atop the rolling prairie hills.

HUNTING AND FISHING Hunting of **deer**, **upland game birds**, **red fox**, and **cottontail rabbit** is permitted on the refuge; **waterfowl hunting** is not allowed. The season for upland birds and rabbits opens Dec. 1, following the firearm deer season. Deer hunting is open to archery, state-permitted firearms, and muzzle-loaders. Special regulations are in effect; contact the refuge prior to hunting for details. Nontoxic shot is required for all shotgun hunting.

Fishing is permitted in accord with state regulations; refuge fisheries are temporary and sporadic. Boats are limited to 25 horsepower or less. Contact the refuge for details.

■ **SEASONAL EVENTS:** The refuge celebrates National Wildlife Refuge Week in October and National Youth Fishing Week in June.

Audubon NWR
Coleharbor, North Dakota

Prairie wildflowers, Audubon NWR

Sprawling Lake Audubon, an impoundment on the Missouri River, is the center-piece of 14,738-acre Audubon NWR. A rich array of northern Plains wildlife inhabits the islands and inlets. Eleven smaller refuges, located within 250 miles in central and western North Dakota, are part of the Audubon NWR Complex.

HISTORY

Established in 1957 to offset waterfowl habitat lost to the Garrison Dam, the refuge began as Snake Creek NWR. It was renamed in 1967 to honor the memory of John James Audubon, the renowned painter and naturalist, who in 1843 spent the summer collecting and painting wildlife in this area.

GETTING THERE

From Coleharbor, ND, drive 3 mi. north on US 83, then east for 0.75 mi. to refuge headquarters and Visitor Center.
■ **SEASON:** Refuge open year-round; however, only the refuge entrance road is plowed during winter.
■ **HOURS:** Daylight; Audubon Complex Headquarters and Visitor Center open weekdays, 8 a.m.–4:30 p.m.
■ **FEES:** Free access.
■ **ADDRESS:** 3275 11th St. NW, Coleharbor, ND 58531
■ **TELEPHONE:** 701/442-5474

TOURING AUDUBON

■ **BY AUTOMOBILE:** A well-interpreted 7.5-mile tour route offers sweeping views of the lake and its abundant water-associated birds; tour route open daylight hours; closed during fall hunting season until 2 each day.

■ **BY FOOT:** A one-mile interpretive trail; visitors are also allowed to park along the auto-tour route and walk the prairie or lakeshore.

■ **BY BICYCLE:** Bicycles are allowed on auto-tour route only; the tour route is closed during fall hunting season until 2 p.m. each day.

■ **BY CANOE, KAYAK, OR BOAT:** No boats are permitted on the refuge portion of Lake Audubon; the Audubon State Wildlife Area to the north offers a public boat launch.

WHAT TO SEE

The refuge lies almost dead center in the state, on the glaciated Missouri River Plateau. Steep or rolling hills of mixed-grass prairie with numerous pothole wetlands and permanent lakes are the dominant natural features. A semiarid climate delivers 15.5 inches of precipitation annually.

Lake Audubon is a vast impoundment; many small islands dotting the water are actually the tops of old prairie hills. The lake's depth (60 to 70 feet) and size (15,000-plus acres) generate waves, which inhibit the growth of cattails and other emergent vegetation. Some 12 fish species are present, including walleye, perch, and the occasional sturgeon or salmon.

Natural prairie pothole wetlands and some constructed marshes comprise some 370 acres of the refuge. The development of marshland is a priority, and toward that end, the refuge is building "cutoffs" across shallow lake inlets to reduce waves and foster emergent vegetation.

About 3,000 acres contain planted native grasses and a small amount of native mixed-grass prairie. Western wheatgrass, green needlegrass, and blue grama are among the native grasses; purple coneflower and pasqueflower are representative wildflowers.

All Canada geese are large, but giant Canada geese—a subspecies unique to the region—are extra large. Saved from extinction by the efforts of several North Dakota refuges, these birds are a common sight in bays and open water from spring through fall. American white pelicans, sandhill cranes, gulls and terns in large numbers, tundra swans, shorebirds, and ducks visit Audubon, either during migration or for summer nesting. The piping plover, a threatened species, nests on-site.

Other birds often seen on the refuge include the northern harrier, American kestrel, and red-tailed hawk; the ferruginous hawk is sometimes present but less common. A number of songbirds reside here, including the LeConte's and Baird's sparrows, bobolink, and meadowlark; along pothole edges in the grass-lands look for spotted sandpiper,

American avocet

American avocet, marbled godwit and Wilson's phalarope.

Mammals found on the prairie lands include coyote, red fox, white-tailed deer, raccoon, badger, striped skunk, and a number of rodents; look for three species of ground squirrel, among them the thirteen-lined and Richardson's. Less commonly seen are pronghorn and moose. On very rare occasions an elk can be spied passing through.

ACTIVITIES

■ **CAMPING AND SWIMMING:** Camping is not permitted on the refuge. Camping facilities are available at two state parks, Fort Stevenson and Lake Sakakawea, 15 to 20 minutes from the refuge. Swimming is not permitted on the refuge.

■ **WILDLIFE OBSERVATION:** One of the best times to see Audubon is in the fall, when prairie lands turn from green to yellow and rust, and migrating birds of all kinds—songbirds, shorebirds, and large concentrations of ducks, geese, sandhill cranes, and swans—fill the skies and waters of the refuge. Visitors seeking solitude should ask refuge staff for directions to and advice on wildlife observation possibilities on the many smaller surrounding refuge sites. During every migration, whooping cranes appear either on Audubon or in the immediate area, usually in the company of sandhill cranes.

■ **HIKES AND WALKS:** The mile-long nature trail offers the best experience of Audubon's prairie and native wetlands. Wandering the lakeshore on foot, from stops along the auto-tour route, offers views and many chances to sight wildlife.

■ **SEASONAL EVENTS:** The refuge celebrates National Wildlife Refuge Week in October with special events Audubon maintains an active summertime schedule of programs

HUNTING AND FISHING Fishing is permitted only in winter, through the ice. You may hunt **white-tailed deer** and **upland birds**, including **sharp-tailed grouse, ring-necked pheasant**, and **gray partridge**. Contact the refuge for information on seasons and other regulations.

and events, including waterfowl banding with volunteers. Contact refuge headquarters for more information.

■ **PUBLICATIONS:** The Audubon Complex brochure includes a listing of all associated refuges with recreation opportunities and short sketches of the landscapes; auto-tour guide and bird checklists also available, along with a complete wildlife cheklist and hunting guide.

Des Lacs NWR
Kenmare, North Dakota

Des Lacs River Valley, Des Lacs NWR

The Des Lacs River valley makes a deep north-south crease in the North Dakota prairie. The river lies from 20 feet to 100 feet below the rolling grassland and has excavated a floodplain so flat and broad that the river spreads out to form long narrow lakes connected by extensive wetlands. This refuge is a beautiful ribbon that ties together breathtaking flights of waterfowl, distinctive and picturesque habitats, and unique public-access facilities.

HISTORY

The Plains Indians set up their winter lodges here and hunted the bison, prong-horns, and elk that also sought shelter in the valley. A wealth of beaver and mink drew French trappers, who were so impressed with the unusual river that they named it *Rivière des Lacs*, or "River of Lakes." In 1935, at the height of the Dust Bowl, the Des Lacs Refuge was established by President Franklin Roosevelt by executive order. The 19,500-acre refuge follows the bed of the river for 28 miles from the Canadian border to 8 miles south of Kenmare, North Dakota.

GETTING THERE

Refuge headquarters is 0.5-mi. west of Kenmare, ND, on Ward County Rd. No. 1A.
■ **SEASON:** Refuge open year-round.
■ **HOURS:** Refuge open sunrise to sunset. Headquarters open Mon.–Fri., 7:30 a.m.–4 p.m.
■ **FEES:** Free access.
■ **ADDRESS:** Des Lacs NWR, P.O. Box 578, Kenmare, ND 58746.
■ **TELEPHONE:** 701/385-4046

TOURING DES LACS

■ **BY AUTOMOBILE:** An 11-mile auto tour follows the course of the river for nearly half the length of the refuge. The 6-mile-long Canada Goose Hiking Trail is open to automobiles for two weeks each year in mid-September. Traffic is one-way from south to north.

■ **BY FOOT:** The well-marked and easy to follow Canada Goose Hiking Trail begins on the northwest corner of Kenmare. A new hiking trail at the south end of the refuge (accessible from the auto tour) has two short loops that total about .8 miles.

■ **BY BICYCLE:** Bikes can be ridden on the auto-tour road and the Canada Goose Hiking Trail.

■ **BY CANOE, KAYAK, OR BOAT:** Canoeists are welcome on Upper Des Lacs Lake only. Motorboats are not permitted.

WHAT TO SEE

■ **LANDSCAPE AND CLIMATE** The river-authored Des Lacs' landscape continues the slow production of new editions. Although summers are short and winters cruel in North Dakota, the sheltering river valley does take some of the bite out of the cold northern winds.

■ **PLANT LIFE** At many places within the river valley, the Des Lacs has spread itself so thin that the great expanses of open water are rarely more than 2 to 3 feet deep. The water is so consistently shallow throughout the refuge that there is no panfish or game fish worth drowning a worm for. Five thousand acres of marsh lie within the valley and are managed for waterfowl. Remnants of the original prairie cling to the valley's hillsides; here and there wooded coulees drive a wedge into the sides of the river basin. Cooperative farming and haying are permitted on parts of the refuge. Grass and alfalfa are planted to provide nesting cover for waterfowl and nongame birds. Cattle graze sections of the prairie, acting as stand-ins for long-gone bison, whose grazing improved the health of the native grasses and plants.

■ ANIMAL LIFE

Birds The refuge offers a king-sized Whitman's sampler of more than 250 bird species. The relatively rare Baird's sparrow and Sprague's pipit, both prairie birds, can be seen and heard in the refuge's remnant grasslands. Sharp-tailed grouse find the refuge to their liking, and birders flock to the blind overlooking the grouse's spring dancing grounds. The male grouse arrive on the dancing grounds before dawn. As dawn breaks, the males lower their heads, extend their wings, stick their tails in the air, and vigorously pump their legs. One dancing male grouse is interesting, but a field full is real entertainment. Warblers, flycatchers, and other songbirds find refuge in the green ash, American elm, and box

Sharp-tailed grouse, mating dance

elder growing in the wooded coulees. Marsh birds are plentiful, and nesting raptors include merlin, Swainson's and ferruginous hawks, and northern harriers.

If the variety of birds delights visitors, the numbers of waterfowl stagger the imagination. Every fall thousands of ducks and geese pour into the valley; some 400,000 snow geese show up here in mid-October. Canada geese number 25,000 to 30,000 at the same time. Tundra swans and bald eagles add to the fall spectacular. In late spring large flights of American white pelicans setting down in the wetlands and lakes; good numbers stay the summer. Large contingents of waterfowl arrive during the spring migration but don't equal the fall count.

Mammals The variety of habitats supports a wide range of bird species and mammals. The fur-bearing animals (beaver and mink) that lured the first trappers to the valley continue to flourish here. The muskrat is commonly seen swimming at any hour of the day. Muskrats eats cattails, grasses, and mussels. Like the beaver it builds a cone-shaped lodge above water, out of mud and sticks, with the entrance underwater. While it swims, the muskrat's head appears wedge-shaped; the large beaver head, on the other hand, looks square in the water. White-tailed deer are present, and an occasional moose wanders into the refuge. But it is the birdlife that really exploits every wrinkle in the habitat.

Muskrat

ACTIVITIES

Eleven miles of refuge road paralleling the river present motorists with intimate views of the landscape and wildlife. A hiking trail on the southern end of the refuge winds through a variety of habitats. Tasker's Coulee, on the west side of the refuge, is popular with birders and boasts a picnic ground and launching ramp with access to the Middle Des Lacs Lake (no motorized boats permitted). Neither camping nor swimming is permitted. The refuge celebrates National Wildlife Refuge Week in October with special events.

J. Clark Salyer NWR
Upham, North Dakota

Riparian wetlands, J. Clark Salyer NWR

Out on the high plains, a Big Sky landscape rolls on to a distant horizon. Clean, bracing air blows out of the Rocky Mountains and Canada, visible to the north—a flannel shirt feels good on a summer morning. There is no dramatic descent into the shallow Souris River valley, though change of another sort is quite apparent. Trees. Forests. Hardwood forests of oak, hickory, basswood, and ash, blanketing the zigzagging course of the river. A woodland oasis in the ocean of grass.

J. Clark Salyer NWR, North Dakota's largest refuge, preserves 75 splendid miles of the Souris River and its native forests, oxbow lakes, and marshlands. There is plenty of prairie, too, giving this refuge outstanding natural diversity. Opportunities for exploring Salyer are equally diverse, and the rewards—in wildlife and far-flung beauty—are worth the effort it takes to get here.

HISTORY

The sodbusters arrived in 1900 with ideas of growing cash crops in a land poorly suited for it. They set to work dredging and draining the Souris River's fertile marshlands. Over the ensuing two decades most of them left. In 1935, the refuge was established with the goal of reviving the Souris marshlands; a series of low dikes were constructed on the river and native marsh vegetation was reintroduced. The man for whom the site is now named, J. Clark Salyer II, was a biology teacher from Minot who served as chief of the Division of Wildlife Refuges in the USFWS from 1934 to 1961.

One of three "Souris Loop" refuges, 58,700-acre J. Clark Salyer, along with Des Lacs and Upper Souris, preserve a great swath of North America's historic waterfowl breeding grounds. Wetland drainage for agriculture has taken a toll here, as in other places, but the quantity and species diversity of waterfowl born each year across north-central North Dakota is amazing.

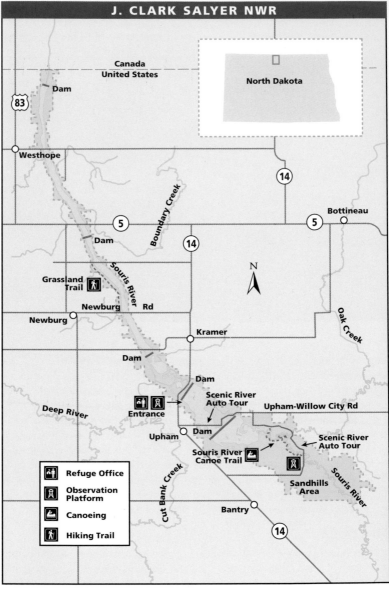

J. CLARK SALYER NWR

GETTING THERE

From Minot, ND: Travel east on US 2 for 40 mi., turning left (north) onto ND 14 at Towner; continue 26 mi. to refuge headquarters on right, 3 mi. north of Upham.

■ **SEASON:** Refuge open year-round.
■ **HOURS:** Daily, 5 a.m.–10 p.m.
■ **FEES:** Free access.
■ **ADDRESS:** P.O. Box 66, Upham, ND 58789-0066
■ **TELEPHONE:** 701/768-2548

TOURING J. CLARK SALYER

■ **BY AUTOMOBILE:** The 22-mile Scenic Trail passes through all major habitats, twice crossing the Souris River. A brochure interprets 18 points of interest along the route. The Grassland Trail, a 5.5-mile, two-track lane with 7 interpreted stops (open May–mid-Sept.), is 10 minutes (by vehicle) north of refuge headquarters; refuge staff can point the way.

■ **BY FOOT:** Grassland Trail, only lightly traveled by vehicles, is also a good destination for hikers. Visitors on foot can walk any length of the 22-mile Scenic Trail, the refuge auto tour, which features two observation towers. Both routes are open to cross-country skiing in winter. At the south end of the refuge, in the Sandhills area, hiking cross-country is encouraged.

■ **BY BICYCLE:** Both Grassland and Scenic trails are open to biking. Scenic Trail is in good condition from early May through September; mud can be a problem at other times.

■ **BY CANOE, KAYAK, OR BOAT:** The Souris River Canoe Trail, part of the National Recreation Trail system, takes canoeists down the slow, meandering Souris, traversing marshes and richly forested bottomlands. A 5.5-mile route takes about 2 to 3 hours, and a 13-mile route takes 5 to 7 hours. The canoe trail is highly recommended; a brochure has more information.

WHAT TO SEE

■ **LANDSCAPE AND CLIMATE** Salyer lies within North Dakota's Drift Prairie, a broad, glaciated band of rumpled hills, prairie wetlands, and shallow, glacier-scoured valleys. In portions of this region and much of the Missouri Coteau to the west, a single square mile may contain more than 270 wetlands. Large and small blocks of receding glaciers here were overlaid with soil and other "drift" materials, which served to insulate them and create the water-holding depressions known as potholes. A similar process took place on the coteau, or ridge, to the west.

The Souris River valley once was a shallow glacial lake; its ancient beach remains today as the Sandhills area on Salyer's southern end. The Souris (French for "Mouse") today drains 240,000 square miles in Canada and North Dakota. It flows in the shape of a horseshoe, beginning in Canada, then looping down and back up for 360 miles through North Dakota before returning to Canada. Salyer encompasses almost all of the Souris's final 75 miles in the United States.

Shallow and slow-moving, the Souris flows north through the heart of Salyer, meandering widely across its namesake valley. Several large oxbow lakes are here, river water stranded in old channels after the Souris changed its course. Five dikes allow refuge management to mimic natural cycles of flooding and drying; behind each dike the impounded river forms deeper, colder pools. The Souris on the whole is shallow and has always been subject to great fluctuations in water level; native fish communities, as a result, are scant.

The region's climate features cold and lengthy winters with average low temperatures of -1 degree to -5 degrees Fahrenheit. The average growing season is just 98 to 106 days. Summers are cool with an average daily high in the mid- to upper 60s; average high temperatures range from the upper 70s to low 80s. Annual snowfall averages 30-40 inches, with a yearly accumulation of 16-17 inches of precipitation. Nearly 80 percent of all precipitation occurs from April to September.

■ **PLANT LIFE**

Bottomland hardwood forest North Dakota is best known for its pothole-studded grasslands, but its native bottomland hardwood forests are a sight to behold. Along the Souris River are deep stands of green ash, oak, and American elm, and scattered cottonwoods, with an understory of western snowberry. The Souris River valley represents the westernmost reach of this forest type. Willows also flourish in the wetter areas along marsh and river edges.

Aspen parklands On the south end of the refuge, formerly open grasslands have been appropriated by the opportunistic aspen, which spreads primarily by cloning itself. A "parent" tree's root system sends up shoots that become saplings, and in short order a few trees become a large clump. Refuge management targets younger stands for removal; the old, mature stands are here to stay.

Wetlands Central North Dakota lies in the heart of "the Duck Factory," the most prolific waterfowl breeding grounds in North America. Wetlands of varying size, depth, and duration are the biological turbines of this factory. Salyer's nearly 30,000 acres of wetlands include all of the major prototypes. Each wetland type serves the critical needs of duck families through the year, as follows:

Temporary wetlands—These are simply low spots, depressions, or dimples in the landscape; they collect snowmelt or spring rains, warm rapidly, and harbor a protein-rich broth of insect larvae and plant life. Often called "pair ponds," these are the first wetlands visited by returning waterfowl in spring. A male and female stake out a puddle, recuperate from migration, and prepare for the ritual of breeding.

Seasonal wetlands—Here is bona fide aquatic vegetation, such as arrowleaf and reed canary grass, though the wetland may go dry by mid- to late summer. Waterfowl nest in the protective cover of cattails, sweet clover, or white top grass surrounding these wetlands. The drake leaves the hen at this point; she will assume sole duties of incubation and raising young.

Permanent wetlands—This is the classic marsh, with some amount of open water bounded by a labyrinth of cattails, sedges and bulrushes, where ducklings follow their mothers soon after hatching. At Salyer, the sloughs, marshes, and some oxbow lakes are all representative of permanent wetlands. Some 50 natural and manmade islands provide additional nesting and resting areas for waterfowl and other water-associated birds. The largest, and the most open areas—including the five diked pools—serve as "staging" areas for waterfowl, places where ducks gather in large flocks from late August to ice-up, preparing for fall migration.

Lesser scaup

Sandhills and wild roses, J. Clark Salyer NWR

Mixed-grass prairie Salyer features about 18,000 acres of native grasslands. Mixed-grass prairie features tallgrass species found as far east as Ohio, along with shortgrass prairie species which become dominant about 200 miles west. Big bluestem and switchgrass, more typical of the east, coexist with such western varieties as needlegrass and western wheatgrass. A splendid assortment of wildflowers—spiderwort, leadplant, purple prairie clover, and golden aster—take turns coloring the prairie spring through fall.

Much of the native prairie here has been overwhelmed by aspen, western snowberry, and nonnative grasses such as smooth brome and Kentucky bluegrass. Intensively managed cattle grazing and prescribed burning are the best options for preventing further degradation; management burns from 500 to several thousand acres of prairie each year to control further encroachment.

Sandhills On the south end of the refuge is a Sandhills area, the long-ago beach of glacial Lake Souris. Sandhills bluestem and prairie sandreed are native grasses here, accompanied by many wildflowers, including prairie wild rose, purple coneflower, and silvery lupine.

■ ANIMAL LIFE

Birds Yes, it is possible to see ducks almost anywhere, but no other place in the United States approaches the species diversity and abundance of North Dakota's Duck Factory; seeing them here by the thousands, on their ancestral grounds in this vibrant, far-flung landscape, one can best appreciate their wildness and place in the natural world. A remarkable 17 species of ducks nest here, from the northern shoveler, blue-winged teal, and common goldeneye to the canvasback, ring-necked, and American wigeon. Add to this five species of grebes, a thriving colony of double-crested cormorants, Canada geese, and four species of herons, including the little blue and black-crowned night-heron, and it is easy to believe that Salyer is a hectic place for water-dependent birds from spring through fall.

During spring and fall migration the numbers can reach beyond comprehension; flocks of up to 250,000 ducks pass through, along with 150,000 brilliantly white snow geese; tundra swans and sandhill cranes, too, are present in large numbers during this time, and the rare whooping crane may be seen occasionally.

The woodlands support a wealth of songbirds—the eastern phoebe, great crested flycatcher, sedge and marsh wrens, and veery nest here; spring migrants include the gray-cheeked thrush, indigo bunting, scarlet tanager, western wood pewee, and a bevy of warblers: the black-throated green, Cape May, palm, Canada, Tennessee, Connecticut, and orange-crowned, among many others.

North Dakota's famous grassland sparrows survive here—the LeConte's, Baird's, sharp-tailed, and grasshopper. Visitors seeking sparrows are encouraged to purchase a cassette tape of bird songs to become familiar with the signature call of each species, as they are reclusive and difficult to identify by sight. The refuge staff can also assist with information on their preferred territories on the prairie. Many other prairie birds are readily encountered, including the western and eastern kingbird, horned lark, sharp-tailed

LeConte's sparrow

grouse, and upland sandpiper. The northern harrier and Swainson's hawk may be seen in flight, working the fields.

Mammals The Souris River's woodlands and willow thickets harbor a great abundance of animal life. Mammals such as moose, white-tailed deer, beaver, gray and fox squirrels, mink and muskrat, and red fox are present; moose favor the river corridor's willow thickets, as do beaver and muskrat. White-tailed deer may be encountered most anywhere.

The grasslands and scattered aspen parks are home to the Franklin's and Richardson's ground squirrel, white-tailed jackrabbit, and the occasional mule deer.

Reptile and amphibians This region of the country is tough going for reptiles and amphibians, though a few species are notable. The wood frog and northern chorus frog enliven spring and early summer evenings with their calls. The tiger salamander is also present in the river and associated marshlands, an important food source for cormorants and white pelicans. Along wetland and forest edges, watch for the plains garter snake. The western painted turtle is also fairly common.

ACTIVITIES

■ **CAMPING:** Camping is not permitted on the refuge. Many of North Dakota's small towns feature beautiful little campgrounds within their city limits—Upham, 2 miles away, is available for tent camping; Kramer City Park, 6 miles away, has RV hookups.

■ **WILDLIFE OBSERVATION:** Salyer is large, and touring its two well-interpreted auto routes—either by vehicle or bicycle—provides an efficient means of getting acquainted prior to exploring specific areas. The 22-mile route begins at refuge headquarters and traverses the Souris River with its associated marshlands and forests, ending in the Sandhills area; two observation towers and a picnic site are along this route. True to its name, Grassland Trail, a five-mile route, offers the best experience of Salyer's prairie and associated wildlife, and panoramic views of the Souris valley and river below; wildflowers are another treat here, coloring the roadsides and grasslands in April and May.

Canoeing the Souris is an excellent way to see all manner of birdlife, and possibly moose, beaver, and other more elusive mammals; muddy roads may limit access to the river prior to May, but spring and summer, meaning June and July, are ideal months for sighting wildlife.

Waterfowl begin returning here in late March; early April brings the snow geese and largest migratory flocks; the process in fall is often more spread out, though very large concentrations of ducks and geese are present from early October through early November. Songbirds such as warblers migrate through from late April to mid-May in spring; breeding species remain through late July and early August. Fall migration for songbirds, too, is less concentrated, with September usually the best month. Spring and fall migration, especially when shorebirds are passing through, provide an outside chance for sighting either a peregrine falcon or merlin; the gyrfalcon and prairie falcon are seen occasionally in winter.

■ **PHOTOGRAPHY:** Spring and early summer offer vivid prairie colors, including emerald-green grasslands dotted with wildflowers and butterflies, and nearly 20 species of ducks in vivid breeding plumage. Salyer's riverbottom forest in its fall colors is a wonderful sight; the best window of opportunity for this is late September through mid-October. Male sharp-tailed grouse perform their courtship dances in late March or early April; refuge staff can assist with dates, optimal sites, and procedures for photographing them. Remember the two observation towers—both can provide memorable images.

■ **HIKES AND WALKS:** The Sandhills area is open to cross-country travel, with much to be seen and enjoyed spring through fall. Wildflowers bloom in spring and early summer; grassland songbirds sing, and wild turkeys, grouse, and coyotes may be spotted. Views from atop the sandhill ridge are terrific. Though Grassland Trail is open to vehicles, this two-track route is ideal for walking as there is almost no traffic. In addition to getting a firsthand experience of the prairie, from July 15 to September 15 hikers can leave the trail and wander down to the Souris River for a walk along its banks.

HUNTING AND FISHING Fourteen public fishing areas are open to fishing during state seasons. A fishing brochure is available at refuge headquarters. Much of the refuge is open at various times to hunting. Check with the refuge headquarters for regulations.

■ **PUBLICATIONS:** Bird checklist; interpretive brochures for Grassland Trail, Scenic Trail, and Salyer Canoe Trail; general visitor information brochure; brochures on hunting and fishing.

Lake Ilo NWR
Dunn Center, North Dakota

Redhead duck, Lake Ilo NWR

The sparsely populated plains of North Dakota are an especially fitting backdrop for the ancient wonders of Lake Ilo NWR. This 4,043-acre refuge, a mixture of grasslands, spring-fed creeks, wetlands, and open water, holds a secret that is 11,000 years old—ancient campsites, work areas, and some 58,000 artifacts belonging to prehistoric people. Wildlife viewing is quite good here, but the real story of this refuge is the part its landscape played in the history of human settlement in North America.

HISTORY

Lake Ilo was formed in 1936 when the Works Progress Administration (WPA) constructed a dam near the confluence of Murphy and Spring creeks. Three years later, President Franklin D. Roosevelt authorized the Lake Ilo NWR. The archaeological riches here were discovered in 1989, when Lake Ilo was drawn down for repairs on the dam and refuge personnel stumbled upon a tipi ring in the exposed lakebed. They immediately notified the state historic preservation office, and what followed was an intensive seven-year survey of the area by a team of researchers from several universities and the USFWS. A wide range of artifacts have since been catalogued, many of which are on display at refuge headquarters.

GETTING THERE

From the city of Dickinson, ND, on I-94, drive north on ND Hwy 22 for 32 mi. to the town of Kildeer, ND; turn right (east) onto ND Hwy 200 and continue 7 mi. to refuge entrance on right.

■ **SEASON:** Refuge open year-round.

■ **HOURS:** Daily, sunrise to sunset; refuge headquarters are open Mon.–Fri., 8 a.m.–4:30 p.m. However, there is currently only a two-person staff at the headquarters, so the office closes frequently when staff members are out in the field.

■ **FEES:** Free access.
■ **ADDRESS:** Lake Ilo NWR, P.O. Box 127, Dunn Center, ND 58626
■ **TELEPHONE:** 701/548-8110

TOURING LAKE ILO

■ **BY AUTOMOBILE:** Refuge roads access Lake Ilo, prairielands west of the lake that are closed to foot travel, and Lee Paul Slough, a good wildlife area. Roads open year-round.

■ **BY FOOT:** Trails include a 1-mile interpretive trail, which winds along the lakeshore; the first 0.5 mile is compacted gravel and wheelchair-accessible. All refuge roads are open to foot travel; the eastern half of the site, including Lake Ilo County Park, is open to foot travel anywhere.

■ **BY BICYCLE:** Bicycling is allowed along main refuge roads only.

■ **BY CANOE, KAYAK, OR BOAT:** Boating on Lake Ilo for wildlife observation and fishing only; motorized craft must be run at idle speed. An all-weather boat launch is on site. Much of the lake's western reaches are closed to entry by watercraft; no landing allowed on islands. Still a very productive means of seeing the refuge and its wide array of water-associated wildlife, especially birds.

WHAT TO SEE

■ **LANDSCAPE AND CLIMATE** It is no coincidence that Lake Ilo, with a record of almost continuous human occupancy for 11,000 years, is near the south-ernmost limits of the Wisconsin glacier's advance into North Dakota. When those earliest of settlers arrived here, the mile-high ice fields are thought to have been about 500 miles to the northwest. Today's semiarid climate and mixed-grass prairie evolved in the wake of the glaciers. Average annual rainfall is 16.8 inches; summers are dry and hot, winters cold.

■ **ARCHAEOLOGY** A fascinating story of humankind lives on here. At refuge headquarters are interpretive displays and exhibits of spear points, pottery shards, hearth stones, and other items excavated on site. One reason for Ilo's importance to early people was its supply of Knife River flint, a glasslike stone that made superb hunting implements. Visitors will learn about hunting and gathering methods, including the glorious Ice Age beasts inhabiting the region; travel, trade, and eco-nomic exchange of early people; and the many questions still unanswered about their arrival and disappearance.

■ **PLANT LIFE**
Open Waters Lake Ilo covers nearly one-fourth of the refuge at 1,240 acres. It is a shallow impoundment with a maximum depth of just 15 feet, though it supports a diverse population of native fish—northern pike, Iowa darter, brook stickleback, and white sucker, among others. Spring Creek and Murphy Creek deliver Lake Ilo's water supply; cattails, bulrushes, smartweed, pondweed, and duckweed are found along its margins and shallows.
Wetlands Wetlands are a mixture of ephemeral prairie pools, which fill and dry over the first weeks of spring, to a number of constructed marshes. Lee Paul Slough is a productive 145-acre marsh of cattails, sedges, smartweed, and pondweed. Man-made wetlands are listed as "semipermanent," meaning that most years they hold some amount of water spring through late summer; the refuge manipulates water levels to create mudflats and other habitat for shorebirds and waterfowl.
Grasslands Ilo's grasslands feature about 1,200 acres of the original stuff—

native mixed-grass prairie untouched by a plow. Grasses include big and little bluestem, blue grama, prairie sandreed, western wheatgrass and needlegrass; silver sage, western yarrow, goldenrod, yellow coneflower, orange globe mallow, and sageworts are among the many wildflowers. Prairie restoration is in progress; each year, old fields of nonnative grasses or croplands are replanted with native species; the refuge aims to return 332 acres to its original state.

Humanmade About 50 acres remain in cropland, with about half the annual output left standing for wildlife. Some 63 acres of old shelterbelts and native shrubs are scattered over the eastern half of the site. Trees include green ash, Siberian elm, Rocky Mountain juniper, ponderosa pine, and wild plum, with thickets of buffaloberry. These introduced habitats support a great many wildlife species. Several islands in Lake Ilo, built when the lake was drawn down, have proven extremely beneficial for waterfowl—the year after they were installed, two islands accounted for some 550 ducks born on the refuge. More islands are planned, including one management hopes will become a nesting site for the piping plover, a threatened shorebird native to the region.

■ **ANIMAL LIFE**

Birds A long list of water-associated birds appears at Lake Ilo; the greatest numbers and diversity of species appear during spring and fall migration, though many are present in summer. Nesting waterfowl include the ruddy duck and northern pintail; the ring-necked duck and snow goose are seen during migration. A great blue heron rookery is just east of Lake Ilo Park. The American bittern, black-crowned night-heron, black tern, American avocet, and eared grebe all nest on site; during migration, notable shorebirds include the ruddy turnstone, Baird's sandpiper, lesser golden plover, and dunlin. The American white pelican is a com-

mon sight spring through fall. The lake's insect life draws a number of swallows and flycatchers, including the purple martin, bank swallow, Say's phoebe, and least flycatcher.

Songbirds plying the marshes, shelterbelts, and shrubs include the orchard and Baltimore oriole, yellow-headed blackbird, orange-crowned warbler, common yellowthroat, Swainson's thrush, eastern bluebird, long-eared owl, ovenbird, swamp sparrow, pine siskin, cedar and bohemian waxwings, warbling vireo, and purple finch.

Ilo's mixed-grass prairie is home to those shy and uncommon grassland specialists—the chestnut-collared longspur, the Sprague's pipit—and several sparrows: Baird's, LeConte's, grasshopper, and sharp-tailed; all nest here. The brown thrasher,

Black-crowned night-herons

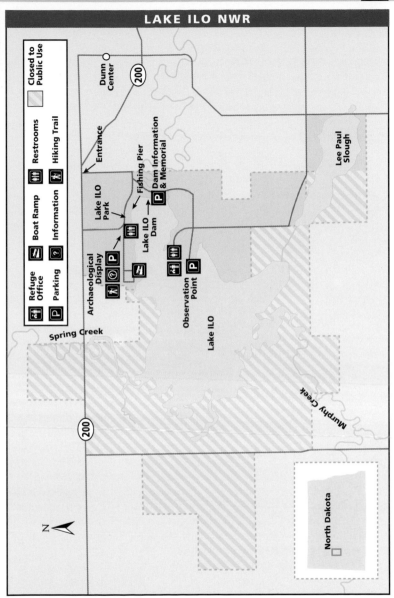

LAKE ILO NWR

spotted towhee, sharp-tailed grouse, ring-necked pheasant, and yellow-breasted chat nest here as well. Burrowing owls are present but rarely seen; the short-eared owl is a bit more widespread and may be encountered spring through fall in the evenings.

Mammals The uplands are the province of many rodents—prairie and meadow voles, western jumping mice, and northern pocket gophers among them—as well as such carnivores as the badger, coyote, striped skunk, red fox, and long-tailed weasel. The pronghorn and mule deer are uncommon though sighted occasionally. White-tailed deer may be seen in most any habitat. Beaver, muskrat, mink, and raccoon are found along wetland and lake margins.

ACTIVITIES

■ **CAMPING:** Camping is not permitted on the refuge. Excellent camping is available nearby at the Little Missouri State Park, located 37 miles north of Kildeer.

■ **WILDLIFE OBSERVATION:** Bald eagle sightings continue to rise at Lake Ilo. A total of 43 eagles were counted on the refuge in 1998, including one day in which 25 birds occupied the refuge while waiting out bad weather to the north. The last whooping crane sighting here occurred in 1995; refuge staff say a whooper or two appear every few years in spring or fall.

Walk or drive the county road west of Lake Ilo for grassland wildlife; for water-associated birds, the observation point offers a good view of two large islands; Lee Paul Slough is a prime area for wetland species. An unusually diverse mix of songbirds favor trees, shrub thickets, and shelterbelts.

Cedar waxwing

■ **PHOTOGRAPHY:** Depending on weather, Ilo's prairie is dressed in green and its wildflowers are blooming from mid-May through late June. On calm summer mornings, sunrise over the lake is a beautiful sight; midday light in summer tends to be harsh and flat.

■ **HIKES AND WALKS:** Explore along refuge roads year-round; Lake Ilo Park features several newly constructed trails that may be circumnavigated on foot. Be sure to wander a bit in the grasslands and trees on the eastern half of the refuge and amble along Lake Ilo's shoreline out on the scenic point west of refuge headquarters. From the parking area at the fishing pier, check out the archaeological display, and then follow the interpretive trail along the lakeshore to the Lake Ilo dam.

■ **SEASONAL EVENTS:** The refuge celebrates National Wildlife Week in October with special events.

■ **PUBLICATIONS:** Up-to-date literature on public-use guidelines, archaeological findings, and interpretation; a current and very helpful all-in-one wildlife checklist.

HUNTING AND FISHING: There is no hunting allowed on the refuge.

Long Lake NWR
Moffit, North Dakota

Sandhill cranes

Several thousand roosting cranes spread over a field resemble nothing so much as a living carpet made up of rippling shades of dark and light. A closer look reveals thousands of sandhill cranes on their migratory journey to the south. In late October as many as 20,000 of these magnificent birds, each standing 4 feet tall and sporting a 7-foot wingspan, stop over at Long Lake before continuing on their migrations. On the wing, with their sinuous necks held straight out in front and their long legs pointing straight back, sandhill cranes resemble winged javelins. Their wing beats are slow, steady, and graceful, and their cry is soft but powerful and carries for miles over the prairie. Even in the years that sandhill cranes make no spring stopovers here, they may be seen making long Vs high overhead as they head north. Cranes are just one of the many wonders to be seen at this 22,310-acre refuge, which lies astride the continent's great central migratory flyway.

HISTORY

Long Lake attracted Plains Indians and early European settlers. Both camped and hunted along the shores of this bountiful, 18-mile lake. Along with a fine reputation for attracting waterfowl though, the lake had an unfortunate history of botulism outbreaks that killed thousands of birds. A bacterial toxin produces the botulism, which paralyzes birds' nervous systems. In an effort to halt the botulism and through the personal interest of President Herbert Hoover the Long Lake NWR was created in 1932. Civilian Conservation corps workers built dikes that divided the lake into three units. The corps also constructed small check dams in ravines creating small ponds, built 19 duck islands in the lake to encourage waterfowl nesting, and built the refuge's headquarters building. Through water-level manipulation, the refuge has had some success in halting the local botulism epidemics.

GETTING THERE

From Bismarck drive about 24 mi. east on I-94 to Exit 182, turn south and drive 10 mi. to Moffit. South of town turn east at the refuge sign.

■ **SEASON:** The refuge is generally open to public entry for wildlife observation and hiking. Visitor should contact refuge headquarters for guidance to best areas for viewing, and to avoid conflict with planned management activities.

■ **HOURS:** Visitor Center hours are Mon.–Fri., 7:30 a.m.–4 p.m.; restrooms and information open 24 hours.

■ **FEES:** Free access.

■ **ADDRESS:** Long Lake NWR, 12000 353rd St. SE, Moffit, ND 58560

■ **TELEPHONE:** 701/387-4397

TOURING LONG LAKE

■ **BY AUTOMOBILE:** Public roads border and cross the refuge, providing many vantage points for scanning the refuge and observing wildlife.

■ **BY FOOT:** There are no established trails, but birders and wildlife photographers may obtain permission from staff to hike within specific areas.

■ **BY BICYCLE:** Biking is not permitted, but miles of public roads surrounding the refuge are open to bicyclists.

■ **BY CANOE, KAYAK, OR BOAT:** Watercraft with outboard motors of 25 horsepower or less are permitted on Unit 1 of Long Lake from May through September, but there is no boat-launching ramp on Unit 1.

WHAT TO SEE

■ **LANDSCAPE AND CLIMATE**

The 16,000-acre Long Lake dominates the refuge. The lake sits in the midst of thousands of acres of rolling prairie-land about 20 miles east of the Missouri River. Summers are warm, and as can happen on the prairies, heat waves can push thermometers into the 90s. Winters are long, hard, and punctuated with deep cold snaps and dangerous blizzards that come howling out of Canada.

■ **PLANT LIFE** The lake's shallow depth allows waterfowl and cranes to feed on the lakebed's aquatic plants, and countless more dine on the duck-weed floating on the surface. Much of

Cattails

the lake is bordered by extensive marshland filled with bulrushes and cattails that offers plenty of shelter and nesting opportunities for waterfowl, nongame birds, reptiles, amphibians, and small mammals. Long Lake NWR contains some shrub plantings and small trees, but most of the land in the refuge is divided between cropland and prairie.

Five hundred acres of cropland are planted with wheat, alfalfa, corn, millet, and sunflowers. The crops serve as cover and nesting habitat, and are served up as food for the migrating waterfowl and resident wildlife. The grasses, various

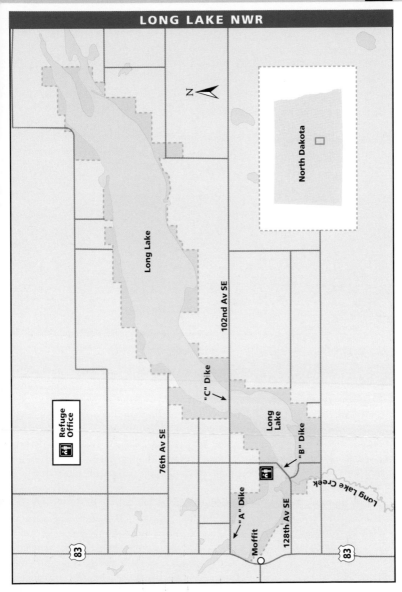

clovers, and wildflowers making up the native prairie are kept healthy and free of brush and trees by periodic haying and grazing.

■ **ANIMAL LIFE** The refuge's marsh contains an abundance of life. Reptiles and amphibians live out most of their lives hidden away in rushes, cattails, and other water plants. A variety of specialized birds live within the refuge's prairie, and beavers can sometimes be spotted in open water, but what are 10,000 seagulls doing so far from either ocean or even the Great Lakes?

Birds Seagulls are only the first of many avian surprises to be found at Long Lake. The normal habitat for the Franklin's gull is the open country and prairie lakes

Ferruginous hawk

found in the middle of the continent, and every September 10,000 or more clamorous Franklin's gulls descend on the refuge. October brings 20,000 Canada geese with snow, blue, and white-fronted geese mixed in with them. Add to the party 25,000 ducks from a dozen different species and the sandhill cranes mentioned above, and the skies of the refuge are crowded and colorful every fall. Large groups of sandhills should be carefully scanned for the occasional whooping crane traveling with the group. Preceding the waterfowl and cranes, shorebirds often move through the refuge in great numbers in late August and early September.

Bird numbers and species in the fall are always great spectacles but the spring show can be even better. So much so that *Wildbird Magazine* named it one of the ten best spring birding sites in North America. In addition to everything seen in the fall, look forward to seeing a bounty of prairie birds and 20 species of sparrows including the rare Baird's sparrow. The great prairie birds of prey, ferruginous and Swainson's hawks, nest on the refuge, as does the great horned owl; the latter sometimes subleases a nest from one of the hawks. Add nesting phalaropes, avocets, and a multitude of marsh birds, and the refuge simply comes alive with birds every spring.

Mammals White-tailed deer are regularly seen in the prairie. Muskrats, beavers, and mink reside in the refuge's wetlands. White-tailed jackrabbits live in the prairie. The "jack" is not a rabbit but a hare because its young are born with their eyes open and completely furred. The hind feet of a white-tailed jackrabbit are 5 inches long and propel the animal at a cruising speed of 20 miles an hour. When in danger the hare lays its ears back and rockets across the landscape at up to 45 miles an hour. What it is usually trying to outdistance are foxes and coyotes. Long Lake is also home to badgers. The low-slung, powerful animal is a world champion digger. It preys on burrowing mammals. Squirrels, prairie dogs, gophers, and other diggers all run out of the tunnel when pursued by a badger.

ACTIVITIES

■ **CAMPING:** Camping is not permitted within the refuge. The nearest public campground is the General Sibley Campground (701/222-1844), in Bismarck.

■ **WILDLIFE OBSERVATION AND PHOTOGRAPHY:** Birding is at its best here in April, May, September, and October. But with the large number of nesting birds, a trip should not disappoint from spring through fall. Birding can be profitable on any of the public roads bordering or crossing the refuge, and birders can ask permission to walk parts of the refuge. Portable photography blinds are permitted on the refuge with prior approval from staff. In addition to numerous chances for close portrait work on wildlife, photographers should check out the stunning panoramic view of the southern end of the refuge from atop the Bluff Picnic Area (a mile east of ND 83 on the north side of the lake).

> **HUNTING AND FISHING Northern pike** and **bullheads** are pulled from Long Lake. Seasons vary for **pheasant**, **sharp-tailed grouse**, **partridge**, and **white-tailed deer**. Contact the refuge for more information concerning specific seasons.

■ **SEASONAL EVENTS:** The refuge celebrates National Wildlife Week in October with special events.

SATELLITE REFUGES

■ **Florence Lake NWR** Two other refuges are administered from Long Lake. The 1,900-acre Florence Lake NWR lies 45 miles northwest of Long Lake. Created in 1935, the refuge is managed for waterfowl production and improved wetland habitat. Birding, photography, and hiking are permitted. Hunting is not permitted. The refuge can be reached by driving about 30 miles north of I-94 from Exit 182 on ND 14.

■ **Slade NWR** Slade NWR was acquired in 1941 through a bequest from George T. Slade. The 3,000-acre refuge contains 900 acres of marsh and open water and is rich in birdlife. Large numbers of shorebirds, marsh birds, and waterfowl call at the refuge. In 1968 a giant race of Canada geese were reintroduced to the area and have thrived. Visitors should check in at the Long Lake NWR Visitor Center before a visit. Slade is reached by driving 4 miles south of Dawson on Highway 3 and then following the signs.

Lostwood NWR
Kenmare, North Dakota

Mixed-grass prairie wildflowers, Lostwood NWR

The best place names originate in a story, and so it is with Lostwood. Early settlers maintained a homestead on what is today the southern end of this 27,000-acre refuge. Just as they do today, a healthy stand of American elms grew along the shores of Lower Lostwood Lake. As winter approached, the settlers cut down some of these elms, the first step in making a good stack of firewood. The felled trees were piled nearby, and then a snowstorm moved in, burying the logs, which were never recovered until the following spring. *Lost wood.* Did it really happen? No one knows, though the name and story endure.

Much endures at Lostwood. As one of the nation's largest, richest, and least disturbed prairie biomes remaining in public hands, it is a place for walking, a place to feel free. Tucked into every dimple and wrinkle and basin in the grasslands are potholes—the signature prairie wetlands—glittering in the sun, strips and circles and crescents of dark blue upon the expanse of green, hundreds upon hundreds of them. Wildflowers in spring and summer add strokes of purple, red, yellow, and white; butterflies and songbirds flit across the land; a Sprague's pipit skylarks overhead, proclaiming a small piece of this place as its own. As a visitor, it is easy to feel that way, too.

HISTORY

North Dakota's Coteau region was spared the first wave of settlers because of its poor soils and prairie wildfires. Not until 1900 through 1910 did ranchers and farmsteaders appear, raising cattle and plowing under the mixed-grass prairie to plant crops. Some of the present-day Lostwood refuge was grazed, and a few of its many wetlands were drained, but almost all of its prairie managed to escape the plow. By the time Lostwood was declared a refuge in 1935, only about 30 percent of its nearly 27,000 acres had been converted to nonnative plantings. These areas are now being restored to native grasslands. Once thought extinct, giant

Canada geese were reintroduced here in 1964 and today maintain a viable nesting population.

In 1975, Congress established the 5,577-acre Lostwood Wilderness Area. Lostwood is administered as a part of the Des Lacs Complex, which includes the Des Lacs refuge to the east and the Lostwood and Crosby Wetland Management Districts.

GETTING THERE

From Minot, ND: Travel northwest on US 52 for 39 mi., turning left (west) onto ND 50 at town of Coulee; continue west 15 mi., turning right (north) onto ND 8; drive about 6 mi. north to refuge headquarters on left. From Williston, ND: Follow US 2 north and then west for 72 mi., turning left (north) onto ND 8 at town of Stanley; drive north 20 mi. to refuge headquarters on left.

■ **SEASON:** Refuge open year-round from 7:30 a.m.–4 p.m. Mon–Fri.
■ **HOURS:** Dawn to dusk.
■ **FEES:** Free access.
■ **ADDRESS:** 8315 Highway 8, Kenmare, ND 58746
■ **TELEPHONE:** 701/848-2722

TOURING LOSTWOOD

■ **BY AUTOMOBILE:** The self-guided auto-tour route is 7 miles long and marked with eight interpretive stops. The auto-tour route is open from late May (or as soon as the road becomes passable after winter) through late September, closing on the Friday before the opening of waterfowl hunting season.
■ **BY FOOT:** Walking is by far the best way to experience Lostwood. Visitors can hike on a designated trail outside Lostwood Wilderness. Foot travel along the auto-tour route is possible. Lostwood Wilderness is open year-round to hiking, skiing, and snowshoeing.
■ **BY BICYCLE:** Bicycles are permitted on the auto-tour route, a maintained gravel and dirt road.
■ **BY CANOE, KAYAK, OR BOAT:** No boating is allowed on refuge waters.

WHAT TO SEE

■ **LANDSCAPE AND CLIMATE** Lostwood lies within the Missouri Coteau, a narrow, meandering scarp 12 to 19 miles wide, extending from North Dakota's extreme northwest corner to its southern midsection. Dividing the humid Central Lowlands to the east from the semiarid Missouri Plateau farther west, the Coteau, or ridge, represents a change in relief of just 100 to 200 feet, though in the wide-open plains a watchful traveler heading west can recognize it on the horizon.

The Wisconsin glacier plowed dead into the Coteau on its southwesterly course 10,000 years ago. Pushing up and over the scarp, the glacier shoved many tons of "drift"—primarily soil and rock—ahead of it, great quantities of which were left behind. As the glacial ice gradually began to melt, drift material became more concentrated at the surface and served to insulate the ice. Long after glacial ice had melted from other areas of the state, it remained across the Coteau region. In the several thousand years following, drift material settled, forming the hills, knobs, and—thanks to the ice—the almost limitless wetlands and lakes covering the Missouri Coteau today.

Lostwood's climate is not for the timid. In this semiarid region, normal temperature extremes range from 100 degrees Fahrenheit in summer to -40 in winter. Annual precipitation averages 16.6 inches, but variation is the norm: One

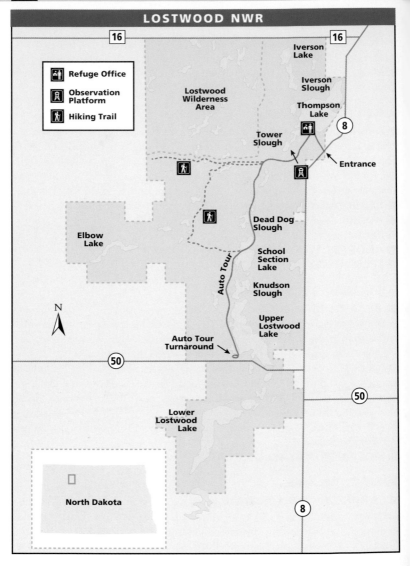

winter may bring no snow at all, while in the next snow might fall from October through May. The wettest months are May and June; violent thunderstorms in July and August bring hail or brief drenching rains. Winds of 30 to 40 miles per hour are a fact of life, especially through spring and fall.

■ PLANT LIFE

Wetlands The term "pothole lake" is a catchall phrase used to describe the thousands of waters, large and small, dotting this glaciated region. Though many appear broad and open, like a small lake or large pond, all "potholes" at Lostwood and elsewhere are true wetlands, not lakes, including the six to eight potholes at Lostwood that were long ago named as lakes. None are more than 10 feet deep, and all are subject to boom-and-bust cycles of drying, refilling, stagnating, and drying again. The smallest, most ephemeral wetlands are just 4 to 6 feet deep and fill with water from snowmelt and early spring rains; they endure for two or so weeks before drying up. The next class of wetlands is no deeper but survives longer, often for eight or so weeks. The six deepest potholes—Upper and Lower Lostwood lakes, and Elbow, Thompson, Iverson, and School Section lakes—have not dried out since the early 1900s.

Dried-up wetlands may seem like a loss, but the fascinating thing here is how the drying process actually produces a healthier, more fertile piece of water when it fills again. The reason has to do with geography and soil. All potholes here are linked to ground water hydrology: some actively feed the ground water, while others are fed by it. Potholes on the upper reaches of hills and ridges receive rain and snowmelt. Deeper potholes, tucked into the bottom of knolls and hills, collect their water from what seeps downhill. Because the soil here is heavily laced with sodium and calcium, the water accumulating in the lowest, deepest wetlands is very heavy with salt. Lostwood Lake, for example, has a higher level of salinity than any ocean.

Things are fine in the pothole for a while: There is all manner of aquatic life, including brine shrimp and

PRESCRIBED BURNING A prescribed burn at Lostwood is a tightly choreographed event. Beginning in spring and continuing through summer and fall, as many as five or six parcels will go up in flames rising 10 to 15 feet high. In the days leading up to a burn, weather conditions and moisture levels on the prairie are monitored frequently. A plan is worked out for each parcel. Fire is set along a secured boundry on the downwind side, and allowed to burn back away from the firebreak. When a sufficient "black line" is formed, the flank areas are burned; once these have developed blacklines, a "headfire" is set. This technique is known as a "surround" fire. Wind is both necessary and a potential problem. Ideal conditions include some amount of second-tier winds to pull smoke upward and carry it off, and lower level winds to move the fire along the desired route. Most burns don't begin until 10 a.m. and ideally are finished by mid-afternoon; any later than that, grasses and other materials may become too damp as evening approaches, causing smoke to settle to the ground instead of rising.

fairy shrimp, which love saltwater, along with many species of snails, insect larvae, and emergent vegetation. But the longer the water sits, the less productive it becomes. Oxygen levels drop, aquatic life dwindles, and the pothole offers little food for shorebirds and other wildlife. It goes bust. At the end of this cycle it may dry out entirely. Aquatic plants go dormant, withering into the exposed, mucky bottom; insects and shrimp lay eggs in the mud and die. The pothole waits for a good year of rain and snow; the freshwater triggers an immediate rebirth. As invertebrates and vegetation flourish, water-associated birds and other wildlife move in again.

The process is played out for potholes of all shapes and sizes at Lostwood year after year. It is a wildly dynamic system, forever swinging one way, then another; in the end, however, it is remarkably stable.

Mixed-grass prairie

In ecological terms, North America's prairies are still reeling from the disappearance of bison and wildfires. For nearly ten thousand years, grazing and burning played critical roles in the nutrient cycle of grasses and wildflowers and fended off

Prairie lilies, Lostwood NWR

shrubs or trees that might otherwise gain a toehold. Lostwood's glorious mixed-grass prairie, 75 percent of which has never been touched by a plow, offers a vivid example of the challenges faced by land managers in maintaining prairie lands in their natural state.

With the exception of the single, storied elm grove, no trees or shrubs grew here at the time of settlement. By 1938, aspen trees had colonized 100 acres; by 1969 the total reached 375 acres; and by 1985, more than 300 wetland areas and 475 upland acres were claimed by aspen. Western snowberry, a native shrub, also has advanced rapidly. Absent at the turn of the last century, it occupied 24 percent of Lostwood's uplands in 1935; by 1985 the total had doubled. Trees and shrubs introduce one more foreign element—shade. Nonnative grasses, including Kentucky bluegrass and smooth brome, love cooler, damper sites and compete with native species.

To keep aspen and snowberry at bay, Lostwood began a prescribed burning program in 1978 and maintains the most aggressive managed-fire regime in the region. A number of areas have been fired four or five times; six to nine burns, ranging in size from 17 to 5,600 acres, were planned for 1999. It is a never-ending battle. In burned areas, the prairie remains rich and diverse, with all native plant species present. Grasses—such as needle-and-thread, blue grama, and prairie junegrass—occupy the driest areas. On slopes and damp sites, western wheatgrass, big bluestem, and prairie dropseed are dominant. Wildflowers are diverse and abundant. Blanketflower, purple coneflower, milk vetches, blazing stars, pasqueflowers, and Canada anemone are only a few.

■ **ANIMAL LIFE**

Birds Birds are the special attraction at Lostwood. North Dakota has a well-established reputation among serious birders for its uncommon grassland songbirds, including the chestnut-collared longspur, Sprague's pipit, Baird's sparrow, grasshopper sparrow, LeConte's sparrow, and sharp-tailed sparrow. All of these prairie-dependent species nest at Lostwood; the Sprague's pipit, along with Baird's and grasshopper sparrows, are common to abundant. The longspur, LeConte's, and sharp-tailed sparrows are uncommon to rare, depending upon yearly moisture levels.

A wide array of shorebirds inhabit the grasslands and wetlands spring through fall. Large, showy species—such as the Wilson's phalarope, willet, American avocet, and marbled godwit—all nest on site and may be seen by most any visitor. The rare piping plover, a threatened species, nests here as well. During spring and fall migration there are many others: white-rumped sandpiper, greater and lesser yellowlegs, red-necked phalarope, black-bellied plover, and Hudsonian godwit.

In the heart of pothole country, ducks are abundant through every season but winter. Twelve species nest here, among them the ruddy duck, canvasback, northern pintail, and green-winged teal. Other water-dependent species here include giant Canada geese, eared and horned grebes, and the American coot.

Lostwood's raptor community has experienced a shift of species over the years, paralleling changes on the prairie. The ferruginous hawk, a large, strikingly colored bird that nests on the ground in open grasslands, has become scarce as aspen and shrub cover has increased. The more adaptable red-tailed hawk did not occur at Lostwood until the 1950s; today it is a fixture of the refuge's aspen groves. The Swainson's hawk, too, was formerly a common sight and today is seen infrequently, though a visitor who invests the time will often spot one.

With timing and a great deal of luck, several rare birds of prey may be seen. Between late April and mid-May, peregrine falcons follow migrating shorebirds through the refuge; the merlin is seen at times in winter, as well as during migration; the gyrfalcon, too, is a rare visitor in fall and winter. Golden eagles often arrive in fall to shadow the large flocks of migrating waterfowl.

Mammals The vast majority of prairie mammals are burrowers, denners, or ground-huggers; foraging and hunting in the knee-high prairie, they are invisible much of the time, though their chirps and chatter join in with the abundant birdsong. Three ground squirrel species are common: the Richardson's, thirteen-lined, and Franklin's; the last is a recent newcomer to the shrubby areas of the refuge. The meadow jumping mouse and meadow vole are abundant; the northern grasshopper mouse and olive-backed pocket mouse are rare.

Baird's sparrow, Lostwood NWR

Dining on the above creatures is the typical array of grassland carnivores: the badger, coyote, least weasel, long-tailed weasel, and striped skunk. White-tailed deer, rare before the 1940s, are common today; elk, mule deer, moose, and pronghorn are rarely sighted.

ACTIVITIES

■ **CAMPING:** Camping is not permitted on the refuge. Primitive and developed camping is available at the Powers Lake Municipal Campground, a pretty spot about 24 miles southwest of the refuge in the town of Powers Lake.

■ **SWIMMING:** There is no swimming allowed in the refuge waters.

■ **WILDLIFE OBSERVATION:** Determined to identify those rare grassland sparrows? Some advance preparation helps. Purchase a tape or CD of birdsongs and become familiar with them—these birds are secretive and most birders locate them

HUNTING AND FISHING
Fishing is not allowed in the refuge waters. You may, however, hunt **white-tailed deer** and **upland game birds**, including **sharp-tailed grouse** and **ring-necked pheasant**.

by hearing. The Sprague's pipit may also be found by watching the skies: Male pipits spend hours "skylarking," circling and fluttering high in the air while singing, then plummeting toward earth, then doing it again. Visitors are permitted to walk 100 yards into the grasslands along the auto tour; Baird's sparrows favor these roadside areas. For chestnut-collared longspurs, explore the south end of the auto tour; at the turnaround area, park and listen awhile. Refuge staff are more than willing to help; if they have time, they will even accompany visitors to likely spots. At the least, they know specific areas favored by each species.

■ **PHOTOGRAPHY:** The sweeping panorama of the prairie can be difficult to capture on film, especially in full sun; instead aim for a tighter composition—a single wetland or ridge, for example. The observation tower just inside the entrance is a fine place to photograph Tower Slough and its birdlife. A sharp-tailed grouse viewing blind, available on a reservation basis, allows close-up views of male grouse performing their courtship dances in April. Lostwood is an outstanding site for wildflower photographs; colors are deepest in the early-morning and late-afternoon hours.

■ **HIKES AND WALKS:** The circular main trail is a good starting point. The eastern side of the trail features grasslands maintained with prescribed burning; on the western side are huge stands of snowberry shrubs, a look at what the entire site might be like without fire, although this will steadily change as the area is burned. Also along the way, look for large "rub rocks" once utilized as back-scratchers by the region's vast bison herds: Near these rocks are bowl-shaped depressions in the ground, where the great beasts took dust baths. Tipi rings from Native American campsites are scattered here and there; within about 100 yards of the observation tower, a sharp-eyed visitor walking into the grass to the north will discover three such rings.

■ **PUBLICATIONS:** A very useful checklist of all vertebrate species (birds, mammals, reptiles, and amphibians); a leaflet for the auto tour's 12 interpreted stops; introductory brochure to site with map.

Sully's Hill NWR
Fort Totten, North Dakota

American bison on grassland range

The richly forested hills and coulees are the first indication that Sully's Hill is a unique place, an oasis of sun-dappled woodlands amidst the rolling expanses of rangeland, farm fields, and prairie. A slow drive through these woodlands, interspersed with bright open meadows, reveals the hulking figures of bison and, with some luck, a meandering cow or bull elk, the bull's massive gnarled antlers all but invisible against the forest backdrop.

Down at Sweetwater Lake, near the refuge Visitor Center, is the other reason Sully's Hill is such a pleasure to visit. In an outdoor amphitheater, entertainment is offered on a regular basis throughout the summer. On this night there is a talk on owls of North America, complete with several living examples. On the following night, a "living history" program interprets the early history of the region that is today the preserve. Later in the summer is a kayaking seminar; a Lakota Indian Buffalo and Eagle Dance; a seminar on wildflowers. Almost every day of the week, May through September, something is going on here—fun things, informative things, hands-on things for all ages. Sully's Hill is a hotbed of conservation and natural history programming.

HISTORY

Sully's Hill lies within the heart of the Spirit Lake Sioux Indian Nation; *Minnewaukan,* or "spirit water," was the name the Sioux bestowed on the sprawling body of water that the preserve overlooks and that settlers later renamed Devils Lake. The high ground on the preserve was the scheduled site of a meeting between a cavalry unit from Illinois and General Alfred Sully in 1865. The cavalry camped on the hilltop in advance of Sully's arrival; when the general failed to show up, soldiers named the hill after him. Sully did eventually arrive, and two years later the army established nearby Fort Totten, one of a string of military outposts protecting settlers on the overland route between Minnesota

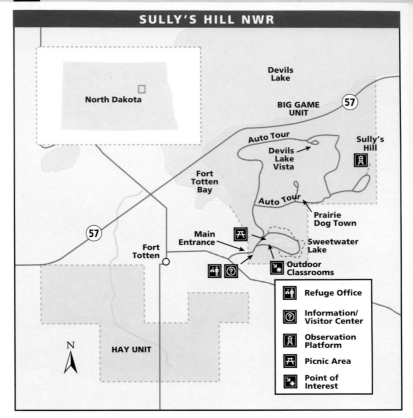

SULLY'S HILL NWR

and Montana. Among the best-preserved sites in North Dakota, Fort Totten today is a state historic area and a fascinating place to visit.

Interestingly, the story of Sully's Hill as a wildlife preserve intersects with the annihilation of the plains bison. By 1884 the animals were extirpated from North Dakota; by 1895 it was estimated that perhaps 20 wild bison in all roamed the United States, with some 250 left in Canada. One of the earliest parcels set aside as public lands in the United States, Sully's Hill was first designated a national park by President Theodore Roosevelt in 1904. In subsequent years, captive herds of bison and Rocky Mountain elk were established on the 1,674-acre preserve. In 1931 Congress authorized the transfer of Sully's Hill to the refuge system, where it was to serve primarily as a big-game preserve.

Sully's Hill has always been popular as a place for picnicking and for visitors who come to see bison, elk, and white-tailed deer; by the late 1990s, it was quickly evolving into an important regional conservation learning center. Utilizing two outdoor classrooms—the amphitheater and nature trail—Sully's Hill offers an endless schedule of events, to excellent response. In just eight months in 1998 and 1999, more than 3,500 people including area residents and school groups, enjoyed presentations here.

GETTING THERE

From the city of Jamestown, ND, on I-94, travel north 83 mi. on US 281, turning right (east) onto ND 57. Continue 6 mi. through town of Fort Totten to the refuge entrance.

- **SEASON:** General season is May through October, with weather a limiting factor; if planning to visit early or late in the season, call headquarters for an update.
- **HOURS:** 8 a.m. until sunset.
- **FEES:** Auto-tour fee is $2 per vehicle; season pass is $12.
- **ADDRESS:** P.O. Box 286, Fort Totten, ND 58335
- **TELEPHONE:** 701/766-4272

TOURING SULLY'S HILL

- **BY AUTOMOBILE:** A 4-mile self-guided auto tour open May through October (weather permitting), winds through the preserve, with opportunities for viewing free-roaming bison, elk, deer, and lots of other wildlife.
- **BY FOOT:** A mile-long interpreted nature trail, a portion of which is wheelchair-accessible; also a short trail climbing Sully's Hill, taking visitors to an observation tower. The Devils Lake Vista, another scenic overlook, is wheelchair-accessible. Plenty of snow in winter provides great opportunities for cross-country skiing near Sweetwater Lake.
- **BY BICYCLE:** Bicycles not permitted.
- **BY CANOE, KAYAK, OR BOAT:** Boating not permitted.

WHAT TO SEE

- **LANDSCAPE AND CLIMATE** Sully's Hill lies within the Drift Prairie region of North Dakota, a wide band of moraine hills, prairie wetlands, and shallow, glacier-scoured valleys. Devils Lake, immediately to the north of the preserve, is a dramatic piece of glacial work; encompassing some 10,000 acres in a wet year, this landlocked basin is the largest natural lake in North Dakota. The "hill" that is Sully's Hill is a massive pile of rock and debris scooped out by the glacier as it tilled the earth. Elevations across the preserve range from 1,450 feet to more than 1,700 feet.

The rolling hills of the region in presettlement days featured unbroken mixed-grass prairie—a transition grassland encompassing species found farther east and west—and tens of thousands of prairie wetlands, known as potholes. As many as half of these wetlands have been filled or drained over the years, and most native prairie is now agricultural land, either grazed by livestock or converted to crop fields. Forests were never part of the uplands of this region, though in areas of relief, such as Sully's Hill, some deciduous hardwood forests colonized cooler north-facing slopes and steep drainages.

Bluestem prairie grass

On average, this area of east-central North Dakota receives some 18 inches of precipitation annually, roughly two inches more than falls in the westernmost reaches of the Drift

Prairie. Winter (or at least winterlike temperatures) can last five months. Summers are a bit milder and wetter than exist farther west. Snowfall at Sully's Hill averages 50 inches per year.

■ PLANT LIFE

Wetlands Sweetwater Lake is the highly scenic backdrop for the preserve's amphitheater and outdoor classrooms. A shallow, 12-acre permanent wetland, it is surrounded by mature forest with minimal emergent vegetation on the margins.

Also accessible to the east and north of the preserve is the mother of all prairie potholes, Devils Lake, a shallow, alkaline body of water given to great fluctuations in size. A long arm of the lake, called Fort Totten Bay, enters the eastern side of the preserve. In years of normal water levels there are mudflats, wet meadows, and emergent vegetation; during high water, the bay and wetlands become open water, and move upslope to flood some of the woodlands.

Development has made a dent in Devils Lake's once-extensive habitats, though it remains an important stopping point for immense numbers of shorebirds and large flocks of waterfowl. Secluded within the rolling terrain of the forests here are a small number of seasonal woodland wetlands. These are recharged each spring and are very shallow, lasting only through the first half of the summer, long enough to serve the needs of nesting waterfowl and provide a source of drinking water for the elk and the bison. Cattails and smartweed are representative of the emergent plants in these pools.

Wild bergamot

Forests Eighty percent of Sully's Hill is forested. The array of deciduous trees, native shrubs, and abundant wildflowers here is due in part to the effects of two springs that nourish the lowlands of the preserve. In the bottomland areas is a community of mature basswood and some American elm; this is a climax forest, though sadly Dutch elm disease has taken its toll on the latter species. On drier hillsides and north slopes is a mixture of native green ash, bur oak, and some aspen.

Chokecherry is the dominant understory shrub, producing fruit important to deer, elk, and other wildlife. Buckbrush and buffaloberry are also present. Refuge management performs some regular thinning of the forest to encourage new growth and to maintain open meadows with the native grasses needed by elk and bison.

Grasslands More appropriately described as meadows, Sully's Hill features a number of large and small openings in the forest with a rich complement of wildflowers and native grasses. Green needlegrass, western wheatgrass, sideoats grama, and needle-and-thread are typical grasses here. More than 25 wildflower species bloom in these areas, including such beauties as wild bergamot, joe-pye weed, leadplant, showy milkweed, purple prairie clover, wild strawberry, hawkweed, spotted touch-me-not, goat's beard, and marsh marigold.

■ ANIMAL LIFE

Birds Visitors interested in birds will find Sully's an outstanding site. Its unique native woodlands, combined with wetlands and open meadows, sustain a host of species not seen elsewhere in the region. Forest species—the northern waterthrush, pileated woodpecker, eastern phoebe, great crested flycatcher, indigo bunting, scarlet tanager, eastern wood pewee—make Sully's a special place. Songbirds favoring wetlands and grasslands are present as well; the yellow-headed blackbird, clay-colored sparrow, eastern and western kingbird, common yellowthroat, and eastern bluebird have been sighted.

The preserve supports a sizable nesting population of wood ducks, along with mallards, Canada geese, and lesser numbers of hooded mergansers. During migration, Devils Lake hosts flights of shorebirds such as stilt sandpipers, longbilled dowitchers, and American avocets, along with tundra swans, and concentrations of ducks—teal, gadwall, canvasback, northern pintail, among others.

Mammals For many visitors, the highlight of a trip to Sully's Hill is found along the auto-tour route, where some 25 to 35 bison, and a similar number of Rocky Mountain elk, roam the meadows and rolling woodlands of the preserve's 700-acre enclosure. By no means is this a zoo experience—the animals are wild and the elk in particular prefer to remain unseen. Patience and luck are needed to see them; sightings are not guaranteed. Due to their immensity and grazing habits, bison are easier to spot, though still not a sure thing. White-tailed deer roam the forests and may be encountered as well. Other mammals dwelling here, though seldom sighted, include the gray fox, coyote, mink, and raccoon. (Also plying the woodlands is a sizable flock of wild turkey.)

Another treat is the prairie dog town, located along the tour route. Introduced here in 1975, the colony is thriving, and these amiable little creatures are always busy—grazing, burrowing, or just keeping a sharp eye out for trouble. They are highly social and maintain a complex society, replete with special greetings for family and neighbors, and a series of barks and yips that warn of specific hazards.

Bison calf

Black swallowtail butterfly

Invertebrates In 1996, Sully's Hill was surveyed for its butterfly population; 34 species were identified on-site, including the regal fritillary, a threatened species, and others such as the little wood satyr, northern pearly eye, compton tortoise shell, western tailed blue, monarch, mourning cloak, Harris' checkerspot, and the tawny crescent.

ACTIVITIES

■ **CAMPING:** Camping is not permitted on the refuge. Camping is available 10 miles west of the preserve at Graham's Island State Park.

■ **WILDLIFE OBSERVATION:** Summer is prime time for encounters with woodland songbirds, nesting wood ducks, and the bustling prairie dog colony. A remarkable fall event not to be missed is the bull elk rut. Beginning in early September, the males, or bulls, weighing 600 to 1,000 pounds, grow restless. For the next several weeks they conduct dramatic mating rites, with the bulls "bugling" in an effort to collect a harem of females for breeding. The sound is unforgettable—a high, quavering whistle, the voice of wildness itself, audible for long distances. Other bulls answer, and the ritual occasionally involves visual contact, as bulls size up one another. Preserve staff lead "bugling" tours throughout the month.

■ **PHOTOGRAPHY:** Visitors are allowed to exit vehicles to snap pictures along the tour route but cannot leave the immediate area around the vehicle—sage advice, as bison are potentially lethal. Many opportunities here for good shots of prairie dogs, wildflowers, wood ducks, butterflies, and for the lucky visitor an elk or deer.

■ **HIKES AND WALKS:** The interpreted nature trail takes visitors through the beautiful woodlands surrounding Sweetwater Lake, with prime opportunities for sighting songbirds, wood ducks, possibly beaver and muskrat, as well as butterflies and wildflowers. A section of this trail passes along the enclosure, providing opportunities to sight elk and deer while on foot. Another trail not to be missed is the short walk up to the crest of Sully's Hill, where an observation tower provides panoramic views of Devils Lake and the surrounding landscape.

■ **SEASONAL EVENTS:** From May through the end of September, something is going on almost every day of the week and on weekends. Call the refuge to receive a calendar of events; or check www.r6.fws.gov/refuges/sullys—the refuge web site.

■ **PUBLICATIONS:** Auto-tour guide; bird checklist; butterfly checklist; list of wildflower species; nature trail brochure; general visitor brochure.

HUNTING AND FISHING: Not permitted on the refuge.

Tewaukon NWR
Cayuga, North Dakota

Fawns, white-tailed deer

A mixing point for birds using both the Mississippi and Central flyways, 8,438-acre Tewaukon NWR hosts a vibrant migratory show in spring and fall; Lake Tewaukon and Sprague Lake—part of the Wild Rice River—are a treat for canoes and other small craft.

HISTORY

Early native people named the lake for *Te Wauk Kon*, "The Great Khan" or "Son of Heaven." The refuge was established in 1945 to preserve area wildlife as habitat loss to agriculture intensified. Four dams built on the Wild Rice River in the 1960s created a sprawling lake-and-marshland complex.

GETTING THERE

From Fargo, ND: travel south on I-29 for 60 mi. to ND 11, exit west and continue 27 mi. to the town of Cayuga. Turn south (left) onto County Rd. 12 and drive 5 mi. to refuge entrance.
- **SEASON:** Refuge open year-round.
- **HOURS:** Open from dawn to 10 p.m. daily; refuge headquarters is open weekdays between 8 a.m. and 4:30 p.m.
- **FEES:** Free access.
- **ADDRESS:** 9754 143 1/2 Avenue SE, Cayuga, ND 58103-9754
- **TELEPHONE:** 701/724-3598

TOURING TEWAUKON

- **BY AUTOMOBILE:** The new Prairie Lake Tour encircles Lake Tewaukon, with signed points of interest; the route is closed October 1 through May 1. Limited opportunities on county roads encircling lakes. Park and enjoy the on-site picnic area on east side of Lake Tewaukon.

■ **BY FOOT:** The refuge has no established trails.

■ **BY BICYCLE:** Bicycling is permitted on the road encircling Lake Tewaukon.

■ **BY CANOE, KAYAK, OR BOAT:** Watercraft for fishing is allowed on Sprague Lake and Lake Tewaukon. No jet skiing or motorboats allowed. Fishing for northern pike and walleye is popular in season; canoeing is also a good way to see and photograph refuge wildlife.

Bobolink

WHAT TO SEE

■ **LANDSCAPE AND CLIMATE** The refuge lies on the glaciated Missouri Coteau, a high, rolling plain once cloaked in mixed-grass and tallgrass prairie and riddled with shallow "pothole" wetlands, many of which have been drained and converted to croplands. The area sees an average of 19.4 inches of precipitation yearly, most of it falling between April and August; high winds, hot summer temperatures, and low humidity are other climatic features.

Lake Tewaukon and Sprague Lake are the two major natural riverine lakes formed by the Wild Rice River, though several smaller lakes are linked to them via natural or constructed channels.

■ **PLANT LIFE**

Wetlands Tewaukon's 48 managed wetland pools and sloughs encompass more than 3,000 acres; cattail and hardstem bulrush, sedge grasses, and sago pondweed are present. Prairie potholes account for 110 acres of natural (and seasonal) wetlands.

Grasslands Scattered remnants of native tallgrass prairie occur here; leadplant and coneflower are representative wildflowers, with little bluestem a characteristic native grass. Many areas of former cropland have been reseeded to either native or "tame" grasses.

Human-made Haying, crop production, and many miles of planted shelterbelts are other features of the site. Hay and crops on about 900 acres are farmed by neighboring landowners, with a portion left standing for wildlife.

■ **ANIMAL LIFE** Tewaukon's sprawling marshlands are the focal point for wildlife; the abundance and diversity of ducks here is a bit overwhelming. Twelve species nest on site, including the ruddy duck, canvasback, wood duck, and blue-winged teal. Spring and fall migrations bring tens of thousands more, along with very high concentrations of tundra swans, snow geese, and Canada geese. A rich array of shorebirds is seen during migration as well, including lesser yellowlegs, marbled godwit, and golden plovers. The Cooper's hawk, bald eagle, and peregrine falcon are seen occasionally during migration. White-tailed deer are common, and red fox, coyote, mink, and muskrat may also be seen. The bobolink and upland sandpiper nest in grassland areas and shelterbelts, as do the clay-colored and grasshopper sparrow, western meadowlark, and brown thrasher.

ACTIVITIES

■ **CAMPING:** Camping is not permitted on the refuge. Camping is available at Fort Ransom State Park, northeast of the refuge near the town of Lisbon; contact the refuge for details.

■ **WILDLIFE OBSERVATION:** It's fun to see the big flocks in spring and fall, but another great time to visit is July to see the young of the year; ducklings, pheasant chicks, and white-tailed fawns are active early and late in the day.

■ **PHOTOGRAPHY:** Tewaukon is an outstanding refuge for waterfowl photography, beginning with spring migration and continuing through summer and into fall. Immense skies and waterscapes await the photographer, along with migratory flocks of truly staggering proportions.

■ **HIKES AND WALKS:** On the western shore of Lake Tewaukon, follow the trails out along the peninsula for a leisurely and very scenic walk.

■ **SEASONAL EVENTS:** North Dakota Junior Duck Stamp Contest in May; Tewaukon Field Days in June; wildflower walks in summer; National Wildlife Refuge Week/Open House, October.

Upper Souris NWR
Foxholm, North Dakota

Tundra (whistling) swans

Where North Dakota is flat, it is supremely flat. Where the landscape is broken, rumpled, or bitten away by glaciers, wind, and water, there are places of heart-stoppingly rugged beauty—Pembina Gorge, the Turtle Mountains, and the upper Souris River basin, site of 32,092-acre Upper Souris NWR. A 35-mile-long corridor, the refuge preserves a landscape of ups and downs. The steep-sided prairie hills are bright in the sunlight, with expansive views of the country and river below; down along the river, a series of deep pockets—coulees, draws, and drainageways—hold dense thickets of woodlands. The Souris meanders through the heart of it all, forming oxbows and lush marshlands.

Upper Souris is one of three refuges that make up the "Souris Loop." Along with Des Lacs NWR to the northwest and J. Clark Salyer NWR to the east, these sites preserve more than 100,000 acres of North Dakota's natural heritage. There are similarities, but each refuge holds something unique. It is possible to speed through all of them in a day, but far better to spend at least two days, and ideally three, especially if canoeing is an interest.

HISTORY

In the heart of the Central Flyway and the great waterfowl breeding grounds of the northern plains, Upper Souris was among the many refuges established with proceeds from duck stamps during the Dust bowl years of the 1930s. Jay N. "Ding" Darling, flamboyant political cartoonist and director of the newly created Bureau of Biological Survey, chose North Dakota native J. Clark Salyer as his top aide. Upper Souris was one of three sites Salyer succeeded in purchasing in 1935; another refuge, downstream from here, today bears Salyer's name. The major impoundment of the river is named for Darling.

Upper Souris hosted a Civilian Conservation Corps (CCC) contingent of 250 young men at Camp Maurek. Along with a Works Progress Administration

(WPA) detail, many roads, dikes, fences, and other water-control structures were installed. The diked oxbow marshes on the south end of the refuge are still managed with log structures built by these civilian engineers.

GETTING THERE

From Minot, ND, travel northwest 18 mi. on US 52 to the town of Foxholm; continue north on County Rd. 11 for 7 mi., follow signs, turning right into refuge headquarters.

■ **SEASON:** Refuge open year-round; access limited in late fall and winter.

■ **HOURS:** Open 5 a.m.-10 p.m. daily. Refuge office and Visitor Center with bookstore and exhibits open weekdays, 8 a.m.-4:30 p.m.

■ **FEES:** Free access.

■ **ADDRESS:** 17705 212th Ave. NW, Berthold, ND 58718-9666

■ **TELEPHONE:** 701/468-5467

TOURING UPPER SOURIS

■ **BY AUTOMOBILE:** A 3.5-mile self-guided auto tour is open spring through fall, and closed during winter, wet weather, and deer rifle season.

■ **BY FOOT:** Hiking is permitted year-round in all open public-use areas, along refuge auto tour, and along four hiking trails, each approximately one-half to one mile long; also in areas marked with "No vehicles—foot traffic only" signs; permission required to enter closed areas. The refuge auto-tour route and areas open to ice fishing are open in winter to cross-country skiing; check with refuge headquarters for ice conditions in riverbottom areas.

■ **BY BICYCLE:** Biking is permitted spring through early fall on refuge auto tour only; many state highways and county roads cross refuge lands, including the Souris River; vehicular traffic is moderate to light, making this the preferred option for exploring the area.

■ **BY CANOE, KAYAK, OR BOAT:** Numerous opportunities abound for small craft and canoe, which are permitted between May 1 and September 30 on Lake Darling and upstream from Renville County Park. Beaver Lodge Canoe Trail on the south end of the refuge offers the most solitude and superb scenery. Boat anglers and canoeists may also two areas of Lake Darling and upstream from Renville County Park between May 1 and September 30.

■ **BY HORSEBACK:** The refuge is open to horseback riding by permit only.

WHAT TO SEE

■ **LANDSCAPE AND CLIMATE** Upper Souris lies on the westernmost edge of North Dakota's Drift Prairie, a broad, glaciated band of moraine hills and prairie wetlands. Across this region and the Missouri Coteau, a lengthy escarpment to the west, a single square mile may contain more than 270 wetlands. Large and small blocks of receding glaciers here were overlaid with soil, rock, and other "drift" materials, which insulated the ice beneath to create these unique water-holding depressions known as potholes.

Originating in Saskatchewan, the Souris River flows south into North Dakota, then swings upward again to flow north out of the state; the U-shaped basin drains 240,000 square miles, and flows for 360 miles through North Dakota. The low, long creases and drainages along this portion of the Souris basin, known as coulees, were sculptured over thousands of years by snowmelt, rain, and wind.

This region's climate features cold, lengthy winters, with average low temperatures of -1 to -5 degrees Fahrenheit. The average growing season is just 98 to 106

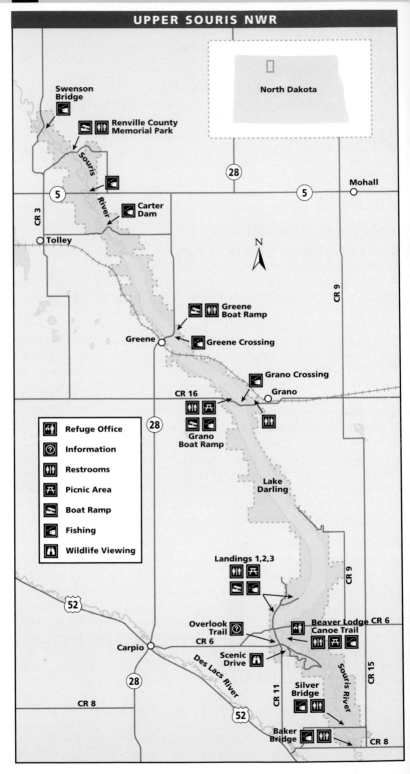

UPPER SOURIS NWR

North Dakota

Swenson Bridge

Renville County Memorial Park

Souris River

CR 3

5

Carter Dam

Tolley

Mohall

5

28

CR 9

N

Greene Boat Ramp

Greene

Greene Crossing

Grano Crossing

Grano

CR 16

28

Grano Boat Ramp

Lake Darling

Refuge Office

Information

Restrooms

Picnic Area

Boat Ramp

Fishing

Wildlife Viewing

Landings 1,2,3

CR 9

Overlook Trail

Beaver Lodge CR 6

Canoe Trail

CR 6

Scenic Drive

52

Carpio

Des Lacs River

CR 11

Souris River

CR 15

28

Silver Bridge

CR 8

52

Baker Bridge

CR 8

days. Summers are mild, with an average daily high in the mid- to upper 70s. Annual snowfall measures about 30 to 40 inches, with a yearly precipitation total of 16 to 17 inches. The majority of the year's precipitation occurs from April to September.

■ PLANT LIFE

Open water The Souris River, lazy, shallow, and meandering, fuels all of Souris's aquatic and wetland habitats. In the upper reach of the refuge it is free-flowing; in the midsection is a 10,000-acre impoundment, Lake Darling. During years of abundant rainfall or snowmelt, the "lake" may be 15 feet deep. Its value for wildlife—especially water-dependent species—rises considerably in dry years, when natural wetlands in other areas become sparse. A two-year water supply is stored here, and the refuge coordinates its cycles of water releases to benefit wetlands on the J. Clark Salyer refuge downriver. In both the free-flowing and impounded segments, the river supports a native fishery of walleye, northern pike, yellow perch, and bullhead. Carp, a serious headache for refuge managers across the nation, have not yet taken hold here, which seems a minor miracle.

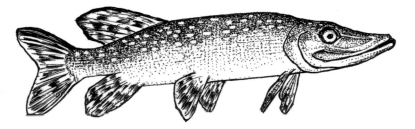

Northern pike

Wetlands The famous prairie pothole wetlands are elsewhere; at Upper Souris, thanks to the CCC, a series of log control structures and dams on the south end of the refuge create marshes, mudflats, and a small amount of wet meadows. Dam 87 holds the river back only a bit, creating some wet margins for cattail and bulrush. Downstream from this structure, Dam 96 impounds more water and has flooded a substantial area of the river bottom. Cattail, bulrush, and tall thickets of phrag-mites are associated with this extensive marsh area. A series of old oxbow marshes parallel the river just south of the refuge headquarters; log structures on these shallow pools assist in developing emergent vegetation and mudflats favored by shorebirds and waterfowl.

Grasslands Upper Souris features 18,900 acres of the real stuff—native mixed-grass prairie, the vast majority of which has never been touched by the plow. It car-pets the rolling hills adjoining the river on both sides, a mixture of such native grasses as little bluestem, green needlegrass, blue grama, and western wheatgrass. In years with adequate rainfall, the prairie sends up a fine display of wildflowers. Purple and yellow prairie coneflowers, blanketflower, goat's beard, dotted blazing star, and prairie clover are among the species found here. Refuge grasslands are maintained with a combination of prescribed burning and grazing. A visit in fall will dispel the notion that only trees put on a color show—though less immedi-ately dramatic, prairie grasses produce soft hues of gold, yellow, and red that are especially beautiful early and late in the day.

Forests "Woodlands" is probably more accurate to describe the lovely stands of

HERBAL THIEVERY The nation's growing appetite for natural remedies, including echinacea, or coneflower, has spawned some decidedly unhealthy behavior. On public and private lands that support native prairie, criminals seeking quick profit are ravaging coneflower populations. It has taken a while, but they are now moving into North Dakota, and refuge managers are deeply concerned.

Using a "cookie cutter" implement with a long shaft, thieves can quickly remove an entire coneflower plant, roots, and all. Sold on the black market, echinacea root fetches $16 to $20 per pound; someone skilled in the practice can make $100 a day, say refuge officials.

With so much untrammeled prairie on North Dakota refuges, it is nearly impossible to catch people in the act, and the damage often remains invisible until fall, when grasses die back and refuge staff are out on hunting patrols. At Chase Lake Wetland Management District, in the south-central region of the state, no fewer than 100 holes have been found where coneflowers once grew.

Visitors who might notice someone digging up wild plants should not approach them. At a minimum, report the time, location, and number of people involved to the nearest law enforcement agency or refuge office. A license plate number or description of a vehicle is even more helpful. And yes, it is OK to call 911.

mature deciduous trees and shrubs that pack themselves into coulees and steep-sided draws flanking the river. Historically the area has been a mixture of American elm and green ash, but Dutch elm disease has taken a heavy toll on the elms, and today ash are dominant. Understory species include a dense mixture of wild plum, juneberry, prairie wild rose, and buffaloberry, all of which yield fruit attractive to wildlife. Closer to the water, willow, too, occupies a few areas of the river corridor, along with occasional stands of mature cottonwood trees planted by the CCC.

■ ANIMAL LIFE

Birds Upper Souris does feature an array of nesting waterfowl species—hooded merganser, canvasback, blue-winged teal, ruddy duck, Canada goose, and red-head, along with several other species—but its value to waterfowl is greatest during other stages in their life cycle. Between mid-July and mid-August, 40,000 to 50,000 ducks gather on the open water and marsh areas of upper Lake Darling to molt, a safe haven for the period in which they cannot fly. And then there's migration. The pulse of activity during spring and fall can be overwhelming, as some 350,000 ducks, swans, and geese stop through in the fall: tundra swans, snow geese, great flocks of gadwall, goldeneye, and pintail, and less-common species such as the white-winged scoter, American black duck, and greater scaup.

By no means is river and wetland birdlife restricted to waterfowl. The great blue heron and double-crested cormorant maintain nesting colonies on site, along with a tremendous variety of swallows (seven species, including the purple martin). In some years, five species of grebes nest here, including the red-necked, eared, horned, western, and pied-billed. American white pelicans grace Lake Darling and impounded marshes from late spring through fall but do not nest on the refuge. The American and least bittern, black-crowned night heron, and little blue heron may also be seen; sora and marsh wrens are abundant. The Virginia and yellow rail probably nest here as well, though they are seen less frequently.

Purple prairie coneflower

Serious birders know of North Dakota's rare grassland songbirds, and Upper Souris is as reliable a spot as any to find them. The marquee species—LeConte's sparrow, Baird's sparrow, sharp-tailed sparrow, chestnut-collared longspur, Sprague's pipit, Savannah sparrow, and grasshopper sparrow—are all present, with most species nesting on site. Sharp-tailed grouse and gray partridge are fairly common as well in the grassland areas; one need not be a world-class birder to locate these and many other lovely birds—the western kingbird, upland sandpiper, rufous-sided towhee, yellow-headed blackbird, western meadowlark, bobolink, and horned lark; all of these species are abundant.

The woodlands of Upper Souris host a rich assortment of nesting species—warbling and red-eyed vireo, ovenbird, cedar waxwing, black-and-white warbler, veery, brown thrasher, willow and least flycatcher, lazuli bunting, and rose-breasted grosbeak. Other species nesting here in limited numbers include the red-headed woodpecker, eastern screech owl, and white-breasted nuthatch.

Hunting marshes and grasslands from above are the raptors. The northern harrier, Swainson's hawk, and red-tailed hawk are all fairly common; ferruginous hawks appear a few times each year.

Mammals Woodland edges are the province of the most easily sighted mammal here, the white-tailed deer. Rare sightings of moose and elk have also occurred. Other species to watch for include fox and raccoon, which rummage through the shrubs and understory in search of berries and other edibles. Red fox, long-tailed weasel, and coyote, elusive species all, may be encountered in any number of habitats. Down in the river basin, along the marshes and streamside areas, the muskrat, beaver, and mink may be seen at work or play. The snowshoe hare is also present.

Mammals in the uplands include the badger and a host of small burrowers: Richardson's ground squirrel, northern pocket gopher, and the meadow and prairie vole.

Reptiles and amphibians A limited variety of reptiles and amphibians inhabit wetlands and woodland floors. The plains garter snake and red-bellied snake may be seen in either habitat; the smooth green snake is probably here though this species is almost never seen. The northern leopard frog, wood frog, western chorus frog, and tiger salamander are present as well.

ACTIVITIES

■ **CAMPING:** Camping is not permitted on the refuge. Camping facilities are available 6 miles west of the refuge in the small town of Carpio and at the far north end of the refuge in a county park.

■ **WILDLIFE OBSERVATION:** They do not show up every year, but whooping cranes put in an occasional appearance at Upper Souris during spring or fall migration. Watch, too, for the occasional pronghorn on the edge of the refuge in neighboring croplands. Beaver Lodge Canoe Trail is notable for sightings of great blue heron, beaver and muskrat, waterfowl, and other marsh wildlife. The uplands bounding the western shore of Lake Darling north of County Road 6 are prime areas in summer for locating Sprague's pipit, Baird's sparrow, sharp-tailed grouse, and gray partridge. For sharp-tailed sparrows and LeConte's sparrows, try Pelican Trail, which originates at the southern end of "A" Pool, southwest of refuge headquarters. June is the prime month to identify grassland songbirds.

Red-necked grebe

UPPER SOURIS HUNTING AND FISHING SEASONS

Hunting	Jan	Feb	Mar	Apr	May	Jun	Jul	Aug	Sep	Oct	Nov	Dec
(Seasons may vary)												
white-tailed deer (using following hunting methods)												
bow	□	□	□	□	□	□	□	□	■	■	■	■
firearm	□	□	□	□	□	□	□	□	□	□	■	□
muzzle-loader	□	□	□	□	□	□	□	□	□	□	□	■
sharp grouse	□	□	□	□	□	□	□	□	■	■	■	■
partridge	□	□	□	□	□	□	□	□	■	■	■	■
pheasant	□	□	□	□	□	□	□	□	□	■	■	■

Fishing	Jan	Feb	Mar	Apr	May	Jun	Jul	Aug	Sep	Oct	Nov	Dec
northern pike	■	■	■	■	■	■	■	■	■	■	■	■
yellow perch	■	■	■	■	■	■	■	■	■	■	■	■
walleye	■	■	■	■	■	■	■	■	■	■	■	■
bullhead	■	■	■	■	■	■	■	■	■	■	■	■

There are several deer-hunting seasons that take place at Upper Souris. An archery season runs from early Sept. through Dec. 31. Overlapping with that season is the rifle season, which occurs over the space of two weeks in early Nov. A special refuge permit is required for this hunt; contact the state Fish & Wildlife Department for details. A muzzle-loading system follows right after the rifle season, running from late Nov. into early Dec. You may also hunt upland game in the fall. There is a sharp grouse and partridge season that runs from the second week in Sept. through Dec., and a pheasant season that runs from the first week in Oct. through Dec.

There are abundant fishing and hunting opportunities on the refuge. Fishing is a year-round activity: In the summer, one-quarter of Lake Darling is open for boat fishing, and there are a dozen areas that are open for shore fishing; in winter all of the refuge waters are open to ice fishing.

■ **PHOTOGRAPHY:** Several on-site viewing blinds are available for visitors interested in photographing the sensational spring courtship displays of sharp-tailed grouse. Fall colors in the woodlands adjacent to the river are lovely and peak in mid-September; spring and fall migration offers photographers an unparalleled opportunity for images of waterfowl, tundra swans, and other species.

■ **HIKES AND WALKS:** For a good experience of the Souris River and its marshlands, follow Oxbow Nature Trail. To sample a different variety of areas, follow the mile-long Cottonwood Trail from its origin at stop 9 on the auto tour; the trail meanders through grasslands up to a scenic overlook of the valley, and continues from there into and out of a wooded coulee.

■ **PUBLICATIONS:** Bird checklist; visitor guide to Beaver Lodge Canoe Trail; general refuge brochure; Prairie Marsh Scenic Drive brochure; hunting and fishing guides; checklist of mammals.

Ottawa NWR
Oak Harbor, Ohio

Waterfowl feeding, Ottawa NWR

At Ottawa NWR, the business is birds. The diked fields, wooded swamps, and vast panorama of restored wetlands and waterfowl habitat leave little doubt as to the refuge's raison d'être. From the carefully managed bird habitat to the ever-present bird population, Ottawa is a haven for winged creatures—and birdwatching heaven.

HISTORY

Ninety-eight percent of Ohio's wetlands have disappeared since the state was settled, a statistic second only to California's in national wetland loss. The Black Swamp alone once stretched from the present site of Port Clinton completely around the west end of Lake Erie and north to the approaches to Detroit. The 300,000 acres of flooded woodlands and marshes were home to an incredible variety of wildlife and served as a bountiful larder for the Ottawa Indians. But with the tribe's removal, by treaty in the early 1800s, Europeans attacked the swamp with ax and shovel. Farm fields replaced wetlands until all that was left of one of the Midwest's greatest swamps were 15,000 acres. The 5,794-acre Ottawa NWR was created in 1961 to provide resting, nesting, and feeding habitat for migratory and other nonmigratory birds. The newly created refuge included a remnant of the original Black Swamp, and work began restoring badly needed wetland habitat. Today, Ottawa NWR and its next-door neighbor Magee Marsh, managed by the Ohio Department of Natural Resources, are together considered the best birding area in Ohio.

GETTING THERE

Ottawa NWR is 16 mi. east of Toledo on OH 2 or 18 mi. west of Port Clinton on OH 2.
■ **SEASON:** Refuge open year-round.
■ **HOURS:** Sunrise to sunset.

■ **FEES:** Free access.
■ **ADDRESS:** Ottawa NWR, 14000 W. State Route 2, Oak Harbor, Ohio 43449
■ **TELEPHONE:** 419/898-0014

TOURING OTTAWA

■ **BY AUTOMOBILE:** No access.
■ **BY FOOT:** The refuge has 7 miles of flat, easy, self-guided hiking trails divided into four loops. The trails, opened for public use in 1981, are part of the National Recreation Trail System. Open from sunrise to sunset, they take hikers and birders through six types of habitat. Cross-country skiers may use the trails in the winter.
■ **BY BICYCLE:** The hiking trails are also open to bicycles. The gravel trails will accommodate any bike with fat tires; touring bikes may have trouble with the rough gravel.
■ **BY CANOE, KAYAK, OR BOAT:** No access.

WHAT TO SEE

■ **LANDSCAPE AND CLIMATE** Except for a small piece of the once great Black Swamp, the landscape at Ottawa NWR has been shaped by human hands for the benefit of birds. Six different habitats are maintained within the refuge, and all are important to the refuge's goal of feeding and sheltering birds.

Lake Erie has a major influence on the weather at Ottawa. Summers in northern Ohio are often hot and humid, but an offshore breeze can moderate the temperature and lower the humidity. During the winter the area around Lake Erie is often much warmer than the frigid air coming down from Canada. The big lake actually warms the Canadian cold fronts as they cross the water—with the result that Ottawa NWR and other lakeside areas can be warmer than sites farther inland. But as winds cross the lake they pick up moisture and drop it in the form of snow on reaching land. This lake effect snow can bury Ottawa in snow.

■ **PLANT LIFE** With the mix of habitats at Ottawa, a wide variety of plant life is a given. Among the plethora of plants found within the refuge, two are noteworthy because of their historical importance within the old Lake Erie marshlands. Pickerelweed is a member of the water hyacinth family. The Ottawas ground the ripe seeds of the plant to make flour and also ate the seeds raw. The American lotus, a member of the water lily family, is ever-present in the refuge's wetlands. (The Ottawas also ate the seeds of this plant.) By midsummer, delicate Queen Anne's Lace covers the meadows and fields at Ottawa; this member of the carrot family is a descendant of the plant named in honor of the patron saint of lace makers.

Pickerelweed

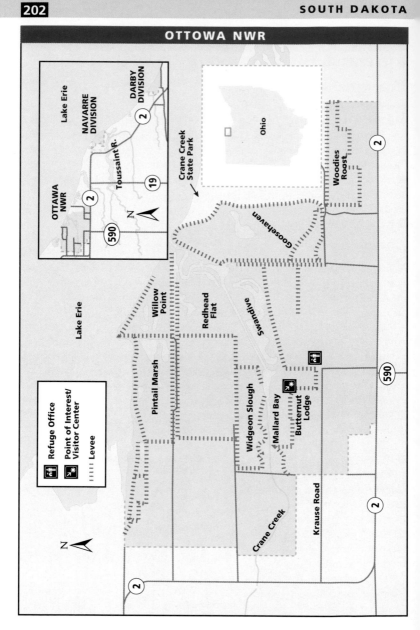

OTTOWA NWR

Wetlands The diked marshes are maintained at a uniform depth and produce a wide variety of plant life on which waterfowl feed. Moist-soil units are marshland that is periodically drained to support and encourage the growth of moist-soil plants. The units are usually flooded in early fall and provide migrating birds with a smorgasbord of succulent plants. The units are then drained in the spring to speed up plant growth. As an added bonus, the muddy units attract shorebirds who are heading south by midsummer. The master plan at Ottawa calls for 20 pools totaling 4,000 acres of permanent marsh plus another 1,000 acres of moist soil.

Open fields The refuge's grasslands and brushy areas produce eye-catching wildflowers, any many birds breed and live within shrubs and meadows. Ringed-necked pheasants, eastern cottontails, a variety of sparrows, and numerous mice and voles that feed hawks and owls are common to the habitat.

Croplands Croplands are an important habitat within the refuge. Local farmers sharecrop the fields, leaving a portion of the harvest as food for migrating waterfowl.

Swampland The small remnants of the Black Swamp were not preserved and maintained for nostalgia's sake. The old woodlands provide nesting and resting sites for numerous migrating and nonmigrating breeding birds. The old-growth hardwoods in the Black Swamp are worth the mile walk that it takes to experience their grandeur.

Open water The last major habitat at Ottawa is the open water of Lake Erie. The aquatic plants found growing on the bottom of open water more than a few feet deep are important food sources for diving ducks.

■ **ANIMAL LIFE** Much of the animal life at Ottawa NWR ultimately ends up supporting the refuge's huge population of waterfowl. Hawks and owls regularly hunt the mice and voles found in meadows and brush. The small fish, crustaceans, frogs, and literally any reptile or amphibian small enough to be eaten by waterfowl or marsh birds have a good chance of ending up as dinner. And to turn the tables, large snapping turtles will prey on young waterfowl.

Birds Ottawa NWR receives 120,000 visitors annually, and birds are the main attraction. Geography plays an especially important part in making the area so popular with birds. The refuge draws large numbers of migrating birds from both the Atlantic and Mississippi flyways. In the fall Ottawa is a rest and feeding stop for birds using both flyways, and it is the fork in the road where the flow of southbound birds splits to follow one flyway or the other. During spring migration birds from both flyways converge on Ottawa before heading further north.

The refuge's choice location is reflected in the number and variety of birds calling here every year. Ottawa's bird checklist notes 274 species as regularly observed; 49 others are listed as rare or accidentals. Wildlife biologists estimate that 70 percent of the population of Mississippi Flyway American black ducks

Canada goose

pass through the Erie marshes and are numbered among large flights of waterfowl that visit the refuge annually. One thousand whistling swans and 4,000 black-crowned night herons also show up here each year. But do not think of Ottawa NWR as just an avian Howard Johnson's and freeway interchange. Huge numbers nest within the refuge, and it is estimated that Ottawa produces 4,000 to 6,000 marsh and water birds, upwards of 2,000 waterfowl, and from 2 to 4 bald eagles annually.

Unlike many fine birding spots that shine only during spring and fall migration, Ottawa can pay visitors dividends almost any time of the year. In the winter, birders can usually count on snow buntings, with Lapland longspurs, snowy owls, and evening grosbeaks occasionally showing up. Open water frequently attracts canvasbacks, scaup, mergansers, and goldeneyes. Bald eagles are present year-round, but look for them to begin nesting in February.

By March waterfowl migration is in full flow, with songbirds joining the northbound stream in April and May. As spring edges into summer the migration ebbs, but with redhead, northern shovelers, wood ducks, screech and great horned owls, and lots of songbirds nesting in the refuge, it never gets dull. In mid-July sandpipers, dowitchers, yellowlegs, plovers, and other shorebirds begin leaving their nesting grounds in the Arctic. July's trickle of shorebirds becomes a full-blown deluge by August, and Ottawa's drained moist-soil units are sometimes filled with thousands of shorebirds probing the mud for food.

As the days grow shorter and cooler, ducks and geese begin winging into the refuge on their journey south. Bald eagle numbers begin increasing at the refuge in late summer until they peak in September. The largest congregation of birds, 25,000 geese and 65,000 ducks, occurs in late October and early November, when waterfowl pack themselves into the refuge to rest and feed before the last push south. Among the thousands of ducks and Canada geese are snow and blue geese and tundra swans. Peregrine falcons often follow the flights of southbound ducks for the same reasons wolves follow migrating caribou.

Mammals White-tailed deer are numerous enough to support a short deer-hunting season. Woodchucks, raccoons, mink, and red fox can often be seen on distant dikes. Fox squirrels, opossum, and skunk also thrive at Ottawa. There are so few natural enemies of the many furbearing animals that trapping is permitted to control their numbers. Muskrat, raccoons, mink, red fox, skunk, and opos-

Muskrat by marsh grasses

Trumpeter swans

sum can be trapped. The number of animals taken by trappers is carefully monitored so that populations can be properly managed.

ACTIVITIES

■ **CAMPING AND SWIMMING:** Neither camping nor swimming is permitted at Ottawa NWR. The closest swimming beach is next door at Crane Creek State
Park, a day-use park that offers a sandy beach stretching along Lake Erie. Back
from the beach are grills and picnic tables. The closest public campground, in
Maumee State Park (419-836-7758), about 10 miles to the west, has 256 camping
sites, all with paved slips and electrical hookups.

■ **WILDLIFE OBSERVATION:** Birding is big business at Ottawa NWR and the
surrounding area. It is estimated that birding at Ottawa and the adjacent Magee
Marsh and Crane Creek State Park contributes $5.6 million to the local economy.
Birding interest mirrors the migration seasons at Ottawa. Birders turn out in
droves to witness the spring and fall spectacle put on by thousands of waterfowl.
Attendance peaks at the refuge in May with the migration of songbirds. Warblers,
vireos, flycatchers, and thrushes often pack the remnants of the once great Black
Swamp. Even the small woodlot next to the parking area can provide plenty of
entertainment.

Hawk-watching can be good in March, April, and the first half of May.
Cooper's hawk, sharp-shinned hawks, red-shouldered and red-tailed hawks,
northern harriers, and broad-winged hawks are all seen in the skies above
Ottawa. Eagles can be seen here anytime of the year, but the best chance for an
eagle sighting occurs in July and August, when immature bald eagles begin gathering in the refuge. The young birds can be seen from the hiking trails.

You don't even have to leave the car to find great birding. A paved road leads
through Magee Marsh, just east of the refuge. Magee Marsh Bird Trail is accessed
from the parking lot of Crane Creek State Park, which also borders the refuge's
east side. The trail is one of the great spots in the Midwest for seeing warblers and
songbirds.

■ **PHOTOGRAPHY:** Ottawa NWR offers plenty of photo opportunities, but nearly all of them require a tele-photo lens. If the dikes make good, solid platforms for camera and tri-pod, they also make photographers highly visible to their subjects. Get-ting close-up views of the wildlife at Ottawa with a regular lens may be difficult—unless your subject is a fat, indolent groundhog who scarcely has the energy to move off the path as you approach.

On the other hand, the Magee Marsh Bird Trail, next door to the refuge, is one of the best places in the Midwest to photograph war-blers and songbirds. The colorful birds are often only a few feet from quiet birders on the trail.

HUNTING AND FISHING A four-day, adult, primitive-weapons **deer** hunt in Jan. is followed by a one-day, juve-nile hunt. **Waterfowl** season is on Mondays, Wednesdays, Fridays, and Saturdays for two weeks in Oct. and two weeks in Dec.

Fishing is not permitted at Ottawa NWR, but **bank fishing** is permitted at the Cedar Point Division, east of Ottawa, from June to Aug. The pub-lic is barred from the division for all activities except fishing.

■ **HIKES AND WALKS:** Most of the refuge's 7 miles of hiking trails run along the top of the dikes, which are great, ready-made platforms from which to search for birds. The dikes also make for dry and sure footing even during the wettest of weather. The trails run in length from the quarter-mile Red Trail to 4.5-mile Blue Trail. The Red Trail circles a small woodlot next to the public parking lot and pre-sents visitors with a sweeping vista of marshland. The Blue Trail plunges into the heart of the refuge, taking hikers and birders for a long walk on the banks of Crane Creek and through a remnant of the Black Swamp before returning to the parking lot. The 2-mile Yellow Trail boasts a wildlife-viewing platform overlooking a diked marsh. Interpretive signs explain points of interest along the trails. All trails begin at the visitors' parking lot.

■ **SEASONAL EVENTS:** The refuge holds two major open houses every year. The first is the International Migratory Bird Day on the second Saturday in May, and the other is during the peak of fall waterfowl migration on the second full week of October. The refuge celebrates National Wildlife Refuge Week in October with special events.

■ **PUBLICATIONS:** A bird checklist, brochure describing the refuge's human and natural history, and an interpretive guide with trail map.

Lacreek NWR
Martin, South Dakota

Black-tailed prairie dog at burrow

Nature operates at Lacreek National Wildlife Refuge with an unwavering constancy. First, last, and always is the wind. It ripples the water of the large pools and creates waves in the shortgrass prairie overlooking the floodings. Every spring and fall birds pass through the refuge in an aviary tidal wave. Pronghorn antelope can usually be seen on distant hillsides. Closer at hand, prairie dogs keep a vigilant lookout for feathered and furred predators. And every year a new crop of waterfowl, numbering in the hundreds, graduates from this prairie nursery. Visit only once, and you will instinctively feel in synch with the constant rhythms that govern Lacreek NWR.

HISTORY

The refuge, created in 1935, has grown to 16,410 acres. Much of this remote acreage was once American Indian tribal land—land that never felt the bite of a plow. Ownership of the land passed into the hands of the U.S. Fish & Wildlife Service, and dams and dikes were employed to create habitat favorable to migrating and nesting waterfowl.

GETTING THERE

Approximately 13 mi. east of Martin on US 18.
- **SEASON:** Refuge open year-round.
- **HOURS:** Refuge, dawn-dusk. Office, 7 a.m.- 3:30 p.m.
- **FEES:** Free access.
- **ADDRESS:** Lacreek NWR, HC5 Box 114, Martin, SD 57551-9410
- **TELEPHONE:** 605/685-6508

TOURING LACREEK

- **BY AUTOMOBILE:** There are 12 miles of roads open to the public and as well

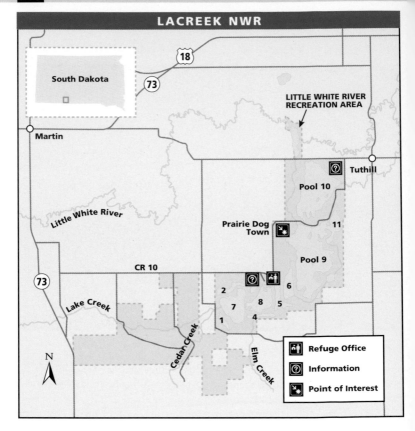

LACREEK NWR

South Dakota

18
73

Martin

LITTLE WHITE RIVER
RECREATION AREA

Tuthill

Pool 10

Little White River

Prairie Dog
Town

11

Pool 9

CR 10

73

Lake Creek

2

7

1

8 5

4

6

Cedar Creek

Elm Creek

N

Refuge Office

Information

Point of Interest

---

as a 4-mile self-guided auto tour that circles Pool No. 8. The speed limit is 35 mph unless otherwise posted.

■ **BY FOOT:** Visitors are welcome to hike all refuge roads and staff will direct hikers to the most interesting areas within the refuge for off-road jaunts.

■ **BY BICYCLE:** All roads open to motorists can be biked.

■ **BY CANOE, KAYAK, OR BOAT:** Watercraft from canoes to speedboats are welcome on the Little White River Recreation Area on the north end of the refuge.

WHAT TO SEE

■ **LANDSCAPE AND CLIMATE** Lacreek lies in a shallow basin on the northern edge of Nebraska's sandhills. Tallgrass prairie has a tenuous grasp on the ancient dunes making up the sandhills, overgrazing or any serious disturbance of the vegetation leaves the door open for the ever-present wind to scour out the sand and create isolated holes in the dunes called blowouts. The grass-covered dunes soak up precipitation like a greedy sponge, and the stored water is returned to the area through hillside springs that flow into numerous small creeks. The refuge is named for Lake Creek, the largest of the spring-fed streams running through the area. Dikes and dams have captured the runoff in 11 pool and marsh water units. Wetlands compromise nearly a third of the refuge's 16,410 acres.

Summers are warm and often hot. Winters can be brutal with severe cold and roaring blizzards, and with spring comes mud.

■ **PLANT LIFE** Refuge habitat includes the open water of the impoundments, 5,000 acres of marsh within the impoundments, upland prairie, and subirrigated (or spring-fed) meadows. The refuge's few trees are found in small woodlots and include elm, green ash, willows, cottonwood, chokecherry, and wild plum. There is even some oak savanna within the refuge. This parklike setting is combination forest and prairie with the trees widely scattered amid pleasant expanses of grasses and wildflowers.

The refuge's extensive open water and marshlands are of critical importance to migrating and nesting waterfowl. The stems, seeds, and roots of a wide variety of marsh plants provide critical food for waterfowl. The algae on and in the water attract herbivorous insects that, in turn, provide plenty of protein for waterfowl and non-game birds. And the abundance of bulrushes and cattails provide nesting material and shelter to a wide variety of birds and other small animals. The upland prairie is a mix of grasses, wildflowers (including asters and goldenrods), and a variety of herbs. Controlled burns are employed to maintain the prairies. Fire kills trees and shrubs, but the thick dense mat of prairie roots sends out new shoots soon after a fire. When bison roamed the prairie they helped maintain prairie habitat through grazing. While trees and shrubs cannot survive grazing, grasses thrive on being grazed or mowed.

The refuge contains forested areas and even some shrubby areas containing chokecherry and plum thickets that are popular with songbirds. To improve upland nesting habitat for ducks, the refuge maintains hayfields near the marshes.

■ **ANIMAL LIFE** Lacreek lies in a rich transition zone between western and eastern flora and fauna. This can be most dramatically seen in the refuge's animal life. White-tailed deer associated with eastern forests are plentiful here, while the western mule deer is also present in small numbers. Pronghorns are occasionally seen in the sand hills framing the refuge. Pronghorns and whitetails are definitely an odd couple and are rarely thought of as sharing the same home range.

Pronghorn antelope

Birds The overlapping of ecosystems and wildlife is also evident in the birdlife at the refuge. Eastern and western meadowlarks, kingbirds, and bluebirds all thrive in the refuge. Waterfowl are abundant. Large numbers nest within the refuge and even larger numbers use it as a layover during spring and fall migration. Spring finds concentrations of 14,000 waterfowl and fall tops that with 22,000 in late October and early November. As many as 5,000 ducks nest in the refuge's wetlands and produce 500 to 4,000 hatchlings a year. Between them, nesting colonies of American white pelicans and cormorants contribute 1,000 young birds annually.

Three races of Canada geese are found here, including giant Canada geese that were successfully introduced in the 1960s. Spring and fall brings the thrilling possibility of spotting whooping cranes that occasionally stop at the refuge during migration.

Ring-necked pheasant

Lacreek was one of the first refuges in which a breeding flock of trumpeter swans was successfully established. Since the 1960s, when they were introduced here, their nesting range has continued to expand. They all return to Lacreek for the winter. In a notable case of localized migration, thousands of ring-necked pheasants and sharp-tailed grouse move into the refuge for the winter. The bird checklist numbers 273 species and indicates that Lacreek is a prime birding site from spring through fall. Shorebirds, birds of prey, good owl diversity, and a surprising number of gulls add to the birding fun.

Mammals In addition to the large grazing animals that are often seen, the refuge shelters an interesting mix of animals. The swift fox, once thought to be on the brink of extinction, lives in the refuge, and its population may be rebounding throughout the northern prairie states. At 4 to 6 pounds, it is the smallest member of the fox family. Nocturnal and shy, it feeds on insects, small mammals, and some fruit. The swift fox is gray to yellowish-gray, has a slender body and a black-tipped tail, and lives in plains, arid foothills, and deserts.

Coyotes, which are usually shy, are commonly spotted here, especially in the morning. Bobcats also call the refuge home. The animal that attracts loads of attention from visitors is the black-tailed prairie dog. The prairie dog town covers 15 acres, lies close to a public road, and is easily observed. The prairie dog population was once estimated to be as high as 600 million and this rodent's range stretched from Texas to Canada. Prairie dog towns once extended for 100 miles or more and contained a million of these highly sociable animals. But ranchers poisoned prairie dogs by the millions and today they survive in refuges, preserves, and government parks.

ACTIVITIES

■ **CAMPING:** Primitive camping (no electricity, flush toilets, or showers), picnicking, and swimming are permitted at the 360-acre Little White River Recreation Area on the north side of the refuge. Fires are permitted in the campground fireplaces or in portable fireplace units.

■ **WILDLIFE OBSERVATION:** Because wildlife is abundant and visitors are few in number, and also because the land is largely undisturbed, Lacreek has garnered the reputation of being a great place for viewing wildlife. With its extensive road system, wildlife viewing is often better from a car than on foot. Parking for observation or photography is encouraged, although the public is asked not to block roads, gates, or bridges. Even during the heat of high summer there is plenty to see if viewing is done in the morning and late afternoon.

■ **PHOTOGRAPHY:** There are plenty of subjects from which a photographer can choose. The prairie dog town and a pelican rookery lie near enough to public roads for the car to serve as a blind. Temporary photo blinds are allowed with written permission. The refuge offers outstanding opportunities for waterfowl photography.

HUNTING AND FISHING Anglers may fish in the recreation area, as well as in some of the refuge pools—check with refuge to see which of the pools are currently open. **Northern pike** is the most sought-after fish, and there are also several ponds that are stocked with **trout**. Ice fishing is permitted during the winter months.

You may hunt **pheasant**, **grouse**, and **deer** in the fall months on the Lacreek refuge. All of the hunts require a refuge permit, which is free and available at the refuge office. The deer season is divided into two, beginning with an archery hunt that starts in Sept. followed by a muzzle-loader hunt in Nov. Contact the refuge for more details.

Lake Andes NWR
Lake Andes, South Dakota

Gadwall

This marsh-fringed lake has nurtured and attracted game since time immemorial. Walk the shore of Lake Andes and watch ducks drift across the water or a Franklin's gull strafing the marsh on graceful wings. Glimpse the wind rippling the prairie grass. You will be following in the footsteps of those who first trod this land 10,000 years ago.

HISTORY

The Sioux and their ancestors camped beside Lake Andes and hunted buffalo, elk, and waterfowl. With the coming of Europeans, iron plows transformed the prairie to cropland, and the lake became regionally famous for its largemouth bass. In 1936, by presidential executive order, the Lake Andes refuge was established with an initial 365 acres. Today, the refuge, which lies 10 miles east of the Missouri River and within the Yankton Indian Reservation, has grown to 5,532 acres.

GETTING THERE

To reach the headquarters, drive 2 mi. north of Ravinia, SD, on a county gravel road, turn west on 291st St. and drive 1.5 mi.
- **SEASON:** Refuge open year-round.
- **HOURS:** Dawn to dusk. Headquarters office hours: 8 a.m.–4:30 p.m., Mon.–Fri.
- **FEES:** Free access.
- **ADDRESS:** Lake Andes NWR Complex, R.R. 1, Box 77, Lake Andes, SD 57356
- **TELEPHONE:** 605/487-7603

WHAT TO SEE

- **LANDSCAPE AND CLIMATE** Lake Andes lies within a prairie pothole landscape and is one of thousands of shallow, marsh-fringed ponds, lakes, and wetlands densely scattered across the Dakotas to central Canada. The lake is many times larger than the usual pothole wetland, but like its smaller brethren, Lake Andes survives at the whim of local precipitation. Dikes divide the lake into three units, but there is no effective way to control the water level, simply because there is no reliable water supply. On the average, Lake Andes dries up once every 20 years. Summers are long and hot. Winters can be milder than in the rest of the state but still brutal.

■ **PLANT LIFE** The 4,700-acre lake is ringed with marshes that give way to rolling prairie. The Owens Bay unit, lying on the east side of the lake, shelters the refuge's greatest diversity of habitats. A free-flowing well ensures a viable marsh, with woods, brush, prairie, and pothole ponds all packed into 832 acres.

The prairie pothole habitat teems with birdlife from spring through fall. Migrating waterfowl and shorebirds make great use of Lake Andes. Within the pothole biome every large body of water and every postage stamp-sized piece of wetland that retains water through midsummer is a fecund breeding ground for waterfowl and marsh birds.

■ **ANIMAL LIFE**

Birds The refuge's bird checklist totals 213 species. Three thousand American white pelicans storm into the refuge in April and May, with a few staying on to nest. The fall often sees 200,000 geese and ducks temporarily ensconced on the lake. Tundra swans, greater white-fronted geese, and snow geese add zest to the fall and spring waterfowl show. In late summer large numbers of shorebirds can often be seen along the muddy fringes of the lake, probing for food with their large bills. Among the 25-plus shorebird species seen here are the visually striking ruddy turnstone, American avocet, black-bellied plover, and the red-necked phalarope. Brush, prairie, and wooded habitats add even more birds to the mix.

Mammals The refuge's mammal population ranges in size from the 200-pound white-tailed deer to the under-one-ounce pigmy shrew. It is especially notable that both white-tailed and mule deer are found here.

The striped skunk and the eastern spotted skunk wander the refuge each night. The eastern spotted skunk is about 5 inches shorter than the striped skunk. The difference in their size makes a big difference in their diets. The smaller species eats birds, eggs, insects, and fruits, while the bigger skunk dines on rats, mice, chipmunks, insects, fruits, and berries.

ACTIVITIES

Behind the refuge headquarters, an easy nature trail slips through the unit's many habitats. The lake can be scanned from several county roads that border or cross the lake. The south and center units of the lake are open to fishing, and the center unit is open to waterfowl hunting. Camping is not permitted on the refuge, but the Army Corps of Engineers Fort Randall Dam campground (605/487-7847) is nearby.

SATELLITE REFUGE

■ **Karl E. Mundt NWR** The Karl E. Mundt NWR, just downstream from the Fort Randall Dam, is administrated by Lake Andes. The refuge preserves one of the last untouched stretches of Missouri River bottomland; it is also a major wintering ground for bald eagles. Eagles perch on cottonwoods lining the bottomlands of the river and swoop in to catch fish. The refuge is off limits to the public, but an observation point just below the dam, adjacent to the Army Corps of Engineers campground, offers a front-row seat for eagle viewing. Eagles begin arriving in late Oct. and peak in Dec. and January, when more than 100 may be in residence.

Sand Lake NWR
Columbia, South Dakota

Wetland, Sand Lake NWR

There is no scarcity of sky out here, and in the rose-tinted light of dawn over Sand Lake, all manner of silhouettes fill it: A great blue heron rows along; a dense, raucous flock of Franklin's gulls hovers and wheels above the water in pursuit of breakfast; a grebe patters across the surface and rises into flight; shorebirds in tight, twisting groups flash low along the lake's edges. High above, borne on wings spanning nearly 10 feet, American white pelicans appear, the birds, perfectly spaced in formation, drifting down toward open water.

It goes like this from late March through October at Sand Lake NWR, a 21,498-acre prairie wetland complex with one of the richest assortments of birdlife to be found anywhere in the region. For travelers headed west, a visit will erase the notion of South Dakota as home to sun-seared Badlands and little more. Water and wildlife abound here, and there's a nice range of access as well. The excellent Visitor Center and developed recreation area with picnic facilities, along with a well-maintained auto tour, offer creature comforts for those who desire them. Visitors seeking exploration and a bit of solitude are allowed to hike in cross-country fashion into grasslands and woodlands.

HISTORY

The grassy plains, forested ravines, and varied waters of this landscape were the hunting and fishing grounds of the Sioux in the days before European settlement. Sica Hollow State Park, about 40 miles east of the refuge, preserves a Sioux holy place where spirits of the dead resided. In 1839, French cartographer Joseph Nicollet worked his way through the region, mapping the landscape between the Mississippi and Missouri rivers. In August 1862, the Minnesota Uprising constituted the first clash between Sioux and European settlers, with outbreaks of violence spreading west into South Dakota. In the wake of these troubles, army units and forts were placed throughout the region, including present-day Sisseton, SD, and along the James River.

Settlers on present-day Sand Lake NWR grazed livestock and grew crops. During the early 1930s, the area was devastated by drought and wind erosion, exacerbated by farming practices and soil types. Following its designation as a National Wildlife Refuge in 1935, Company 2749 of the Civilian Conservation Corps (CCC) set up a work camp at Sand Lake. Over the next four years, enrollees constructed two major dams and seven minor dams; nesting islands for water-fowl were created, and a half-million trees planted. The camp was disbanded in July 1939.

GETTING THERE

From Aberdeen, SD, travel 7 mi. east on US 12, turning left (north) at Bath Corner onto County Rd. 16; continue 20 mi., through Columbia, SD, to turnoff for refuge headquarters, just north of the Columbia Recreation Area.

■ **SEASON:** Open from early April to late Sept. Dates vary according to weather from year to year.

■ **HOURS:** Open daylight hours; Visitor Center open weekdays 8 a.m.-4:30 p.m.; extended weekend hours during spring waterfowl migration and some other special events, and in summer—call ahead for weekend hours.

■ **FEES:** Free access.

■ **ADDRESS:** Sand Lake NWR, Columbia, SD 57433

■ **TELEPHONE:** 605/885-6320

TOURING SAND LAKE

■ **BY AUTOMOBILE:** A 15 mile self-guided auto tour, with 12 interpreted stops, is open between April and September. Northern Rd. is also open to vehicles at this time, when passable.

■ **BY FOOT:** Hiking is permitted in season on 40 miles of refuge roads; a 0.75-mile hiking trail originates at the Columbia Recreation Area; travel on unimproved foot trails also permitted. Some reasonably good opportunities for cross-country skiing.

■ **BY BICYCLE:** Bicycling is permitted on refuge auto tour and Northern Rd. and also on surrounding county roads and state highways. The terrain is level to rolling amid sweeping vistas. It's not the most effective means for viewing wildlife; for enjoying the scenery, however, it is hard to beat and popular with area residents.

■ **BY CANOE, KAYAK, OR BOAT:** No boating is allowed on the refuge due to the abundance of overwater nesting birds here.

WHAT TO SEE

■ **LANDSCAPE AND CLI-MATE** Sand Lake is in north-eastern South Dakota, about four miles from the North Dakota border. The refuge lies in the western edge of a large, shallow plain, the old lakebed of Glacial Lake Dakota, which disappeared some 10,000 years ago. Just 25 miles or so to the west, the plain gives way to the rolling hills of the Missouri Coteau, a

Long-billed dowitcher

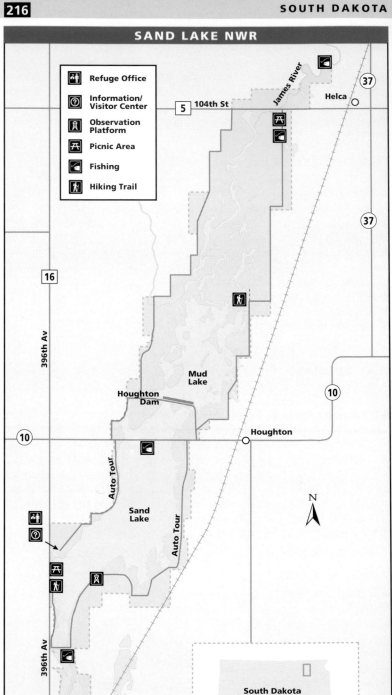

massive glacial moraine dimpled with tens of thousands of prairie "pothole" wet-lands. To the east a short distance is the Prairie Coteau region, another piece of glacial handiwork rising 750 feet above the flat Central Lowlands. Both coteaus, or ridges, extend well into North Dakota and south into Nebraska.

Prior to settlement, both lowlands and surrounding hills featured a matrix of tallgrass prairie interspersed with a tremendous array of wetlands, some perma-nent, many more seasonal or temporary. More than half of these wetlands have been drained and converted to agriculture, by far the dominant land use sur-rounding the refuge today.

Bisected by the 100th meridian, South Dakota marks the transition from the warmer, humid climate of the Mississippi Valley to the semiarid conditions that define the Great Plains. The eastern reaches of the state, including Sand Lake, receive as much as 24 inches of rain annually, nearly double the annual total found west of Pierre, the state capital. Extreme cold in winter and hot, dry sum-mers are not uncommon, but the climate is best characterized as highly variable, with large swings of temperature—from balmy to frigid—occurring through fall, winter, and spring.

■ PLANT COMMUNITIES
Wetlands and open water Few if any wetland complexes left in the region approach the size and diversity of Sand Lake; as a whole, water-associated habi-tats account for more than half of the refuge. Flowing 600 miles through the Dakotas, the James River is the lifeblood of these water-associated habitats. Among the flattest, slowest moving rivers in North America, its "lakes" are merely broad pools in the floodplain. Water levels can vary greatly from year to year—even when water levels are high, winter kills of fish are a part of the natural cycle—and the added control provided by dams only goes so far in maintaining the refuge's preferred matrix of marshes, wet meadows, mudflats, and open water. Looking out across the floodplain from flat ground, it is hard to appreciate just how vast and diverse these marshes are—the dense stands of cattail, phragmites, and bulrush appear as unbroken as grass covering a healthy lawn. From above,

Wilson's phalaropes

however, the view is much different: emergent vegetation appears as a rich mosaic of green within equal amounts of open water. It is a labyrinth of water and deep thickets, ideal for a tremendous variety of birdlife. Sago pondweed and bladderwort are important submergent plants. Wet meadows consist primarily of reed canary grass and cord grass.

Grasslands Sand Lake's 7,417 acres of grasslands are a mixture of nonnative species, including smooth brome and bluegrass, along with some areas reseeded to native species, such as big bluestem, switchgrass, and Indian grass. Other areas are sown with a "dense nesting cover" mixture of sweet clover and alfalfa to facilitate waterfowl nesting. Most of today's grasslands served prior duty as crop fields before the refuge was established. About 1,200 acres today are farmed through cooperative agreements with area landowners. Corn, alfalfa, and grains are produced, with a portion left standing for wildlife. Grasslands are managed with a combination of haying, grazing, and prescribed burns.

Forests Most wooded areas at Sand Lake were introduced by early settlers or in later years by refuge management. Throughout the refuge are shelterbelts of nonnative trees' such as Russian olive and Siberian crabapple, along with green ash. Also present are shrub thickets of cotoneaster, chokecherry, and lilac. Closer to marshes and open water are stands of mature cottonwoods and willows.

■ ANIMAL LIFE

Birds Designated in 1998 as a Wetland of International Importance, Sand Lake is both a migratory stopover and nesting site for a splendid array of water-dependent birds. The refuge supports one of the largest nesting colony of Franklin's gulls in the world. Each spring up to 150,000 pairs take up residence in the dense stands of cattail and bulrush. Assertive, noisy birds, they feed heavily on insects, often in midair; their wariness during nesting season makes them ideal neighbors. Three species of grebe—the eared, western, and Clark's—nest amidst the gulls, as do the black tern and Forster's tern. The white-faced ibis, an incomparably beautiful bird that has declined in the wake of wetland losses, is part of the colony as well. And there are many more: black-crowned night-heron, great egret, cattle egret,

WATER BALLET The abundance of western grebes at Sand Lake provides an exceptional opportunity for visitors to witness their spring courtship ritual, which surely ranks among the most dazzling of any wild creature, bird or otherwise.

The largest of all North American grebes, the western grebe is easy to pick out. Its long, slender neck is bright white along the throat, with a dashing black stripe on the backside, culminating in a black cap and mask over the bird's eyes, which are bright red. Its bill is long and daggerlike, bright yellow.

Between mid-May and mid-July, dozens of western grebes gather in the open water below Houghton Dam. Suddenly a pair rises up, bills pointed skyward, and with a graceful rush they literally dance their way across the water, each bird mirroring the posture and steps of the other in perfect unison. Then another pair joins in, and another. Early morning and late evening are prime dancing hours, though it is not unheard of to see grebes performing in the daytime. Watching from a vehicle parked along the dam works just fine.

double-crested cormorant, and the little blue heron, another species seldom seen in the region.

Waterfowl are present in equally impressive numbers. Nesting species include the gadwall and blue-winged teal, a rare pair or two of American black duck, large numbers of wood ducks, northern shovelers, red head, and ruddy ducks, along with the American wigeon and northern pintail. Waterfowl diversity and numbers reach extremes during spring and fall migration. Sand Lake is an important stopover for snow geese—fall migration is big (250,000 birds) and spring even bigger, when nearly 50 percent of the midcontinent population, a staggering million or so birds, may descend here. Tundra swans may also appear in large numbers during their fall flight, but are uncommon in spring.

A remarkable shorebird community is here, with many species either nesting on site or appearing during migration. Species numbers and diversity are highly dependent upon water levels. Commonly seen birds include the American avocet, willet, Wilson's phalarope, long-billed dowitcher, greater and lesser yellowlegs, marbled godwit, and several sandpipers: upland, pectoral, spotted, stilt, and semipalmated. Present but seen less frequently are the solitary sandpiper, ruddy turnstone, black-bellied and American golden plover, short-billed dowitcher, sanderling, red knot, dunlin, and red-necked phalarope.

Sand Lake's woodlands and grasslands do not lack for wildlife, most notably songbirds. The house wren, orchard oriole, common yellowthroat, western kingbird, brown thrasher, yellow-headed blackbird, American goldfinch, tree swallow, and bobolink are among the more commonly seen species. Less conspicuous but present are several sparrows—the sharp-tailed, clay-colored, swamp, grasshopper, LeConte's—as well as the eastern bluebird, eastern wood pewee, chimney swift, dickcissel, chestnut-collared longspur, warbling vireo, and the black-billed and yellow-billed cuckoo.

Mammals Mammals associated with marshlands or wet meadow areas include mink, muskrat, raccoon, and beaver, any of which may be glimpsed in prime hours, along with such smaller, less visible species as the meadow vole and masked shrew. Along wooded edges and grasslands, white-tailed deer are the most visible

Western grebe

and abundant; coyote, red fox, badger, and a variety of prey species such as the plains pocket gopher and Richardson's ground squirrel, inhabit these same areas.

Reptiles and amphibians Tiger salamanders, northern leopard frogs, western chorus frogs, and the western painted turtle are fairly common throughout the floodplain.

ACTIVITIES

■ **CAMPING AND SWIMMING:** Not permitted. Camping is available at Richmond Lake State Recreation Area, southwest of the refuge, near the city of Aberdeen.

■ **WILDLIFE OBSERVATION:** Though colonial nesting species are found throughout the site, activity is most heavily concentrated in the center of the Sand Lake pool, south of state highway 10. The auto tour, which encircles most of Sand Lake and crosses Houghton Dam at the base of Mud Lake, passes close to water throughout its length. In many areas it is possible to park and walk either closer to the marsh or into woodlands and grassland areas, which yield the most songbird sightings. Some 100 to 200 bald eagles pass through each year from late winter to early spring; in summer, a nesting pair resides just off the refuge. Don't miss the observation tower, also along the auto-tour route, for a fine bird's-eye view of Sand Lake.

> **HUNTING AND FISHING** Waterfowl hunting is permitted in designated areas along the refuge boundary, in accordance with the state-regulated season. There are also special **white-tailed deer** seasons and a late **pheasant** season. Special regulations apply for these hunts; contact the refuge for details.
>
> **Fishing** is permitted at four locations, where county or state roads cross refuge waters; boats are not permitted. **Northern pike** is the most commonly caught species. Contact the refuge for more details.

■ **PHOTOGRAPHY:** Situated on a north-south axis, Sand Lake offers great dramatic potential for images of both sunrise and sunset over the marshlands. Long lenses are standard equipment for shooting nesting gulls, grebes, and other birds—check with refuge staff for tips on the best areas to set up.

■ **HIKES AND WALKS:** Two recreation areas on site offer two different walking experiences. The Columbia Recreation Area, on the southern end of the site, features the popular mowed foot trail with interpretive stops, which traverses mature woodlands, grasslands, and lake-marsh areas for 0.75 mile. North of Mud Lake is the Hecla Recreation Area, accessible in season via the refuge's Northern Road, a well-maintained gravel route that receives far less traffic than the auto tour, making it an ideal hiking trail.

■ **SEASONAL EVENTS:** Eagle Day Celebration held annually in late March, with displays, eagle viewing setups, slide shows, refuge tours, talks, and more; contact refuge Headquarters for dates. International Migratory Bird Day celebration annually in May, with the public invited to join refuge staff conducting bird counts. The refuge celebrates National Wildlife Refuge Week in October with special events. The annual National Audubon Society Christmas Bird Count is popular here—contact the refuge for date. Refuge tours are sponsored by several area groups, including the Aberdeen Parks and Recreation Department and the Glacial Lakes Tourism Association.

Waubay NWR
Waubay, South Dakota

Prairie wildflowers (black-eyed Susans)

Think of it as the last great flourish of the east, with a few resonant overtures from the west. Lush, sun-dappled woodlands are filled with broad trunks of basswood, oak, and elm; songbirds twitter and squirrels chatter, just as they do in distant forests on the far side of the Mississippi. Step out of the trees, however, and the land opens up—the sweep of hills and sky indicate of the great expanse to the west.

The literal translation of the word *waubay* is "a nesting place for birds," a term the Sioux used to describe this region of abundant wetlands, prairie, and woodland thickets. Today, amid crop- and ranchland, 4,650-acre Waubay NWR preserves a swath of the landscape that was. In addition to the refuge, some 40,000 acres in the six surrounding counties comprise the Waubay Wetland Management District, lands that provide vital habitat for a great array of shorebirds, waterfowl, and grassland songbirds.

HISTORY

More than 150 years ago, famed artist George Catlin described this region as "a blue and boundless ocean of prairie." European settlers appeared not long after, and clashes between Sioux Indian culture and settlers moving west would result in the establishment of several military installations in the region, including Fort Sisseton, about 28 miles north of the refuge, today preserved as a state historic park.

By the 1930s, the drought of the Dust bowl and unchecked hunting practices had ravaged waterfowl populations here; giant Canada geese survived only in captive flocks. Waubay was established in 1935, and two years later the geese were reintroduced. The flock has steadily rebuilt itself since then, and today about 15 to 20 pairs of giants nest on the refuge.

GETTING THERE

From Watertown, travel north 31 mi. on I-29 and take Exit 207 onto US 12 west

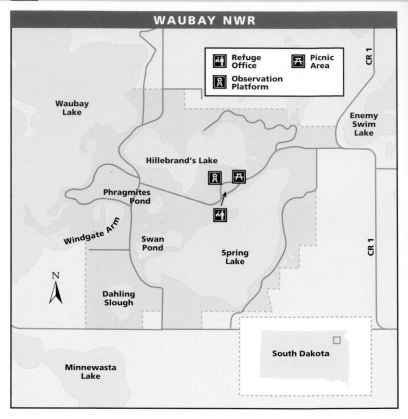

WAUBAY NWR

Refuge Office
Picnic Area
Observation Platform

Waubay Lake

Enemy Swim Lake

Hillebrand's Lake

Phragmites Pond

Windgate Arm

Swan Pond

Spring Lake

N

Dahling Slough

South Dakota

Minnewasta Lake

CR 1

at Summit. Drive west for 5 mi., turning right (north) onto County Road 1; continue 8 mi. to refuge entrance.

■ **SEASON:** Refuge open year-round.

■ **HOURS:** Open daylight hours; refuge headquarters, including a splendid new Visitor Center with many exhibits and displays, is open Mon.–Fri., 8 a.m.–4:30 p.m.

■ **FEES:** Free access.

■ **ADDRESS:** RR 1, PO Box 79, Waubay, SD 57273

■ **TELEPHONE:** 605/947-4521

TOURING WAUBAY

■ **BY AUTOMOBILE:** During normal water levels, an interpreted auto tour traverses the southern reaches of Spring Lake spring through fall.

■ **BY FOOT:** The half-mile Headquarters Loop Hiking Trail and quarter-mile Spring Lake Overlook Trail offer exploration of woodlands, lake, and prairie. In winter—and during normal water levels—a 6-mile cross-country ski trail takes visitors around scenic Hillebrand's Lake.

■ **BY BICYCLE:** Permitted on refuge entrance road only.

■ **BY CANOE, KAYAK, OR BOAT:** No boating permitted on refuge.

WHAT TO SEE

■ **LANDSCAPE AND CLIMATE** Waubay, in northeastern South Dakota, displays the gentle, rolling hills and shallow basins of the Prairie Coteau region, a broad, glaciated band rising 750 feet above the flat Central Lowlands farther east. Formed of mud and gravel left behind by the receding Wisconsin Glacier, the "coteau," or "ridge," extends into North Dakota, and as far south as Nebraska.

The surrounding area, which includes Sand Lake NWR to the northwest, features an exceptionally high density of prairie "pothole" wetlands and shallow prairie lakes. Prior to settlement, these abundant, often seasonal waters were interspersed with tallgrass prairie and occasional pockets of bur oak savanna. At least half of all the original wetlands have been drained and converted to agriculture, by far the dominant land use in the region today.

Bisected by the 100th meridian, South Dakota marks the transition from the warmer, humid climate of the Mississippi Valley to the semiarid conditions that define the Great Plains. The eastern reaches of the state, including Waubay, may receive 22 or more inches of rain annually, nearly double the total found west of Pierre, the state capital. Horrendous cold spells occur in winter, with temperatures plummeting well below zero, topped off by the occasional blizzard. Summers are highly variable—from wet and mild to dry and very hot.

The true meaning of climatic fluctuation, and its effects on wildlife, has been seen here in dramatic proportions in recent years. Beginning in 1994, a wet cycle, the likes of which had never occurred since settlers arrived, delivered four straight years of above-average precipitation to the region. The 200,000-acre Waubay watershed is a closed basin, with no outlet to a river; the result has been a complete remaking of refuge lakes and wetlands. Waubay's 7,000 acres of open water expanded to 25,000 as water levels rose 20 feet in five years. The two shallow prairie lakes on the refuge—Hillebrand's and Spring merged together, isolating refuge headquarters on a wooded island between them. Expanding further, refuge waters then merged with Waubay Lake, which lies outside the western boundary.

Damage to refuge infrastructure has been immense—one road is entirely gone, along with ski and hiking trails, and the sole remaining refuge road has been raised 13 feet to keep up with the water. The other effect has been a near-complete conversion of marshes, sloughs, mud flats, beaches, and shallow, weedy inlets to deep, rippling water. Cropland and a portion of Waubay's prairie have been inundated as well. Refuge lakes, historically too shallow to support a fishery, currently are rich in walleye and yellow perch, courtesy of Waubay Lake.

Prairie lake, Waubay NWR

American avocet

It was tempting to call the event "unprecedented." No one in the region could recall a period of so much water, nor did any historical records indicate it had ever occurred before. Researchers from South Dakota State University studied a number of ancient bur oaks in the area, some of which are 300 to 400 years old. Taking core samples of tree rings and comparing them to available weather data, they concluded that similar wet cycles had occurred at least twice before, in the early 1700s, and again in the 1880s—just about the time settlers arrived.

By no means unprecedented, the story of water at Waubay is an important reminder that the period of "settlement" and occupation of this landscape—of North America as a whole—is so very brief. More surprises lie ahead, including the future of the Waubay watershed. Management has done little to interfere with the process on the refuge aside from maintaining one road so staff can report to work. So an opportunity is here—an unprecedented one—to observe and learn as landscape, climate, wildlife, and plants continue their dynamic relationships.

■ PLANT LIFE

Wetlands and open water The surest way to sterilize a prairie wetland ecosystem is to be consistent. This was the first great lesson learned by refuge managers across the region. Potholes and other wetlands are immensely valuable for wildlife because they fill, evaporate, die out, and recharge. Maintain water at stable levels year after year and the very things that make a wetland worthwhile—rich plant life, invertebrates such as snails and shrimp, and nutrients—dwindle. It is no coincidence that the prairie pothole region accounts for half of all the ducks born in the United States. If ducks thrived on consistency they would live someplace else.

Until the mid-1990s, Waubay featured the full complement of prairie wetlands. The mix included temporary wetlands, mere dimples on grasslands that held water only two or so weeks; and seasonal wetlands, pools from one to three acres in size that filled with rain and snowmelt and held water through mid-June, growing such plants as pondweed, spike rushes, and reed canary grass. Semipermanent wetlands were here, too, deeper, open pools of water surrounded by thick belts of cattail and hardstem bulrush. For all of these wetlands, the annual cycle of filling and drying and recharging proceeded in a manner acceptable to a wide variety of water-dependent birds, most notably ducks, geese, grebes, and shorebirds.

Prior to being inundated, Hillebrand's and Spring lakes were shallow, natural basins, four to six feet deep. Ringed with phragmites, cattails, and other emergent vegetation, and with a number of weedy coves and quiet inlets, these large wetlands had maintained fairly constant water levels throughout the year, over many years. As a result, neither was exceedingly productive for the aforementioned varieties of birds.

The wet cycle has changed everything. Some 1,000 acres of marshes and grasslands are for the time being submerged, incorporated into the new superlake. The number and diversity of nesting waterfowl and shorebirds are somewhat diminished. An entirely different group of water-dependent birds has moved in, taking advantage of new resources—namely sizable fish—never before available here.

Is it a shame or a loss? Not in the least. As sure as the waters rose, they will recede. A drop of just twelve inches will expose new mud flats rich with invertebrates and the shorebirds will reappear. The oxygen-rich water is recharging the lakes, setting the stage for a new burst of aquatic life; the cattails and bulrushes will bide their time.

Grasslands Some 2,000 acres of grasslands at Waubay are a mosaic of native tallgrass prairie and mixed grass prairie. The tallgrass species, including big bluestem and Indian grass, occupy damper sites and the lower reaches of hills, which tend to have better soil. On the higher hills, which tend to be drier and with weaker soil, mixed grass species such as green needlegrass and needle-and-thread are dominant. Including woodland species, about 200 varieties of wildflowers bloom from spring through fall; prairie species include purple prairie clover, lead plant, and black-eyed Susan. Another 500 acres are tame grasses, with a mixture of wheatgrass and alfalfa to provide nesting cover for waterfowl and other birds. A sizable white-tailed deer herd winters on the refuge; some 60 acres of cropland provide winter feed.

Forests Waubay's beautiful mature woodlands provided an important clue about the history of this watershed. The oldest trees here, bur oaks of 300 to 400 years, have remained on exposed high ground despite the great influx of water, which suggests they may have survived it long ago. Samples of tree rings provided further evidence to support this—the trees have been through similar cycles twice. The concentration of wetlands and lakes in this region may also have helped these woodlands endure. Refuge management suspects the prairie wildfires so common before settlement were slowed down by water,

Black-eyed Susan

allowing a uniquely eastern mix of trees to survive. The species here today—basswood, American elm (most all of which are still thriving), green ash, with bur oak dominant—exist on the western edge of their range. Beneath the canopy, decidedly eastern wildflowers such as jack-in-the-pulpit and dutchman's breeches bloom. In the absence of wildfire, other understory species such as wild grape, hack berry, and juneberry have moved in as well.

■ ANIMAL LIFE

Birds The revamped waterscape has been accompanied by a shift in the types of birds using Waubay. Nesting shorebird numbers have diminished, though the American avocet, willet, and marbled godwit continue to raise young in sizable numbers; during spring and fall migration, shorebird numbers and diversity remain high. Waubay was well known as one of the easternmost nesting sites for the red-necked grebe, one of five grebe species here. High water for the moment has eliminated prime nesting and foraging habitats {though they still may be seen and are nesting here}. A decline in nesting numbers of some duck species—most notably redhead and canvasback—has paralleled the decline in emergent vegetation. Mallard, blue-winged teal, and gadwall continue to nest at Waubay in significant numbers. Wood ducks have found the flooded edges of woodlands ideal, and have increased their population. Three years ago, the fish-eating birds—American white pelican, double-crested cormorant, great blue heron, and great egret—began to increase; with the exception of the pelican, all nest on site today. The black, Forster's, and common tern are all readily seen.

Great blue heron

The woodlands support a variety of eastern songbirds—scarlet tanager, rose-breasted grosbeak, indigo bunting—along with many cavity-nesting species, such as the black-capped chickadee, eastern bluebird, tree swallow, northern flicker, and the occasional red-headed woodpecker. The eastern phoebe and willow flycatcher are common, as is the black-billed cuckoo. During spring and fall migration, a fine array of warblers pass through—the Tennessee, blackpoll, orange-crowned, yellow-rumped, ovenbird, and Wilson's are commonly sighted; seen occasionally are the mourning, chestnut-sided, palm, and yellow-breasted chat.

Typical grassland songbirds include the grasshopper sparrow, dickcissel, bobolink, eastern and western kingbird, and, on grassland edges, the clay-colored sparrow.

Mammals The white-tailed deer and muskrat are probably the two most readily encountered mammals here. The muskrat is a favorite meal of the mink, which is also present though fairly elusive. Fox squirrels chatter and forage in the woodlands; the raccoon, striped skunk, red fox, and coyote also inhabit the woodland edges with forays into uplands and lake edges. The prairie is home to the badger and two of its preferred meals—the Franklin's and thirteen-lined ground squirrels. The meadow jumping mouse and masked shrew are also present.

Rarities here include the occasional moose, usually a young bull, wandering south from the Red River Valley in North Dakota, and the fleet-footed pronghorn, which lives in small numbers in the surrounding hills outside refuge boundaries.

ACTIVITIES

■ **CAMPING:** Camping is not permitted on the refuge; excellent facilities are available at Pickerel Lake Recreation Area, six miles north of the refuge on County Road 1.

■ **WILDLIFE OBSERVATION:** When it isn't bitter cold, Waubay in winter offers reliable viewing of northern goshawk and rough-legged hawk, and the occasional snowy owl. Some other notable raptors—the bald eagle, osprey, and peregrine and prairie falcon—are here during spring and fall migration.

■ **PHOTOGRAPHY:** The refuge and surrounding hills are cloaked in emerald green prairie grasses from mid June through mid-July or thereabouts; various wildflowers bloom from late spring through late September. The observation tower near refuge headquarters is a fine spot for panoramic shots.

■ **HIKES AND WALKS:** The influx of water for the time being has greatly limited opportunities for foot travel. A trail to the Spring Lake Overlook remains dry and one of the better places to see refuge prairie lands. Unimproved trails begin near the refuge entrance road and wind south along the eastern boundary, traversing woodlands and prairie. The small trail system around refuge headquarters, with interpreted stops, remains the best place for exploring Waubay's forests.

> **HUNTING AND FISHING** The only hunting allowed on the refuge are various kinds of **deer** hunting through a state lottery. Fishing is not permitted on the refuge.

■ **SEASONAL EVENTS:** The refuge celebrates National Wildlife Week in October with special events.

■ **PUBLICATIONS:** Bird checklist; general visitor information; visitor leaflet on other USFWS lands in South Dakota.

Horicon NWR
Mayville, Wisconsin

Wetland trail, Horicon NWR

Traveling westward on Highway 49, the gently rolling landscape of dairy farms and groomed fields gives little indication of the sights to come. Crest yet another hill, and you'll thrill to the country's largest freshwater cattail marsh, a sea of cattails spread out before you. As the car dips into the valley and traverses the northern end of the marsh, you'll be treated to handsome nature tableaus of water and waterfowl. Birds of all size and feather stalk the reedy edges of marsh pools or float gently across open water.

HISTORY

During the last Ice Age the Wisconsin glacier carved a 14-mile-long-by-6-mile-wide trough in the southeast quarter of the state. As the ice receded, the depression became a shallow lake that filled with vegetation, creating today's 32,000-acre Horicon Marsh. Since the time Neolithic hunters first stalked game in the upper Midwest, the marsh provided a bounty of waterfowl and larger game. When Europeans arrived in the 1840s the marsh was dammed, drained, and neglected, until finally—after 20 years of lobbying—Congress in 1941 protected 21,000 acres as the Horicon National Wildlife Refuge. The other third of the marsh is administered by the Wisconsin Department of Natural Resources.

Since joining the National Wildlife Refuge system the marsh has been recognized as a Wetland of International Importance, a Globally Important Bird Area, and a unit of the Ice Age National Scientific Reserve. Today, the refuge attracts 400,000 visitors annually for the same reason it attracted ancient hunters—for the incredible number and variety of waterfowl.

GETTING THERE

From the junction of US 41 and WI 49, south of Fond du Lac, turn west on WI 49 for 12 mi. to County Rd. Z. Turn south on Z for 3.5 mi. to the Visitor Center. From the junction of highways WI 49 and US 151, when coming from the west, go east on WI 49, 6 mi. to County Rd Z, turn south for 3.5 mi.

■ **SEASON:** Refuge open year-round. Dike Rd., auto tour, and fishing sites open mid-April–mid-Sept.

■ **HOURS:** Sunrise to sunset. Visitor Center, Mon.–Fri. 7:30 a.m.–4 p.m.; weekends early Sept.–early Nov., 9 a.m.–6 p.m.

■ **FEES:** Free access.

■ **ADDRESS:** Horicon NWR, W4279 Headquarters Rd., Mayville, WI 53050

■ **TELEPHONE:** 920/387-2658

TOURING HORICON

■ **BY AUTOMOBILE:** A 3-mile auto tour, in the northwest corner of the refuge, features seven stops with interpretive signs explaining the differing habitat and the wildlife dependent on it. The Main Dike Rd. (3 miles) runs ruler straight into the heart of the marsh and is open to motor traffic. WI 49 crosses the marsh's northern end, and its shoulder is a favorite viewing spot.

■ **BY FOOT:** Three well-maintained hiking trails, totaling 6 miles, lace the northwestern corner of the refuge off WI 49. On the refuge's east side, on Point Rd., the Bud Cook Hiking Area adds 1.5 miles to the refuge's trail system. All trails are open for cross-country skiing in winter.

■ **BY BICYCLE:** Both the 3-mile auto-tour route and the Main Dike Rd. are open to bicycles.

■ **BY CANOE, KAYAK, OR BOAT:** Boating is not permitted in the two-thirds of the marsh controlled by the federal agency. The southern third of the marsh, administered by the Wisconsin DNR, contains several boat-launching ramps. The village of Horicon, at the south end of the marsh, has a canoe livery and raft tours.

WHAT TO SEE

■ **LANDSCAPE AND CLIMATE** The first and lasting impression at Horicon Marsh is of low hills populated by well-groomed farms cupping a grand, oblong expanse of variegated green, here and there dappled with the dark blue of open pools. The thick blanket of vegetation looks impenetrable, yet cattails part as if on cue to frame dark, still pools of water. The Rock River, many small streams, and natural springs, in addition to precipitation, supply the wetlands with water.

Horicon Marsh is not exempt from the Northern Midwest climate. Summers can sometimes be hot and humid, while winter locks the marsh in ice and often buries it under snow. Fall and spring are more often than not cool, crisp, and vibrantly alive with new growth or hillsides splashed with fall colors.

■ **PLANT LIFE** Wetlands cover more than 15,000 acres of the marsh—and nearly every single acre holds cattails. The old, shallow, peat-filled lakebed provides an ideal rooting environment for cattails. Where cattails give way to open water, lily pads vie for their share of the sun. Horicon is a virtual sea of cattails cut by small creeks, open pools, and small

Lily pads

wooded hillocks. Area residents, long awed by this remarkable habitat, have honored it with the nickname "Little Everglades of the North."

A complex of dikes and pumps manipulates the water level in four large impoundments within the marsh. Each year the water level is lowered in some impoundments, creating moist soil units. The muddy, water-saturated fields encourage the growth of smartweed and wild millet. Both are favorite foods of waterfowl.

Horicon is not entirely wetlands. There are 5,000 acres of upland fields and prairie restoration projects and a bare 500 acres of forested land. Most of the trees are scattered among a few small upland woodlots that are great concentrators of songbirds during spring migration. A few trees cluster on small islands within the marsh and add a dramatic flourish to the otherwise vertically challenged landscape.

In spring and summer wildflowers are abundant within woodlots, wetlands, and prairie habitats. The variety of habitats produces not only a wonderful diversity of wildflowers but also a longer bloom season.

■ **ANIMAL LIFE** The simply staggering abundance of wildlife and the facilities and ease of viewing nature's bounty have made Horicon Marsh the top tourist attraction in the two counties in which the marsh lies. Although the marsh boasts a large and varied number of mammals, reptiles, and amphibians, birds steal the show here and account for the vast majority of visitors.

Birds The marsh is one of the finest birding sites in the Midwest. More than 240 bird species have been recorded in the refuge, and more than half that number nest within it. But the bird that put the refuge on the map as a tourist attraction is the Canada goose. The refuge is an important stop for the geese on their semiannual flights between their nesting grounds on Hudson Bay and wintering grounds in southern Illinois. Every fall some 200,000 geese wing into Horicon to feed and rest before continuing their journey south. They are joined at the marsh by thousands of migrating ducks.

The refuge shelters the largest nesting population of redhead ducks east of the

Canada geese

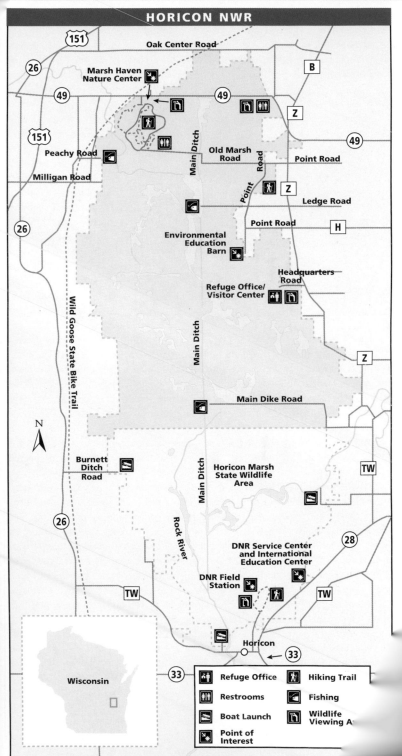

HORICON NWR

Oak Center Road

151

26

49

151

26

Marsh Haven
Nature Center

Peachy Road

Milligan Road

Main Ditch

Old Marsh
Road

Point Road

Point Road

Ledge Road

B

Z

49

49

Z

H

Environmental
Education
Barn

Refuge Office/
Visitor Center

Headquarters
Road

Main Ditch

Z

Main Dike Road

Wild Goose State Bike Trail

N

Burnett
Ditch
Road

Main Ditch

Horicon Marsh
State Wildlife
Area

TW

26

Rock River

DNR Service Center
and International
Education Center

DNR Field
Station

28

TW

TW

Horicon

33

Wisconsin

33

	Refuge Office		Hiking Trail
	Restrooms		Fishing
	Boat Launch		Wildlife Viewing A
	Point of Interest		

Mississippi and, at 1,000 pairs, one of the largest great blue heron rookeries in the Midwest. Other waterfowl and shorebirds commonly seen in the marsh include American black ducks, northern shovelers, and green-winged teals. The "green-winged," North America's smallest dabbling duck, is easily identified by the reddish-brown head and brilliant iridescent green patch behind each eye. Ruddy

Ruddy duck

ducks can usually be seen here in good numbers. The "ruddy," with its webbed feet set well back on its body and a tail that is used as a rudder, is an expert diver. On the downside, it cannot walk upright on land. The ruddy duck dives instead of taking to the air to escape danger. The marsh is also rich in birds, with great egrets, bitterns, sora, rails, and herons regularly seen.

In May, after the last of the geese have moved north, migrating songbirds invade the refuge. The small woodlots, especially those on the auto tour, are powerful magnets for warblers, flycatchers, vireos, woodpeckers, and other woodland birds. The open meadows and prairie restoration projects in the same area attract both eastern and western meadowlarks, bobolinks, and Savannah and field sparrows in addition to numerous other grassland species.

One federal endangered species, peregrine falcons, can often be seen in the refuge. Nesting platforms are provided for two other state-threatened species, Forster's terns and osprey.

Mammals Although birds receive most of the press coverage and public attention, mammals should not be forgotten. The common muskrat, plentiful in the refuge, plays an important part in maintaining desirable marsh habitat. The muskrat eats aquatic plants—and in doing so helps the refuge staff maintain open water for waterfowl. Although muskrats may be trapped within the refuge, permits are closely monitored to ensure that there will always be enough muskrats to maintain open water. Mink, also present, are nearly as aquatic as the muskrats on which they sometimes make a meal. The mink's hind feet are webbed; its diet also includes fish, birds, young waterfowl, and frogs. Cottontail rabbits are plentiful, and white-tailed deer, raccoon, and opossum are commonly sighted. The badger, skunk, and red fox are less often seen, and only the luckiest visitor will catch sight of a coyote or a river otter.

Reptiles and amphibians A variety of turtles inhabit the marsh and are commonly seen sunning themselves on anything that floats. Snapping turtles of prodigious sizes live within the marsh. They commonly grow to 12 inches in diameter (the world's largest, not found here, measured 18.5 inches in diameter and tipped the scales at 86 pounds). Snappers are vicious predators and eat, well, just about everything they want to. Plants, earthworms, other turtles, fish, frogs, snakes, young waterfowl, mammals, and carrion are all food to snapping turtles.

Frogs are numerous and spring into the water, seemingly, from underneath your very footsteps along the edge of the marsh. The most commonly seen snake is the garter snake.

ACTIVITIES

■ **CAMPING:** Horicon NWR does not permit camping, but a number of public and private campgrounds are within a few miles of the refuge. The Fond du Lac Convention and Tourist Bureau (800/937-9123), Horicon Chamber of Commerce (414/485-3200), and Waupun Chamber of Commerce (414/324-3491) can supply information on campgrounds.

■ **WILDLIFE OBSERVATION:** Wildlife viewing is not just good at Horicon, it is spectacular, especially in October and early November, when hundreds of thousands of waterfowl descend on the marsh. A roadside overlook of the refuge at the junction of WI 49 and County Road Z features jaw-dropping views of the waterfowl every fall. In addition to the memorable view of the northern half of the marsh, the pull-off has interpretive displays and public restrooms.

The choicest seat in the house for the fall waterfowl extravaganza is WI 49 where it cuts across the northern tip of the marsh. From the shoulder of the road, and the comfort of a warm car, visitors are treated to close-up views of many waterfowl and the occasional marsh bird. And from the same spot, viewers can

witness an aerial display unmatched in the country when upwards of 200,000 geese darken the sky as they fly out of the refuge in the morning and return in the late afternoon. The sight attracts so many people that 10-mile-long traffic jams are not uncommon on fall weekends.

Waterfowl are not the only birds putting on a show at Horicon. From late April through early June, songbird migrations bring a multitude of smaller birds to the refuge; more than 100 nesting species migrate to and from Horicon from early spring to late fall.

Main Dike Road, which marks the waistline of the refuge, provides close-up views of the middle of a cattail marsh. The auto tour is another way to see a wild variety of wildlife.

Birdwatching

■ **PHOTOGRAPHY:** The view of Canada geese flying in and out of the refuge every morning and evening from W 49 has been named by the U.S. Fish & Wildlife Service as one of the outstanding photographic opportunities in the national refuge system. The auto tour and hiking trails in the northwest corner of the refuge off WI 49 supply nature photographers with plenty of tempting photo opportunities. The refuge's photography blind is just south of the Visitor Center. Photographers must reserve the blind in advance.

■ **HIKES AND WALKS:** Three easy trails at the northwest corner of the refuge give visitors an intimate look at the dynamics of the refuge. Redhead Hiking Trail meanders for 2.5 miles through upland meadows and edges extensive wetlands. Egret Nature Trail, the shortest, leads visitors on a half -mile walk into the marsh on a floating boardwalk. Handicapped-accessible, the boardwalk features a large viewing area equipped with benches, interpretive panels, and spotting scopes. The two-mile Red Fox Nature Trail treats walkers to upland meadows and two woodlots. At the Bud Cook Hiking Area, off Point Road on the east side of the refuge, a half-mile and a one-mile trail meander through uplands habitat.

Several other trails access nonfederal areas of the marsh. On the north side of WI 49, almost opposite the auto tour, the private, not-for-profit Marsh Haven Nature Center includes both an interpretive center and nature trails. From the Wisconsin DNR headquarters, in the village of Horicon, a well-marked hiking trail slips through a small woodland before edging the wetlands. The DNR headquarters' parking lot sits on a hill and bestows a panoramic view of the southern end of the marsh.

■ **SEASONAL EVENTS:** The Horicon Marsh Bird Festival, in early May, includes wildlife activities for children, nature talks, and a reception for the Wisconsin Junior Duck Stamp. National Wildlife Refuge Week Open House in mid-October features slide shows at the auditorium and guided hikes. The Tour de Marsh in late August is a noncompetitive bicycle race and a fund-raiser for charitable organizations.

■ **PUBLICATIONS:** A refuge bird checklist, refuge map, special events calendars, hunting regulations and information, and a general guide with map.

Necedah NWR
Necedah, Wisconsin

Wetland, Necedah NWR

There may be no finer way to while away an afternoon than communing with nature at Necedah NWR. The observation tower overlooking Rynearson Pool No. 1 is a great spot to see a remnant of the Great Central Wisconsin Swamp. The swamp spreads north from the base of the tower until it is interrupted by a tree line near the horizon. On nearly any typical June morning, 4-foot tall sandhill cranes are easily picked out nosing around in the meadowlands, and Canada geese by the dozens poke their heads above the dense marsh. A northern harrier skims the wetlands and meadows looking for its next meal. Look skyward and spy a red-tailed hawk cutting lazy circles in the sky. Closer at hand, pileated woodpeckers rattle pass the tower, and the high-pitched call of the cedar waxwing drifts from nearby trees.

HISTORY

Geography and nature conspired to fashion the perfect wetlands in central Wisconsin. When the last glaciers retreated from the area some 10,000 years ago, they left behind a huge expanse of poorly drained, marshy land interspersed with timbered islands. By the time Europeans arrived on the scene, what was to become known as the Great Central Wisconsin Swamp was a vast complex of peat bogs quartered by sandy ridges, open water, wooded islands, and meadowlands.

The Ho-Chunk, or Winnebagos, looked on the place as a wonderful pantry; European settlers saw it as land going to waste. Beginning in the 1800s the land was drained and lumbered out, and farms were platted. But it was hard to scratch a living from peat bogs and the poor soil of the meadowlands. Few viable farms remained in the area when Franklin Roosevelt signed Executive Order 8065 on March 14, 1939, and created Necedah NWR. The order set apart the land "as a refuge and breeding ground for migratory birds and other wildlife" and signaled the beginning of years of work to restore the land to its former glory.

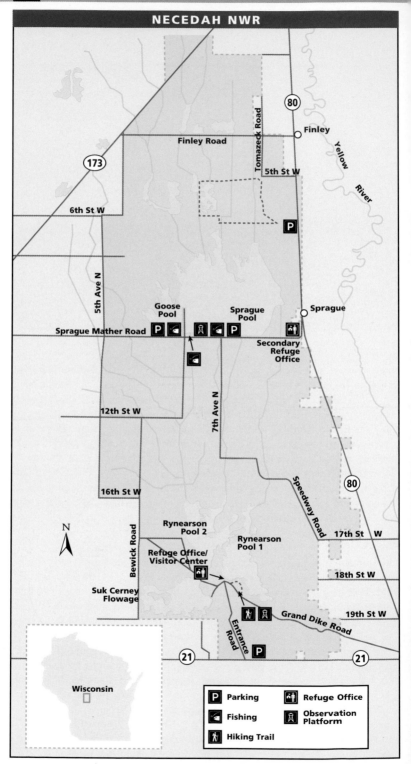

NECEDAH NWR

Finley

Finley Road

5th St W

6th St W

Tomazeck Road

Yellow River

P

5th Ave N

Goose Pool

Sprague Pool

Sprague Mather Road

P | Fishing | Hiking | Fishing | P

Fishing

Sprague

Secondary Refuge Office

12th St W

7th Ave N

16th St W

Speedway Road

17th St W

Bewick Road

Rynearson Pool 2

Rynearson Pool 1

18th St W

Refuge Office/ Visitor Center

Suk Cerney Flowage

Hiking | Observation

19th St W

Grand Dike Road

Entrance Road

P

Wisconsin

P Parking

Fishing

Hiking Trail

Refuge Office

Observation Platform

GETTING THERE

Four mi. west of Necedah on W 21, or 16 mi. east of the junction of W 21 and I-94 on W 21.

■ **SEASON:** Refuge open year-round. No other public use activity is allowed on the refuge during the state gun deer season in Nov.

■ **HOURS:** Refuge, sunrise to sunset. Headquarters office, 7:30 a.m.–4 p.m. weekdays. Call ahead for information on weekend hours.

■ **FEES:** Free access.

■ **ADDRESS:** Necedah NWR, W7996 20th St. West, Necedah, WI 54646

■ **TELEPHONE:** 608/565-2551

TOURING NECEDAH

■ **BY AUTOMOBILE:** Beginning at the observation tower, east of the head-quarters, a 13-mile auto tour (25mph speed limit) uses township roads to reveal the many faces and features of Necedah. At least another 13 miles of township roads traverse the refuge. All are in good condition, and most are kept plowed in winter. Parking is permitted in designated areas only.

■ **BY FOOT:** Three trails totaling 2.1 miles are open to hikers year-round except during deer-hunting season. July 1–Aug. 15 the entire refuge is open for berry-picking. Visitors may snowshoe or cross-country ski anywhere in the refuge between Dec. 12 and March 31.

■ **BY BICYCLE:** Bikers may pedal all of the 26-plus miles of township roads bisecting the refuge. There are no established bike paths.

■ **BY CANOE, KAYAK, OR BOAT:** Nonmotorized craft are permitted on Sprague Mather and Goose pools. Boats with motors are permitted on Suk Cerney Flowage.

WHAT TO SEE

■ **LANDSCAPE AND CLIMATE** Today, woodlands cover much of what was once a rich mixture of meadowlands and wetlands. The meadows were kept free of brush and trees through grazing and fires—both naturally occurring and those set by Native Americans. The present woodlands are the result of modern fire sup-pression efforts. Even after the farms died and the land was abandoned, fires were discouraged, allowing trees to colonize the open land.

   Summers at Necedah are pleasant, often warm. But as the luckless farmers dis-covered, the growing season is short, frost is common, and winters bring plenty of snow and ice.

■ **PLANT LIFE**

Savannah and barrens Settlers, finding it difficult to raise a cash crop on the poor, drought-prone soil, bestowed the name "barrens" on the land that failed them. These "barrens" are now classified as a type of savannah or open woodland, with an understory of grass, wildflowers, and low shrubs. At one time, this type of savannah covered 4.1 million acres in Wisconsin; less than 10,000 acres of the unique habitat remain. Delying its name, Necedah's savannahs were and are any-thing but barren. The grasses, wildflowers, low shrubs, and occasional trees mak-ing up the habitat shelter more than 100 bird species, 44 species of butterflies, and several state and federal endangered and threatened species. Woodlands are being restored to oak barrens. The refuge has also restored 11,000 acres of wetlands—usually in the form of large impoundments. Other wetland habitat includes wet sedge meadows, marshes, numerous small ponds, and 70 miles of ditches used to control water levels.

The most common plants within the oak barrens are sweet fern, blueberry bushes, and goldenrod. A variety of grasses, low fruit-bearing shrubs, wildflowers, and scattered oak and pine trees add to the texture, color, and even the scent of the meadowlands. In late summer, blooming wildflowers turn the meadowlands into a sublime swirl of vibrant colors.

One of the more important plants native to the barrens is wild lupine. Egyptians cultivated the flower and served it as food. Pliny, the Roman scholar and naturalist, claimed that the beans of the plant made one's countenance cheerful and complexion fresh. And the larval stage of the Karner blue butterfly eats only

Beaver

wild lupine; thereby hangs this rare butterfly's existence.

Wetlands The refuge has restored 11,000 acres of wetlands—usually in the form of large impoundments. Other wetland habitat includes wet sedge meadows, marshes, many small ponds, and 70 miles of ditches used to control water levels. Smartweed, arrowhead, water lilies, marigolds and duckweed all grow in the wetlands and provide waterfowl with high-energy food. Soon after it became a refuge the Civilian Conservation Corps planted pine plantations here, but these have been thinned to encourage use by a greater diversity of plants and animals.

■ **ANIMAL LIFE** Although birds are the most conspicuous creatures, many other animals make Necedah special. The state and federally threatened bald eagle, massasauga rattlesnakes, timber wolf, Karner blue butterfly, and Blanding's turtles reside in the refuge.

Birds The refuge leaves no doubt about the importance it places on birds. At the refuge entrance on WI 21, a board tallies the seasonal totals of ducks, geese, and sandhill cranes. The numbers are impressive, easily climbing past the 20,000 plateau for both ducks and geese, and often approaching 2,500 cranes. Necedah is home to the largest concentration of sandhill cranes of any NWR, and their courtship dances draw appreciative audiences from across the Midwest. The birds congregate each spring and fall at the refuge, with the largest numbers peaking in mid-October.

The Canada geese summering at the wetlands are the descendants of a captive flock introduced to the refuge in the 1950s. Another of the refuge's great success stories is the reintroduction of trumpeter swans to the wild. In 1994 eggs were taken from trumpeter swan nests in Alaska and incubated at the Milwaukee Zoo, and the cygnets (young swans) were released at Necedah. The offspring from the hand-reared swans now nest here, and their deep, resounding, buglelike call can be heard throughout the refuge.

A total of 224 bird species are included on the refuge's bird checklist. Joining the Canada geese every year are snow and greater white-fronted geese. The refuge attracts tundra swans, as well as 15 different species of ducks. Common loons, bald eagles, wild turkeys, eastern screech owls, great horned owls, and a variety of raptors nest within the refuge. Warbler and songbird traffic is heavy during spring and fall migration. Although not known as a place to see shorebirds, late spring and early autumn sometimes finds flocks of yellowlegs, a few dowitchers and phalaropes, and a sampling of sandpipers at Rynearson Pools No. 1 and No. 2.

Mammals Mink, otters, and beavers all thrive at the refuge and are most often observed from the area's few bridges. The beaver has done so well that trappers are allowed to take the animal in order to control their population. Squirrels and raccoon are common; and although badgers inhabit the refuge, it is the lucky visitor who sees one. Black bears are occasionally seen, and white-tailed deer are ubiquitous. Necedah marks the southernmost range of the gray wolf in Wisconsin, but it is far more likely that visitors will hear the call of a wolf than see one.

Invertebrates Necedah is home to more than 40 species of butterflies, but one particular butterfly makes this refuge very special. The world's largest population of the rare Karner blue butterfly is found here. The small blue butterfly with a 1-inch wingspan was once plentiful in a narrow band from eastern Minnesota to

New England. Through the destruction of habitat all across its former range, the species may have been wiped out in Ontario, Ohio, Massachusetts, Pennsylvania, and possibly Illinois. The Karner blue produces two broods each year. The eggs of the first brood have overwintered and hatch in April. The larvae feed on upper surfaces of the wild lupine, and in May the larvae pupate; by the end of the month adult butterflies emerge. These adults lay eggs on the lupine in June, and the second brood reaches adulthood in mid-July. Because it is an endangered species, the killing, molesting or destroying of its habitat is a federal crime that carries fines of up to $10,000 and/or a year in jail.

Karner blue butterfly, Necedah NWR

ACTIVITIES

■ **CAMPING:** The refuge does not permit camping but Buckhorn State Park (608/565-2789), about 7 miles south of the Village of Necedah, has 20 camping sites. There are primitive camping sites adjacent to the refuge at the Meadow Valley Wildlife Headquarters Unit.

■ **WILDLIFE OBSERVATION:** Hunting and fishing draw a fair number of people to Necedah every year, but wildlife observation accounts for the vast majority of its 140,000 annual visitors. The best viewing is April through early June and August to early November. The observation tower at Rynearson Pool No. 1 gives a superb view of the pool and grasslands. It takes a while to absorb the view from the tower, but a careful quartering of the expanse should reveal cranes, waterfowl, and birds of prey scattered across the landscape. The tower is a great spot from which to view the cranes' spring and fall courtship dance. Carefully check the shoreline of the pool for otters, mink, and beavers. Rynearson Pools No. 1 and No. 2 fill with geese, ducks, and trumpeter swans every spring and fall.

A wetlands restoration project (completed in conjunction with Ducks Unlimited) on the east side of the Headquarters Road features an observation deck and good views of a pond community. The refuge has two wildlife photo blinds built into the ground near the sandhill crane courtship dancing grounds. Sprague and Goose Pool are good for marsh birds and more waterfowl. Any stand of trees is apt to be filled with warblers and songbirds in May. Wildlife observation can be very rewarding on a slow drive along the many roads bisecting the refuge. Winter birding is often very good. Most of the township roads are drivable except during the worst storms. Horned larks, snow buntings, tree sparrows, redpolls, evening grosbeaks, and rough-legged hawks are all commonly seen on a winter drive.

■ **PHOTOGRAPHY:** Necedah offers unequaled opportunities for photographing sandhill cranes. The refuge has several choice locations to snap the large birds, but the best is the phot blind located adjacent to Rynearson Pool No. 1. Wildflower photo-

THE CHARM OF THE SANDHILL CRANE To see a sandhill crane is to fall under its charm. In flight the crane looks like a bird that has been taught to fly by the Moscow Ballet. It extends its neck straight out in front of its body when flying, unlike great blue herons and egrets, who fly with their necks pulled in close to their body like a kinked hose. The crane balances its long neck in front with legs that extend nearly the same distance from the other end of the body. The bird is kept in flight by the graceful beat of a 7-foot wingspan.

The sandhill crane is equally impressive on the ground. Whether in a field or up to its knees in water, the 4-foot tall, tuxedo-gray bird has an almost stately bearing—even though its rump feathers suggest that it is wearing a bustle, and a red forehead suggests that it just ran headfirst into a door.

The bird lets its hair down when it comes to sex. The sandhill winters in southern Florida, Texas, New Mexico, and Arizona and flies north every spring to breeding grounds that reach from Michigan's Upper Peninsula and northern Wisconsin to the Arctic Circle. On its way north and on its nesting sites, sandhill cranes perform courtship dances. The choreography includes crouching or bowing and graceful 6- to 8-foot leaps into the air that may be repeated so often that the bird begins to resemble a bouncing ball. The leaps are accompanied by the flapping of wings and great yodeling cries that can be heard for miles.

raphy is at its prime in late summer, and fall colors are vibrant here. Necedah presents amateur photographers with plenty of challenges and technical problems, from too much available light to dealing with a flat, nearly limitless landscape.

■ **HIKES AND WALKS:** Of the refuge's three established trails, the shortest is a 0.1-mile stroll from the parking lot to the observation tower overlooking Rynearson Pool No. 1. The trail is a good place to look for woodpeckers and warblers. As the name implies, the mile-long Pair Ponds Trail takes hikers to two ponds on the west side of the refuge. Hikers should watch for waterfowl, shorebirds, marsh birds, reptiles, and amphibians.

Sandhill crane

Lupine Trail is a 1-mile circuit through an oak savannah painted blue when the wild lupine is in bloom. This is the place to be on the lookout for the rare Karner blue butterflies, especially from late May to early June and late July to early August, when the butterfly's two annual hatches occur. The entire refuge is open to hikers and gatherers of wild food from July 1 to August 15.

Although blueberries are the most sought after wild fruits, blackberries and raspberries are also picked. A refuge brochure suggests the best picking sites.

■ **SEASONAL EVENTS:** The refuge celebrates National Wildlife Refuge Week in October with special events.

■ **PUBLICATIONS:** Bird checklist, fishing and hunting regulations, auto-tour guide, and a general introductory brochure with map.

Trempealeau NWR

Trempealeau, Wisconsin

Sand prairie, Trempealeau NWR

Although the great river is out of sight from almost anywhere in Trempealeau NWR, there is an almost tactile sense of being in the presence of the Father of Waters. Indeed, the backwaters of the Mississippi River pinch the refuge's meager share of terra firma into knobby peninsulas and narrow isthmuses. The high wooded bluffs—looming over the refuge on the east and marking the western horizon—announce that this land exists at the river's whim.

HISTORY

The Mississippi may have created Trempealeau's unique and valuable habitats, but human intervention helped preserve them. Beginning in the 1850s, three railroads laid track along the east side of the Mississippi, forming—by accident rather than design—a large triangle enclosing much of the refuge's wetlands. The railroad grades served as dikes, easing sedimentation and reducing pollution within the triangle. Recognizing its special capacity to provide shelter and breeding grounds for migratory birds, President Franklin Roosevelt, by executive order, made the area a National Wildlife Refuge in 1936.

GETTING THERE

From Centerville, WI, take WI 35/WI 54 west for 3.25 mi. to West Prairie Rd. Turn south and drive 1.25 mi. on West Prairie to the refuge entrance. From Winona, Minnesota, cross the Mississippi on W 54. On the east side, turn right at the light and drive 5 mi. east on WI 35/WI 54 to West Prairie Rd. and turn south.

- **SEASON:** Refuge open year-round.
- **HOURS:** Sunrise to sunset. Headquarters, Mon.–Fri., 7:30 a.m.–4 p.m.
- **FEES:** Free access.
- **ADDRESS:** Trempealeau NWR, W 28488 Refuge Rd., Trempealeau, WI 54661
- **TELEPHONE:** 608/539-2311

TOURING TREMPEALEAU

■ **BY AUTOMOBILE:** A 5-mile self-guided Wildlife Drive leads motorists through the refuge's three distinct habitats, to an observation deck, and trailheads; it parallels the Trempealeau River.

■ **BY FOOT:** Two self-guided nature trails—each about 0.5 miles long—explore different habitats within the refuge. Several miles of dikes and service roads (closed to motorists) invite further exploration by hikers.

■ **BY BICYCLE:** Bikes may be ridden on all refuge roads including some that are closed to public vehicles. The Great River State Trail (a bicycle trail) passes through the refuge on Wildlife Drive.

■ **BY CANOE, KAYAK, OR BOAT:** A boat launch gives access to canoes, hand-powered boats, and boats equipped with electric motors.

WHAT TO SEE

■ **LANDSCAPE AND CLIMATE** The classical ecosystems and landscapes found within the floodplain of any large river are present at Trempealeau. Marsh, hardwood swamps, and large open pools account for 4,400 of the refuge's 5,700 acres. The 1,300 acres of dry land are divided between old meadows, brush land, scattered woods, and a few hundred precious acres of sand prairie.

Trempealeau has warm, pleasant summers with temperatures usually in the mid 80s. Winters can be hard with temperatures often falling below zero. The Mississippi and its backwaters freeze solid, and snow blankets the land.

■ **PLANT COMMUNITIES** The most distinctive and horticulturally impor-tant land in the refuge is the 300-plus acres of sand prairie. Little and big bluestem, Indian grass, and sideoats grama are just some of the native grasses growing within the sand prairies. The prairie puts on a flower show from spring through fall, with colorful blooms and grasses that can grow to 8 feet tall. The diverse land-scape includes tree-lined riverbanks and shrubby areas.

The wetlands also vie for equal attention during the summer, when white and yellow water lilies and lotus bloom. Arrowhead and pickerelweed, the latter a member of the water hyacinth family, bloom in abundance in the summer. By midsummer the large pool in front of the observation deck is blanketed by lotus, lily pads, and mats of floating vegetation. The pads provide good cover to the many broods of wood ducks, mallards, and blue-winged teal, while the mats are used as nesting platforms by black terns.

■ **ANIMAL LIFE** Animal life is abundant at Trempealeau NWR. The refuge is a rest and refueling stop on the Mississippi Flyway— one of the most important and heavily traveled bird migration routes in the world. Most of the refuge's 60,000 annual visitors are drawn here by the birdlife. Birds at Trempealeau account for all but one of the species that are listed by the state or federal gov-ernment as threatened. The

Mallard

Blanding's turtle may be threatened in the state and scarce in the rest of Wisconsin, but it is commonly seen here throughout the summer.

Birds The refuge's bird checklist totals more than 250 birds, with new species still being added. In October, upwards of 50 eagles converge on the refuge to rest and feed before continuing south. In March, it is not uncommon to have more than a hundred eagles dining on winter-killed fish while waiting for the ice to break up on the upper Mississippi. For the last several years, at least one pair of eagles has set up housekeeping in nests that can reach 7 to 8 feet in diameter and measure up to 12 feet deep. State or nationally threatened birds that nest or pass through the refuge include osprey, Forster's tern, peregrine falcon, and the great egret.

Huge flights of ducks and geese call on the refuge each fall as the birds head south for the winter. Included in the fall gathering are 600 to 900 tundra swans, which arrive here in mid-October and leave just before the freeze-up. Spring

migration begins in March with the arrival of waterfowl. In April, birds of prey and vultures join the northward stream of birds flowing up the Mississippi, and by mid-May songbirds flood the refuge. Other nesters at Trempealeau include yellow-headed blackbirds, sora, Virginia rails, and the crow-sized pileated woodpecker, which sports a punk rocker's red hairdo. (The creator of Woody the Woodpecker modeled Woody's laugh after the pileated's call.) American white pelicans were sighted at Trempealeau during almost every summer in the 1990s. Prairie nesters at the refuge include eastern meadowlarks, grasshopper sparrows, and dickcissels.

Mammals The refuge is home to many of the most common small mammal species found throughout the Midwest, includ-

Pileated woodpecker

ing skunk, raccoon, woodchuck, and muskrat. No matter how common, white-tailed deer are always an enjoyable and frequent sight at Trempealeau. The gray fox breeds within the refuge in Jan. or Feb., and two months later three to five kits are born. Red fox, coyotes, and the gray fox are all more commonly seen in the winter, when they come down to the refuge from the hills. River otters are best seen in the winter, when they play in the water or slide on the ice. Beavers and muskrats are plentiful and may be trapped, with a permit.

ACTIVITIES

■ **CAMPING AND SWIMMING:** Neither camping nor swimming is permitted in the refuge, but Perrot State Park, just to the south, contains 96 campsites (608/534-6409).

■ **WILDLIFE OBSERVATION:** From early spring through late fall, wildlife

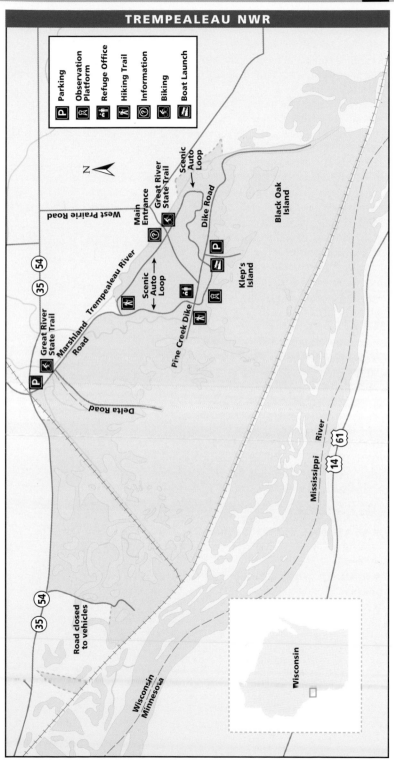

observation is a favored activity at Trempealeau. A large observation deck with two mounted scopes—one wheelchair-accessible—overlooks an immense pool and provides a front-row seat for the show on the busy Mississippi Flyway. An incredible number of birds can be seen just from the deck in the course of a year. The observation deck and the boat-launching basin are the best places to look for eagles.

The refuge's many trails and roads lead to a variety of different habitats and viewing opportunities. Pine Creek Dike is rife with birdlife, and other dikes pay equally good dividends. Best wildlife viewing at the refuge is March through May and Sept. through early Nov. Fall sees the largest concentrations of birds at Trempealeau and the largest influx of visitors who come to enjoy the spectacle.

■ **PHOTOGRAPHY:** Although Trempealeau has no photo blinds, wildlife photography can be productive, especially from a car on the wildlife drive. Even a modest telephoto lens offers the promise of snapping a few eagle portraits in October and March. If you're stealthy and quiet, you may even capture close-ups of birds along the Pine Creek Dike. The refuge also presents a unique opportunity to photograph the many grasses and flowers common to the uncommon sand prairie.

■ **HIKES AND WALKS:** The first of the self-guided nature trails starts near the observation deck and takes the inquisitive on a jaunt through a quiet, wooded area that quickly becomes a pulse-pounder when surprised ducks rocket up through the trees. The trail through the sand prairie begins with a living display of labeled plants commonly found on the prairie; it then circles through a moving sea of grass dappled with wildflowers. There is a shorter, wheelchair-accessible loop of the half-mile prairie trail. Kiep's Island, reached by a narrow isthmus, awards hikers with an assortment of striking views. In the winter, cross-country skiers (no groomed trails) and snowshoers may explore the entire refuge.

■ **SEASONAL EVENTS:** National Wildlife Refuge Week—the second week in October—is celebrated with nature walks, motor tours, and nature crafts for children.

■ **PUBLICATIONS:** Refuge brochure with map, bird checklist, and sand prairie brochure.

HUNTING AND FISHING There is a nine-day firearm **deer** season in Nov. and an archery deer season in Dec. The handicapped have their own deer season. No other hunting is allowed. Fishing is permitted—from shore and boat—but some areas may be closed to anglers. **Bullheads** are the fish most often taken, but **northern pike** and **panfish** are also hooked. Ice fishing is permitted in season.

Appendix

NONVISITABLE NATIONAL WILDLIFE REFUGES

Below is a list of other National Wildlife Refuges in the Northern Midwest. These refuges are not open to the public.

Michigan Islands NWR
c/o Shiawassee NWR
6975 Mower Rd.
Saginaw, MI 48601
517/777-5930

Mille Lacs NWR
c/o Rice Lake NWR
Rte. 2, Box 67
McGregor, MN 55760
218/768-2402

Bone Hill NWR
c/o Kulm WMD
P.O. Box E
Kulm, ND 58456-0170
701/647-2866

Dakota Lake NWR
c/o Kulm WMD
P.O. Box E
Kulm, ND 58456-0170
701/647-2866

Half-way Lake NWR
c/o Valley City WMD
11515 River Rd.
Valley City, ND 58072-9619
701/845-3466

Hobart Lake NWR
c/o Valley City WMD
11515 River Rd.
Valley City, ND 58072-9619
701/845-3466

Johnson Lake NWR
c/o Arrowwood NWR
7745 11th St. SE
Pingree, ND 58476
701/285-3341

Lake Otis NWR
c/o Audubon NWR
RR 1, P.O. Box 16
Coleharbor, ND 58531
701/442-5474

Lost Lake NWR
c/o Audubon NWR
RR 1, P.O. Box 16
Coleharbor, ND 58531
701/442-5474

McLean NWR
c/o Audubon NWR
RR 1, P.O. Box 16
Coleharbor, ND 58531
701/442-5474

Pretty Rock NWR
c/o Audubon NWR
RR 1, P.O. Box 16
Coleharbor, ND 58531
701/442-5474

Shell Lake NWR
c/o Des Lacs NWR
P.O. Box 578
Kenmare, ND 58746-0578
701/385-4046

Stoney Slough NWR
c/o Valley City WMD
11515 River Rd.
Valley City, ND 58072-9619
701/845-3466

Tomahawk NWR
c/o Valley City WMD
11515 River Rd.
Valley City, ND 58072-9619
701/845-3466

White Lake NWR
c/o Audubon NWR
RR 1, P.O. Box 16
Coleharbor, ND 58531
701/442-5474

Karl E. Mundt NWR
c/o Lake Andes NWR
38672 291st St.
Lake Andes, SD 57356-6838
605/487-7603

West Sister Island NWR
c/o Ottawa NWR
14000 West State Rte. 2
Oak Harbor, OH 43449
419/898-0014

FEDERAL RECREATION FEES

Some—but not all—NWRs and other federal outdoor recreation areas require payment of entrance or use fees (the latter for facilities such as boat ramps). There are several congressionally authorized entrance fee passes:

■ ANNUAL PASSES

Golden Eagle Passport Valid for most national parks, monuments, historic sites, recreation areas and national wildlife refuges. Admits the passport signee and any accompanying passengers in a private vehicle. Good for 12-months. Purchase at any federal area where an entrance fee is charged. The 1999 fee for this pass was $50.00

Federal Duck Stamp Authorized in 1934 as a federal permit to hunt waterfowl and as a source of revenue to purchase wetlands, the Duck Stamp now also serves as an annual entrance pass to NWRs. Admits holder and accompanying passengers in a private vehicle. Good from July 1 for one year. Valid for *entrance* fees only. Purchase at post offices and many NWRs or from Federal Duck Stamp Office, 800/782-6724, or at Wal-Mart, Kmart or other sporting good stores.

■ LIFETIME PASSES

Golden Access Passport Lifetime entrance pass—for persons who are blind or permanently disabled—to most national parks and NWRs. Admits signee and any accompany passengers in a private vehicle. Provides 50% discount on federal use fees charged for facilities and services such as camping, or boating. Must be obtained in person at a federal recreation area charging a fee. Obtain by showing proof of medically determined permanent disability or eligibility for receiving benefits under federal law.

Golden Age Passport Lifetime entrance pass—for persons 62 years of age or older—to national parks and NWRs. Admits signee and any accompanying passengers in a private vehicle. Provides 50% discount on federal use fees charged for facilities and services such as camping, or boating. Must be obtained in person at a federal recreation area charging a fee. One-time $10.00 processing charge. Available only to U.S. citizens or permanent residents.

For more information, contact your local federal recreation area for a copy of the *Federal Recreation Passport Program* brochure.

VOLUNTEER ACTIVITIES

Each year, 30,000 Americans volunteer their time and talents to help the U.S. Fish & Wildlife Service conserve the nation's precious wildlife and their habitats. Volunteers conduct Fish & Wildlife population surveys, lead public tours and other recreational programs, protect endangered species, restore habitat, and run environmental education programs.

The NWR volunteer program is as diverse as are the refuges themselves. There is no "typical" Fish & Wildlife Service volunteer. The different ages, backgrounds, and experiences volunteers bring with them is one of the greatest strengths of the program. Refuge managers also work with their neighbors, conservation groups, colleges and universities, and business organizations.

A growing number of people are taking pride in the stewardship of local national wildlife refuges by organizing non-profit organizations to support individual refuges. These refuge community partner groups, which numbered about 200 in 2,000, have been so helpful that the Fish & Wildlife Service, National Audubon Society, National Wildlife Refuge Association, and National Fish & Wildlife Foundation now carry out a national program called the "Refuge System Friends Initiative" to coordinate and strengthen existing partnerships, to jump start new ones, and to organize other efforts promoting community involvement in activities associated with the National Wildlife Refuge System.

For more information on how to get involved, visit the Fish & Wildlife Service Homepage at http://refuges.fws.gov; or contact one of the Volunteer Coordinator offices listed on the U.S. Fish & Wildlife General Information list of addresses below or the U. S. Fish & Wildlife Service, Division of Refuges, Attn: Volunteer Coordinator, 4401 North Fairfax Drive, Arlington, VA 22203; 703/358-2303.

U.S. FISH & WILDLIFE GENERAL INFORMATION

Below is a list of addresses to contact for more inforamation concerning the National Wildlife Refuge System.

U.S. Fish & Wildlife Service Division of Refuges
4401 North Fairfax Dr., Room 670
Arlington, Virginia 22203
703/358-1744
Web site: fws.refuges.gov

F & W Service Publications:
800/344-WILD

U.S. Fish & Wildlife Service Pacific Region
911 NE 11th Ave.
Eastside Federal Complex
Portland, OR 97232-4181
External Affairs Office: 503/231-6120
Volunteer Coordinator: 503/231-2077
The Pacific Region office oversees the refuges in California, Hawaii, Idaho, Nevada, Oregon, and Washington.

U.S. Fish & Wildlife Service Southwest Region
500 Gold Ave., SW
P.O. Box 1306
Albuquerque, NM 87103
External Affairs Office: 505/248-6285
Volunteer Coordinator: 505/248-6635
The Southwest Region office oversees the refuges in Arizona, New Mexico, Oklahoma, and Texas.

U.S. Fish & Wildlife Service Great Lakes-Big Rivers Region
1 Federal Dr.
Federal Building
Fort Snelling, MN 55111-4056
External Affairs Office: 612/713-5310
Volunteer Coordinator: 612/713-5444
The Great Lakes-Big Rivers Region office oversees the refuges in Iowa, Illinois, Indiana, Michigan, Minnesota, Missouri, Ohio, and Wisconsin.

U.S. Fish & Wildlife Service Southeast Region
1875 Century Center Blvd.
Atlanta, GA 30345
External Affairs Office: 404/679-7288
Volunteer Coordinator: 404/679-7178
The Southeast Region office oversees the refuges in Alabama, Arkansas, Florida, Georgia, Kentucky, Lousiana, Mississippi, North Carolina, South Carolina, Tennessee, and Puerto Rico.

U.S. Fish & Wildlife Service Northeast Region
300 Westgate Center Dr.
Hadley, MA 01035-9589
External Affairs Office: 413/253-8325
Volunteer Coordinator: 413/253-8303
The Northeast Region office oversees the refuges in Connecticut, Delaware, Massachusetts, Maine, New Hampshire, New Jersey, New York, Pennsylvania, Rhode Island, Vermont, Virginia, West Virginia.

U.S. Fish & Wildlife Service Mountain-Prairie Region
P.O. Box 25486
Denver Federal Center
P. O. Box 25486
Denver, CO 80225
External Affairs Office: 303/236-7905
Volunteer Coordinator: 303/236-8145, x 614
The Mountain-Prairie Region office oversees the refuges in Colorado, Kansas, Montana, Nebraska, North Dakota, South Dakota, Utah, and Wyoming.

U.S. Fish & Wildlife Service Alaska Region
1011 East Tudor Rd.
Anchorage, AK 99503
External Affairs Office: 907/786-3309
Volunteer Coordinator: 907/786-3391

NATIONAL AUDUBON SOCIETY WILDLIFE SANCTUARIES

National Audubon Society's 100 sanctuaries comprise 150,000 acres and include a wide range of forest habitats. Audubon managers and scientists use the sanctuaries for rigorous field research and for testing wildlife management strategies. The following is a list of 24 sanctuaries open to the public. Sanctuaries open by appointment only are marked with an asterisk.

EDWARD M. BRIGHAM III ALKALI LAKE SANCTUARY*
c/o North Dakota State Office
118 Broadway, Suite 502
Fargo, ND 58102
701/298-3373

FRANCIS BEIDLER FOREST SANCTUARY
336 Sanctuary Rd.
Harleyville, SC 29448
843/462-2160

BORESTONE MOUNTAIN SANCTUARY
P.O. Box 524
118 Union Square
Dover-Foxcroft, ME 04426
207/564-7946

CLYDE E. BUCKLEY SANCTUARY
1305 Germany Rd.
Frankfort, KY 40601
606/873-5711

BUTTERCUP WILDLIFE SANCTUARY*
c/o New York State Office
200 Trillium Lane
Albany, NY 12203
518/869-9731

CONSTITUTION MARSH SANCTUARY
P.O. Box 174
Cold Spring, NY, 10516
914/265-2601

CORKSCREW SWAMP SANCTUARY
375 Sanctuary Rd. West
Naples, FL 34120
941/348-9151

FLORIDA COASTAL ISLANDS SANCTUARY*
410 Ware Blvd., Suite 702
Tampa, FL 33619
813/623-6826

EDWARD L. & CHARLES E. GILLMOR SANCTUARY*
3868 Marsha Dr.
West Valley City, UT 84120
801/966-0464

KISSIMMEE PRAIRIE SANCTUARY*
100 Riverwoods Circle
Lorida, FL 33857
941/467-8497

MAINE COASTAL ISLANDS SANCTUARIES*
Summer (June–Aug.):
12 Audubon Rd.
Bremen, ME 04551
207/529-5828

MILES WILDLIFE SANCTUARY*
99 West Cornwall Rd.
Sharon, CT 06069
860/364-0048

NORTH CAROLINA COASTAL ISLANDS SANCTUARY*

720 Market St.
Wilmington, NC 28401-4647
910/762-9534

NORTHERN CALIFORNIA SANCTUARIES*

c/o California State Office
555 Audubon Place
Sacramento, CA 95825
916/481-5440

PINE ISLAND SANCTUARY*

P.O. Box 174
Poplar Branch, NC 27965
919/453-2838

RAINEY WILDLIFE SANCTUARY*

10149 Richard Rd.
Abbeville, LA 70510-9216
318/898-5969 (Beeper: leave message)

RESEARCH RANCH SANCTUARY*

HC1, Box 44
Elgin, AZ 85611
520/455-5522

RHEINSTROM HILL WILDLIFE SANCTUARY*

P.O. Box 1
Craryville, NY 12521
518/325-5203

THEODORE ROOSEVELT SANCTUARY

134 Cove Rd.
Oyster Bay, NY 11771
516/922-3200

LILLIAN ANNETTE ROWE SANCTUARY

44450 Elm Island Rd.
Gibbon, NE 68840
308/468-5282

SABAL PALM GROVE SANCTUARY

P.O. Box 5052
Brownsville, TX 78523
956/541-8034

SILVER BLUFF SANCTUARY*

4542 Silver Bluff Rd.
Jackson, SC 29831
803/827-0781

STARR RANCH SANCTUARY*

100 Bell Canyon Rd.
Trabuco Canyon, CA 92678
949/858-0309

TEXAS COASTAL ISLANDS SANCTUARIES

c/o Texas State Office
2525 Wallingwood, Suite 301
Austin, TX 78746
512/306-0225

BIBLIOGRAPHY AND RESOURCES

Birds

Powers, Tom. *Great Birding in the Great Lakes,* Davison, Mich.: Walloon Press, 1998.

Terres, John K. *Audubon Society Encyclopedia of North American Birds*, Avenel, N.J.: Wings Books, 1995.

Tessen, Daryl D. *Wisconsin's Favorite Bird Haunts*, 3rd Edition, De Pere, Wis.: Wisconsin Society for Ornithology, 1989.

Thomson, Tom. *Birding in Ohio*, Bloomington, Ind.: University of Indiana, 1994.

Botany

Aaseng, et. al. *Minnesota's Native Vegetation: A Key to Natural Communities,* Biological Report No. 20, Version 1.5, St. Paul, Minn.: Minnesota Dept. of Natural Resources, 1993.

Benyus, Janine. *A Field Guide to Wildlife Habitats of the Eastern United States.* New York: Simon and Schuster, 1989.

Benyus, Janine. *A Field Guide to Wildlife Habitats of the Western United States.* New York: Simon and Schuster, 1989.

Coffey, Timothy. *History and Folklore of North American Wildflowers,* New York: Houghton Mifflin, 1993.

Ladd, Doug and Frank Oberle. *Tallgrass Prairie Wildflowers,* Helena, Mont.: Falcon Press, 1995.

Madson, John and Frank Oberle. *Tallgrass Prairie,* Helena, Mont.: Falcon Press, 1993.

Madson, John. *Where The Sky Began: Land of the Tallgrass Prairie,* Boston: Houghton Mifflin Co., 1982.

Sutton, Anne and Myron Sutton. *National Audubon Society Nature Guides, Eastern Forests,* New York: Knopf, 1985.

Field Guides

Collins, Henry Hill, Jr. *Harper & Row's Complete Field Guide to North American Wildlife, Eastern Region,* New York: Harper & Row, 1981.

Duda, Mark Damian. *Watching Wildlife: Tips, Gear and Great Places for Enjoying America's Wild Creatures,* Helena, Mont.: Falcon Press, 1995.

Knue, Joseph. *North Dakota Wildlife Viewing Guide,* Helena, Mont.: Falcon Press, 1992.

Niering, William A. *Audubon Society Field Guide to North American Wildflowers, Eastern Region,* New York: Knopf, 1979.

Peterson, Roger Tory. *A Field Guide to the Birds East of the Rockies,* 4th Edition, Boston: Houghton Mifflin Co., 1980.

Peterson, Roger Tory. *Peterson Field Guides: Western Birds,* Boston: Houghton Mifflin Co., 1961.

Shepherd, Lansing. *The Smithsonian Guides to Natural America: The Northern Plains,* New York: Random House, 1996.

Stokes, Donald and Lillian. *Stokes Field Guide to Birds, Eastern Region,* Boston: Little, Brown, 1996.

Tilden, J. W. and Arthur C. Smith. *Western Butterflies,* Boston: Houghton Mifflin Co., 1986.

Whitaker, John, Jr. *National Audubon Society Field Guide to North American Mammals,* New York: Knopf, 1996.

Mammals

Grassy, John and and Chuck Keane. *National Audubon Society First Field Guide to Mammals,* New York: Scholastic Books, 1998.

Kurta, Allen. *Mammals of the Great Lakes Region,* Ann Arbor, Mich.: University of Michigan Press, 1995.

Nelson, Richard. *Heart and Blood: Living with Deer in America,* New York: Knopf, 1997.

Petersen, David. *Racks: A Natural History of Antlers and the Animals That Wear Them,* Santa Barbara, Ca.: Capra Press, 1991.

Rue, Leonard Lee III. *Sportman's Guide to Game Animals,* New York: Harper & Row, 1972.

General

Ambrose, Stephen. *Undaunted Courage: Meriwether Lewis, Thomas Jefferson, and the Opening of the American West,* New York: Simon and Schuster, 1996.

Brandon, William. *Indians,* Boston: Houghton Mifflin Co., 1987.

Farb, Peter. *Face of North America: The Natural History of a Continent,* New York: Harper and Row, 1963.

Halpern, Daniel, Ed. *On Nature: Nature, Landscape, and Natural History,* San Francisco: North Point Press, 1986.

McKibben, Bill. *The End of Nature,* New York, Doubleday, 1989.

Noss, Reed and Robert L. Peters. *Endangered Ecosystems: A Status Report on America's Vanishing Habitat and Wildlife,* Washington. D.C.: Defenders of Wildlife, 1995.

Stewart, Frank. *A Natural History of Nature Writing,* Washington, D.C.: Island Press, 1995.

Wilson, Edward O. *Consilience: The Unity of Knowledge,* New York: Knopf, 1998.

GLOSSARY

Accidental   A bird species seen only rarely in a certain region and whose normal territory is elsewhere. *See also* occasional.

Acre-foot   The amount of water required to cover one acre one foot deep.

Alkali sink   An alkaline habitat at the bottom of a basin where there is moisture under the surface.

Alluvial   Clay, sand, silt, pebbles and rocks deposited by running water. River floodplains have alluvial deposits, sometimes called alluvial fans, where a stream exits from mountains onto flatland.

Aquifer   Underground layer of porous water-bearing sand, rock, or gravel.

Arthropod   Invertebrates, including insects, crustaceans, arachnids, and myriapods, with a semitransparent exoskeleton (hard outer structure) and a segmented body, with jointed appendages in articulated pairs.

ATV   All-Terrain-Vehicle. *See also* 4WD and ORV.

Barrier island   Coastal island produced by wave action and made of sand. Over time the island shifts and changes shape. Barrier islands protect the mainland from storms, tides, and winds.

Basking   The habit of certain creatures such as turtles, snakes, or alligators to expose themselves to the pleasant warmth of the sun by resting on logs, rocks or other relatively dry areas.

Biome   A major ecological community such as a marsh or a forest.

Blowout   A hollow formed by wind erosion in a preexisting sand dune, often due to vegetation loss.

Bog   Wet, spongy ground filled with sphagnum moss and having highly acidic water.

Bottomland   Low-elevation alluvial area, close by a river. Sometimes also called bottoms.

Brackish   Water that is less salty than sea water; often found in salt marshes, mangrove swamps, estuaries, and lagoons.

Breachway   A gap in a barrier beach or island, forming a connection between sea and lagoon.

Bushwhack   To hike through territory without established trails.

Cambium   In woody plants, a sheath of cells between external bark and internal wood that generates parallel rows of cells to make new tissue, either as secondary growth or cork.

Canopy   The highest layer of the forest, consisting of the crowns of the trees.

Carnivore   An animal that is primarily flesh-eating. *See also* herbivore and omnivore.

Climax   In a stable ecological community, the plants and animals that will successfully continue to live there.

Colonial birds   Birds that live in relatively stable colonies, used annually for breeding and nesting.

Competition   A social behavior that organizes the sharing of resources such as space, food, and breeding partners when resources are in short supply.

Coniferous   Trees that are needle-leaved or scale-leaved; mostly evergreen and cone-bearing, such as pines, spruces, and firs. *See also* deciduous.

Cordgrass   Grasses found in marshy areas, capable of growing in brackish waters. Varieties include salt-marsh cordgrass, hay, spike grass, and glasswort.

Coteau   A term used in the Midwest for a highland landform. *See also* Drumlin.

Crust   The outer layer of the Earth, between 15 to 40 miles thick.

Crustacean   A hard-shelled, usually aquatic arthropod such as a lobster or crab. *See also* arthropod.

DDT   An insecticide (C14H9Cl5), toxic to animals and human beings whether ingested or absorbed through skin; particularly devastating to certain bird populations, DDT was generally banned in the U.S. in 1972.

Deciduous   Plants that shed or lose their foliage at the conclusion of the growing season, as in "deciduous trees," such as hardwoods (maple, beech, oak, etc.). *See also* coniferous.

Delta   A triangular alluvial deposit at a river's mouth or at the mouth of a tidal inlet. *See also* alluvial.

Dominant   The species most characteristic of a plant or animal community, usually influencing the types and numbers of other species in the same community.

Drumlin   A long ridge or hill composed of glacial till.

Ecological niche   An organism's function, status or, occupied area in its ecological community.

Ecosystem   A mostly self-contained community consisting of an environment and the animals and plants that live there.

Emergent plants   Plants adapted to living in shallow water or in saturated soils such as marshes or wetlands.

Endangered species   A species determined by the federal government to be in danger of extinction throughout all or a significant portion of its range (Endangered Species Act, 1973). *See also* threatened.

Endemic species   Species that evolved in a certain place and live naturally nowhere else. *See also* indigenous species.

Epiphyte   A type of plant (often found in swamps) that lives on a tree instead of on the soil. Epiphytes are not parasitic; they collect their own water and minerals and perform photosynthesis.

Esker   An extended gravel ridge left by a river or stream that runs beneath a decaying glacier.

Estuary   The lower part of a river where fresh-water meets tidal salt water. Usually characterized by abundant animal and plant life.

Evergreen   A tree, shrub, or other plant whose leaves remain green through all seasons.

Exotic   A plant or animal not native to the territory. Many exotic plants and animals displace native species.

Extirpation   The elimination of a species by unnatural causes, such as over-hunting or fishing.

Fall line   A line between the piedmont and the coastal plain below which rivers flow through relatively flat terrain. Large rivers are navigable from the ocean to the fall line.

Fauna   Animals, especially those of a certain region or era, generally considered as a group. *See also* flora.

Fledge   To raise birds until they have their feathers and are able to fly.

Floodplain   A low-lying, flat area along a river where flooding is common.

Flora   Plants, especially those of a certain region or era, generally considered as a group. *See also* fauna.

Flyway   A migratory route, providing food and shelter, followed by large numbers of birds.

Forb   Any herb that is not in the grass family; forbs are commonly found in fields, prairies, or meadows.

4WD   Four-wheel drive vehicle. *See also* ATV.

Frond A fern leaf, a compound palm leaf, or a leaflike thallus (where leaf and stem are continuous), as with seaweed and lichen.

Glacial outwash Sediment dropped by rivers or streams as they flow away from melting glaciers.

Glacial till An unsorted mix of clay, sand, and rock transported and left by glacial action.

Gneiss A common and rather erosion-resistant metamorphic rock originating from shale, characterized by alternating dark and light bands.

Grassy bald A summit area devoid of trees due to shallow or absent soil overlying bedrock (ledge).

Greentree reservoir An area seasonally flooded by opening dikes. Oaks, hickories, and other water-tolerant trees drop nuts (mast) into the water. Migratory birds and other wildlife feed on the mast during winter.

Habitat The area or environment where a plant or animal, or communities of plants or animals, normally live, as in an alpine habitat.

Hammock A fertile spot of high ground in a wetland that supports the growth of hardwood trees.

Hardwoods Flowering trees such as oaks, hickories, maples, and others, as opposed to softwoods and coniferous trees such as pines and hemlocks.

Herbivore An animal that feeds on plant life. *See also* carnivore and omnivore.

Heronry Nesting and breeding site for herons.

Herptiles The class of animals including reptiles and amphibians.

Holdfast The attachment, in lieu of roots, that enables seaweed to grip a substrate such as a rock.

Hot spot An opening in the earth's interior from which molten rock erupts, eventually forming a volcano.

Humus Decomposed leaves and other organic material found, for instance, on the forest floor.

Impoundment A man-made body of water controlled by dikes or levees.

Indigenous species Species that arrived unaided by humans but that may also live in other locations.

Inholding Private land surrounded by federal or state lands such as a wildlife refuge.

Intertidal zone The beach or shoreline area located between low and high tide lines.

Introduced species Species brought to a location by humans, intentionally or accidentally; also called nonnative or alien species. *See also* exotic.

Lichen A ground-hugging plant, usually found on rocks, produced by an association between an alga, which manufactures food, and a fungus, which provides support.

Loess Deep, fertile, and loamy soil deposited by wind, the deepest deposits reaching 200 feet.

Magma Underground molten rock.

Management area A section of land within a federal wildlife preserve or forest where specific wildlife management practices are implemented and studied.

Marsh A low-elevation transitional area between water (the sea) and land, dominated by grasses in soft, wet soils.

Mast. A general word for nuts, acorns, and other food for wildlife produced by trees in the fall.

Meander A winding stream, river, or path.

Mesozoic A geologic era, 230-65 million years ago, during which dinosaurs appeared and became extinct, and birds and flowering plants first appeared.

Midden An accumulation of organic material near a village or dwelling; also called a shell mound.

Migrant An animal that moves from one habitat to another, as opposed to resident species that live permanently in the same habitat.

Mitigation The act of creating or enlarging refuges or awarding them water rights to replace wildlife habitat lost because of the damming or channelization of rivers or the building of roads.

Moist-soil unit A wet area that sprouts annual plants, which attract waterfowl. Naturally produced by river flooding, moist-soil units are artificially created through controlled watering.

Moraine A formation of rock and soil debris transported and dropped by a glacier.

Neotropical New world tropics, generally referring to central and northern South America, as in *neotropical* birds.

Nesting species Birds that take up permanent residence in a habitat.

Occasional A bird species seen only occasionally in a certain region and whose normal territory is elsewhere.

Oceanic trench The place where a sinking tectonic plate bends down, creating a declivity in the ocean floor.

Old field A field that was once cultivated for crops but has been left to grow back into forest.

Old-growth forest A forest characterized by large trees and a stable ecosystem. Old-growth forests are similar to precolonial forests.

Omnivore An animal that feeds on both plant and animal material. *See also* carnivore and herbivore.

ORVs Off-Road-Vehicles. *See also* 4WD and ATV.

Oxbow A curved section of water (once a bend in a river) that was severed from the river when the river changed course. An oxbow lake is formed by the changing course of a river as it meanders through its floodplain.

Passerine A bird in the *Passeriformes* order, primarily composed of perching birds and songbirds.

Peat An accumulation of sphagnum moss and other organic material in wetland areas, known as peat bogs.

Petroglyph Carving or inscription on a rock.

Photosynthesis The process by which green plants use the energy in sunlight to create carbohydrates from carbon dioxide and water, generally releasing oxygen as a by-product.

Pictograph Pictures painted on rock by indigenous people.

Pit and mound topography Terrain characteristic of damp hemlock woods where shallow-rooted fallen trees create pits (former locations of trees) and mounds (upended root balls).

Plant community Plants and animals that interact in a similar environment within a region.

Pleistocene A geologic era, 1.8 million to 10,000 years ago, known as the great age of glaciers.

Pothole A bowl-shaped depression formed by glacial ice, as small as a table or large as a parking lot, now a wetland; a "pothole lake" is a wetland, not a lake.

Prairie An expansive, undulating, or flat grassland, usually without trees, generally on the Plains of mid-continent North America. In the southeast, "prairie" refers to wet grasslands with standing water much of the year.

Prescribed burn A fire that is intentionally set to reduce the buildup of dry organic matter in a forest or grassland, to prevent catastrophic fires later on or to assist plant species whose seeds need intense heat to open.

Proclamation area An area of open water beside or around a coastal refuge where waterfowl are protected from hunting.

Rain shadow An area sheltered from heavy rainfall by mountains that, at their higher altitudes, have drawn much of the rain from the atmosphere.

Raptor A bird of prey with a sharp, curved beak and hooked talons. Raptors include hawks, eagles, owls, falcons, and ospreys.

Rhizome A horizontal plant stem, often thick with reserved food material, from which grow shoots above and roots below.

Riparian The bank and associated plant-life zone of any water body, including tidewaters.

Riverine Living or located on the banks of a river.

Rookery A nesting place for a colony of birds or other animals (seals, penguins, others).

Salt marsh An expanse of tall grass, usually cordgrass and sedges, located in sheltered places such as the land side of coastal barrier islands or along river mouths and deltas at the sea.

Salt pan A shallow pool of saline water formed by tidal action that usually provides abundant food for plovers, sandpipers, and other wading birds.

Scat Animal fecal droppings.

Scrub A dry area of sandy or otherwise poor soil that supports species adapted to such conditions, such as sand myrtle and prickly pear cactus, or dwarf forms of other species, such as oaks and palmettos.

Sea stack A small, steep-sided rock island lying off the coast.

Second growth Trees in a forest that grow naturally after the original stand is cut or burned. *See also* old growth.

Seeps Small springs that may dry up periodically.

Shorebird A bird, such as a plover or sandpiper, frequently found on or near the seashore.

Shrub-steppe Desertlike lands dominated by sagebrush, tumbleweed, and other dry-weather-adapted plants.

Slough A backwater or creek in a marshy area; sloughs sometimes dry into deep mud.

Spit A narrow point of land, often of sand or gravel, extending into the water.

Staging area A place where birds rest, gather strength, and prepare for the next stage of a journey.

Successional Referring to a series of different plants that establish themselves by territories, from water's edge to drier ground. Also, the series of differing plants that reestablish themselves over time after a fire or the retreat of a glacier.

Sump A pit or reservoir used as a drain or receptacle for liquids.

Swale A low-lying, wet area of land.

Swamp A spongy wetland supporting trees and shrubs (as opposed to a marsh, which is characterized by grasses). Swamps provide habitat for birds, turtles, alligators, and bears and serve as refuges for species extirpated elsewhere. *See also* extirpated.

Test The hard, round exoskeleton of a sea urchin.

Threatened species A species of plant or animal in which population numbers are declining, but not in immediate danger of extinction. Threatened species are protected under the Endangered Species Act of 1973. *See also* endangered.

Tuber A short, underground stem with buds from which new shoots grow.

Understory Plants growing under the canopy of a forest. *See also* canopy.

Vascular plant A fern or another seed-bearing plant with a series of channels for conveying nutrients.

Vernal pool Shallow ponds that fill with spring (vernal) rains or snowmelt and dry up as summer approaches; temporary homes to certain amphibians.

Wader A long-legged bird, such as a crane or stork, usually found feeding in shallow water.

Wetland A low, moist area, often marsh or swamp, especially when regarded as the natural habitat of wildlife.

Wilderness Area An area of land (within a national forest, national park, or a national wildlife refuge) protected under the 1964 Federal Wilderness Act. Logging, construction, and use of mechanized vehicles or tools are prohibited here and habitats are left in their pristine states. Designated Wilderness is the highest form of federal land protection.

Wrack line Plant, animal, and unnatural debris left on the upper beach by a receding tide.

ACKNOWLEDGEMENTS

The authors are most grateful to refuge managers, biologists, and other staff who met every request for printed materials, every interview, and seemingly endless phone calls with patience, good humor, and loads of information.

—John Grassy and Tom Powers

ABOUT THE AUTHORS

An editorial consultant for the *Smithsonian Guides to Natural America*, John Grassy also wrote the National Audubon Society's *First Field Guide to Mammals* and its *Regional Guide to the Rocky Mt. States.*

Tom Powers is the author of many birding, camping, and general outdoors guides to the Great Lakes region.

PHOTOGRAPHY CREDITS

We would like to thank the U. S. Fish & Wildlife Service for letting us publish photos from their collection, as well as the other contributing photographers for their wonderful imagery. The pages on which the photos appear are listed after each contributor.

Daniel B. Gibson: 5, 185, 203

John & Karen Hollingsworth: ii-iii, 4, 6, 14, 18, 20, 21, 22, 33, 38, 45, 48, 56, 58, 68, 70, 73, 82, 84, 86, 90, 95, 101, 104, 111, 114, 126, 131, 140, 142, 145, 147, 151, 153, 156, 157, 159, 162, 163, 164, 174, 176, 180, 181, 183, 187, 200, 204, 205, 214, 217, 223, 226, 228, 235, 239, 242, 244

Gary Kramer: xiv, 7, 8, 23, 24, 26, 30, 34, 36, 42, 43, 46, 54, 65, 71, 76, 93, 102, 107, 109, 117, 123, 124, 130, 133, 136, 138. 148, 166, 168, 171, 188, 192, 207, 209, 212, 219, 232, 241

Omni-Photo Communications: 62, 91, 96, 197, 198, 233

William Palmer: 189

U.S. Fish & Wildlife Service: 19, 31, 51, 63, 78, 99, 119, 146, 150, 190, 221, 224, 230

NATIONAL AUDUBON SOCIETY
Mission Statement

The mission of National Audubon Society, founded in 1905, is to conserve and restore natural ecosystems, focusing on birds, other wildlife, and their habitats for the benefit of humanity and the earth's biological diversity.

One of the largest, most effective environmental organizations, Audubon has more than 560,000 members, numerous state offices and nature centers, and 500+ chapters in the United States and Latin America, plus a professional staff of scientists, lobbyists, lawyers, policy analysts, and educators. Through our nationwide sanctuary system we manage 150,000 acres of critical wildlife habitat and unique natural areas for birds, wild animals, and rare plant life.

Our award-winning Audubon magazine, published six times a year and sent to all members, carries outstanding articles and color photography on wildlife and nature, and presents in-depth reports on critical environmental issues, as well as conservation news and commentary. We also publish Field Notes, a journal reporting on seasonal bird sightings continent-wide, and Audubon Adventures, a bimonthly children's newsletter reaching 500,000 students. Through our ecology camps and workshops in Maine, Connecticut, and Wyoming, we offer professional development for educators and activists; through Audubon Expedition Institute in Belfast, Maine, we offer unique, traveling undergraduate and graduate degree programs in Environmental Education.

Our acclaimed World of Audubon television documentaries on TBS deal with a variety of environmental themes, and our children's series for the Disney Channel, Audubon's Animal Adventures, introduces family audiences to endangered wildlife species. Other Audubon film and television projects include conservation-oriented movies, electronic field trips, and educational videos. National Audubon Society also sponsors books and interactive programs on nature, plus travel programs to exotic places like Antarctica, Africa, Australia, Baja California, Galapagos Islands, Indonesia, and Patagonia.

For information about how you can become an Audubon member, subscribe to Audubon Adventures, or learn more about our camps and workshops, please write or call:

National Audubon Society
Membership Dept.
700 Broadway
New York, New York 10003
212/979-3000
http://www.audubon.org/audubon

JOIN THE NATIONAL AUDUBON SOCIETY—RISK FREE!

Please send me my first issue of AUDUBON magazine and enroll me as a temporary member of the National Audubon Society at the $20 introductory rate—$15 off the regular rate. If I wish to continue as a member, I'll pay your bill when it arrives. If not, I'll return it marked "cancel," owe nothing, and keep the first issue free.

____ Payment Enclosed   ____ Bill Me

Name _____

Street _____

City _____

State/zip _____

Please make checks payable to the National Audubon Society. Allow 4–6 weeks for delivery of magazine. $10 of dues is for AUDUBON magazine. Basic membership, dues are $35.

Mail to:

NATIONAL AUDUBON SOCIETY
Membership Data Center
PO Box 52529
Boulder, CO 80322-2529